THEY SHALL
NOT PASS!

For the fallen

THEY SHALL NOT PASS!

THE BRITISH BATTALION AT JARAMA
— THE SPANISH CIVIL WAR —

Ben Hughes

First published in Great Britain in 2011 by Osprey Publishing,
Midland House, West Way, Botley, Oxford, OX2 0PH, UK
44-02 23rd Street, Suite 219, Long Island City, NY 11101, USA
E-mail: info@ospreypublishing.com

A CIP catalogue record for this book is available from the British Library

ISBN: 978 1 84908 549 6

Page layout by Bounford.com, Cambridge, UK
Index by Alison Worthington
Cartography by Peter Bull
Typeset in Charter ITC
Originated by United Graphics Pte, Singapore
Printed in China through Bookbuilders

11 12 13 14 15   10 9 8 7 6 5 4 3 2 1

Osprey Publishing is supporting the Woodland Trust, the
UK's leading woodland conservation charity,
by funding the dedication of trees.

www.ospreypublishing.com

Front Cover: 'They Shall Not Pass', created by Lorenzo
Goñi for the United Socialist Party. (Imperial War Museum
PST 8648)

CONVERSION TABLE

1 millimetre (mm)	0.0394 in.
1 centimetre (cm)	0.3937 in.
1 metre (m)	1.0936 yards
1 kilometre (km)	0.6214 miles
1 kilogram (kg)	2.2046 lb
1 inch	2.54cm
1 foot	0.3048m
1 yard	0.9144m
1 mile	1.609km

CONTENTS

AUTHOR'S NOTE

The following account is compiled entirely from first hand sources. In the days, weeks and months after the battle, several volunteers wrote diaries, memoirs, letters or newspaper articles detailing their experiences. Four decades later the Imperial War Museum began a series of interviews which added a wealth of detail to the existing accounts. Whilst I am confident that what follows is an accurate description of the events of 12–14 February 1937, memories fade and some veterans may have embellished their exploits. Furthermore, although they largely agreed on what happened, precisely when each particular event occurred, and in which particular order, proved far more difficult to ascertain.

The scope of any work of non-fiction is limited to the sources available. Whilst the British participants at Jarama left copious material, the Nationalist sources are sparse. The reasons are various. Although they won the war, the Nationalists lost the battle for hearts and minds that followed and therefore the market for their memoirs has been limited. Furthermore, after Franco's death, Spain underwent a period of deliberate forgetting (*el pacto del olvido*) and as the veterans entered their twilight years, the desire to record their reflections was lacking. Finally, although several of the British veterans were well read and educated and predisposed to writing about their experiences, the men they faced at Jarama were from different backgrounds. The vast majority of the Spaniards who made up the bulk of the rank and file of the Foreign Legion were barely literate and the Moors who fought alongside them were even less well equipped to leave a written record.

They Shall Not Pass! is a micro-history. The narrative is constructed from a worm's eye point of view. It is not an account of 'great men' whose decisions altered the course of history. Instead, it aims to immerse the reader in the lives of a select number of 'ordinary' individuals over a brief period of time. As such, it inevitably overlooks the contributions of others, chief amongst whom are the Spaniards themselves.

On a related note, in an attempt to make the characters come to life from limited resources, I have included references to individual's ages. However, in several cases, whilst the year of birth was possible to ascertain, I was unable to find the exact date. Where this was the case, I have assumed that the individual's birthday occurred before the start of the battle. Therefore, a volunteer whose year of birth was 1900, is assumed to have been 37 on 12 February rather than 36. Although this supposition is unsatisfactory, it avoids over complicating the text.

One of the problems facing any writer of history is the use of terminology. Truth is always more complex than fiction and applying labels to the various groups of men involved at Jarama is fraught with difficulty. Nevertheless, I have chosen to make a few generalizations to avoid becoming bogged down in detail. 'The British' were not all British; amongst the 'Republicans' were communists, socialists and anarchists; and those they fought were certainly not all fascists. For the benefit of objectivity I have chosen to use the less emotive epithet of Nationalists for the enemies of the British Battalion. Even though the volunteers referred to them as 'Fascists' in their letters and memoirs, to label the Moroccan mercenaries and professional soldiers of the Foreign Legion in such a way would be to do them a disservice.

This project would not have been possible without the cooperation of numerous archivists and librarians in England, Spain and Russia. I would also like to thank Kate Moore, Emily Holmes and Philip Smith at Osprey; Richard Baxell, the author of the meticulously well researched *British Volunteers in the Spanish Civil War*; Jane and Dave Hughes, Tim Dalrymple, Jamie Cowper and Julia Winslet for their comments on various drafts and DeeDee Cunningham for her invaluable insights into her great uncle Jock, to my mind the greatest of all the unsung British heroes at Jarama.

LIST OF ILLUSTRATIONS

13. The British Battalion on parade behind the front line at Jarama. (Topfoto)

14. Moorish Infantry, Spain 1937. The British feared and demonized the dreaded Moors they faced at Jarama. (Keystone Images)

15. T26 tank. The Russian-built T26 was the most advanced tracked vehicle operating on either side during the Spanish Civil War. (Keystone Images)

16. The Sunken Road. (Author's Collection)

17. A view from the Sunken Road looking west towards the ridgeline. (Author's Collection)

Between pages 192 and 193

18. William Ball. At twenty years old, Ball was one of the youngest volunteers to join the British Battalion. (Image courtesy of the Marx Memorial Library)

19. Walter Gregory recovering from the wound he suffered at Jarama. (Image courtesy of the Marx Memorial Library)

20. George Nathan, a veteran of the Great War. (Image courtesy of the Marx Memorial Library)

21. John 'Bosco' Jones. Before travelling to Spain, Jones had fought Oswald Mosley's Black Shirts at the battle of Cable Street, the British Union of Fascists' biggest defeat. (Image courtesy of the Marx Memorial Library)

22. Donald Renton. The political commissar of the 2nd Company, Renton was wounded then captured on the second day. (Image courtesy of the Marx Memorial Library)

23. A well-earned break. Members of the British Battalion resting behind the lines at Jarama, 1937. (Image courtesy of the Marx Memorial Library)

24. Wounded from Jarama. Walter Gregory, the 3rd Company's runner, is second from the right in the bottom row. (Image courtesy of the Marx Memorial Library)

25. Members of the 2nd Company captured at Jarama on 13 February 1937. James Maley is second on the right, partially obscured next to him is Jimmy Rutherford. George Leeson is fifth from the right. Harry Fry, the company commander, stands two places to Leeson's right. Bert 'Yank' Levy is standing alone on the left wearing a cap. Two places to Levy's right is Tommy Bloomfield and beside him is Donald Renton. (Image courtesy of the Marx Memorial Library)

26. Burial of a British soldier amongst the olive groves. (IWM HU 34695)

LIST OF MAPS

PREFACE

According to the historian A.J.P. Taylor, socialists seeking admittance to heaven in the aftermath of the Second World War were asked just one question: 'What was the turning point in the battle against fascism?' Those who replied Stalingrad were banished without further discussion. Any who named the Battle of Britain were given a second chance, but only the enlightened few who answered 'on the banks of the Jarama' were immediately ushered inside.[1] This near-forgotten struggle, which took place in February 1937 amongst the olive groves south-east of Madrid, proved for the first time that fascism and its ilk, which up until then had steamrollered all opposition from the Rhineland to Addis Ababa, could in fact be stopped. Although the Republicans would lose the Civil War, their efforts, and those of the international volunteers who fought alongside them, paved the way for the more celebrated victories that followed. Without them, twentieth-century history might well have taken a very different path indeed.

Spain: February 1937

INTRODUCTION

Many contemporaries saw the Spanish Civil War as a straight fight between fascism and communism. The truth was far more convoluted. In fact the conflict's origins stretch back to the early nineteenth century, long before either doctrine existed. Ever since the Napoleonic invasion of 1808 had overthrown King Ferdinand VII and given rise to the Cortes (or Spanish parliament), those who believed in progressive ideals had been locked in a struggle with the reactionary forces of old Spain, spearheaded by the monarchy, the church and the landowning elite. In the years that followed the picture grew ever more complex: the 1830s saw the birth of Basque Nationalism; forty years later, Bakunin's anarchist movement was enthusiastically adopted by thousands of disenfranchised peasants in Andalucía, Catalonia and Extremadura; and at the turn of the twentieth century Catalans began to call for independence and the industrial proletariat of Madrid, Barcelona, Bilbao and Santander found a voice with the foundation of the Socialist Party and the establishment of the trade unions.[1] In the 1920s and 1930s these divisions came to a head. The period was punctuated by the rapid rise and fall of coalition governments of both the left and the right. Coups, assassinations and uprisings became commonplace and three further forces emerged: the Carlist Requetés, armed defenders of the traditional role of the church; the Falange, a fascist paramilitary organization inspired by Mussolini's Black Shirts; and the Spanish Communist Party. Although relatively insignificant before the conflict, the last of these would rapidly gain influence once hostilities began.

15

In July 1936 two of the country's senior generals, Emilio Mola and José Sanjuro, sought to put an end to the uncertainty. Their plan was to use elements of the armed forces to overthrow the Republican government of Manuel Azaña, a 'Popular Front' of loosely allied centre and left-wing parties. Having won just 34 per cent of the vote in the general election earlier that year, Azaña's government had only the flimsiest of mandates to rule. The generals, however, were overconfident. They thought the left would crumble swiftly, considered the people an undisciplined rabble and believed the government only needed a push to collapse entirely. On 18 July they put their plan into effect. Although the coup was successful in some areas, people's militias, backed by elements of the security services, defeated the rebellious military in the key cities of Madrid, Valencia and Barcelona. Fearing destruction, the generals united with the Falangists, Monarchists and Conservatives under the loosely defined banner of nationalism. In the chaos that ensued, 50,000 were executed by death squads working for both sides. A front line later emerged, splitting Spain in two. Starting midway across the Pyrenees, it cut south through Aragon, turned west at the mountain stronghold of Teruel, skirted Madrid and then proceeded south-west to the Portuguese border, terminating just south of the city of Badajoz. The government controlled the majority of the population, over half the armed forces and the country's entire industrial output. The Nationalists, on the other hand, held one trump card: Francisco Franco's Army of Africa. Made up of Moroccan *regulares* (regulars) and the *tercios* (battalions) of the Foreign Legion, it was an elite force, tempered in the ashes of Spain's final colonial war. As they were on the far side of the Gibraltar straits and the Republicans controlled most of the navy, however, the generals had no way of deploying them. Help was needed. It would come from abroad.

Mussolini was the first to offer his support. Within weeks of the coup Italian planes were on their way to Tetúan, the capital of Nationalist Morocco. Later, Hitler also became involved. Enthused by a Wagner recital he had just attended, the Führer named the operation to aid the Spanish Nationalists *Unternehmen Feuerzauber* (Operation *Magic Fire*). Twenty Junkers transports, the first detachment of the Condor Legion (an elite unit of Wehrmacht and Luftwaffe volunteers), were soon on their way to Morocco.[2] On arrival, the German pilots were met by an extraordinary sight. Thousands of Moors, 'wearing flowing *Chilaba* robes ... red fezzes or tightly wound turbans', had gathered at the airport. Others were camped in the hills beyond. 'Unencumbered, by German efficiency ... [the Moors] stormed the planes' as soon as they touched down, piling into the back until an adjutant cried "*Voll*" – the signal for the pilot to take off for Seville.'[3] Thus began the first military air-bridge in history.

Meanwhile, in Britain, Stanley Baldwin's Conservative government concentrated on attracting signatories for its international policy of Non-Intervention. Like many Conservatives in the mid-1930s, including Winston Churchill, Baldwin saw communism as a greater threat than fascism. He was content to turn a blind eye to Hitler's and Mussolini's excesses whilst hoping they would help keep Stalin in check. Although denying arms to both Azaña's democratically elected government and the rebellious generals, Non-Intervention effectively played into the latter's hands. Whilst Franco *et al* were receiving aid from both Hitler and Mussolini, who although joint signatories to Baldwin's pact had no qualms about breaking their promises, the Republicans were poorly supplied. Forced to rely on unscrupulous arms dealers, Republican Mexico and the half-hearted and intermittent support of the French Popular Front headed by Léon Blum, their armies would prove no match for the Nationalists in the opening exchanges of the war.

Around 14,000 men, 44 pieces of artillery, 90 machine guns and 500 tons of ammunition and stores were taken across the Straits of Gibraltar by German and Italian planes and blockade-defying Nationalist launches. Franco, who had flown from Morocco on 6 August, marshalled his troops in Seville before sending them north under Lieutenant Colonel Juan Yagüe y Blanco. With that the advance on Madrid began.[4] Led by a column of 3,000 men, Yagüe's troops punched their way through isolated units of the people's militias, advancing 500 miles in a matter of weeks. At each captured town, scores of suspected Reds were rounded up and shot. On 11 August Merida fell. Then came the city of Badajoz, which proved the Nationalists' sternest test yet. Nevertheless, it too was captured after a day's fierce fighting breached the walls that had held Wellington's redcoats at bay for three weeks over a hundred years before. The reprisals that followed were atrocious.

Hundreds were executed in the bullring. The shots rang out for weeks, both day and night. By the time the Nationalists had finished, the floor was said to run ankle deep with blood.[5]

With the Republicans seemingly at his mercy, Franco committed a strategic mistake. Rather than finishing his enemies with an attack on the capital, his troops were diverted to relieve the besieged garrison of Toledo. Trapped in the Alcazar, an ancient fortress *cum* palace built on a commanding height above the banks of the river Tagus, the Nationalists had been holding out since the rebellion began. It is thought that Franco's motivation for this move was political: by saving these well-publicized heroes, who had been a much-needed focus for Nationalist pride since the failures at Madrid, Barcelona and Valencia, he was able to boost his popularity at a time when he was merely the junior element of the triumvirate leading the rebellion. If politics was indeed his motivation, the move proved remarkably astute. After driving off the encircling militia and massacring those left behind, the Army of Africa lifted the siege on 27 September, two months after it had begun. Amidst a flurry of publicity, photos of Franco flooded the right-wing press. It was the perfect publicity coup. From that point on he became the *de facto* head of the Nationalists.

By the time Franco got round to attacking the capital, Azaña's ineffectual government had been replaced by a wartime cabinet headed by Largo Caballero, a socialist leader inappropriately nicknamed the Lenin of Madrid. His appointment stiffened the people's resistance against the Nationalists and their hopes were given a further boost in November with the arrival of the first consignment of Russian aid. Although Stalin's interest in Spain was self-serving and his policies would lead to a civil war within the Civil War, he was also the only national leader to supply up-to-date military aid to the Spanish government on a large scale. T26 tanks, biplane and mono-wing fighters, bombers, advisors, small arms and ammunition were followed by the first International Brigades, volunteer units organized by the Comintern, a body originally conceived to spread the revolution beyond Russia's borders, which had since been bent to Stalin's will. As the columns advanced down the Gran Via, Madrillenos spilled out of their houses to yell '*No Pasarán!*' (they shall not pass) and '*Viva Los Rusos!*', unaware that they were actually cheering Germans,

French, Belgians and Poles. Some of the most intense fighting of the war followed. For seven days, the 4th and 6th *banderas* (battalions) of the Foreign Legion battled Polish anti-fascists for control of the Clinical Hospital, a prominent building caught on the front line. Whilst the Poles occupied the upper floors, the Legion held the basement. Countless bayonet charges were made up the staircase. Each was repulsed by showers of grenades.

Amongst the Internationals were a handful of British pioneers. Too few to form their own unit, nineteen fought with the 4th Section of the Commune of Paris Battalion, whilst a group of twenty-one were with the German Thaelmann Battalion, in the XII Brigade.[6] According to one of their number, Esmond Romilly, a young aristocrat who had rebelled against his conservative upbringing, the British were made up of a variety of types. Amongst them were 'Lorrimer Birch, a brilliant scientist and Oxford graduate, [a] sincere and wholehearted communist; Joe Gough, [an] unemployed Luton humorist; [and] Tich, an ex-sergeant of the Buffs, with a kind heart, and first class ability as a quartermaster'.[7] Also present was a tough young Scot named Jock Cunningham, who would play a decisive role at Jarama. In November 1936 the fighting grew increasingly bloody. As the Moors tried to cross the streets below, the British poured volleys of rifle fire upon them, hiding behind stacks of library tomes which swiftly became riddled with bullets. 'I ... had the Everyman series around my window,' one later recalled.[8]

On 23 November after his troops had suffered 50 per cent casualties, Franco called off the offensive.[9] The direct assault on Madrid had failed. In the next three months the Nationalists would concentrate on encircling the capital and cutting it off from resupply. The change in tactics would prove effective. Whilst the chaotic nature of street fighting had been a great leveller, the militias could not match the Army of Africa's organization in the open field. In the weeks to come road after road leading out of Madrid would be severed.

At the end of November the Nationalists attacked the Corunna Road to the north-west of the capital. The offensive began with an artillery bombardment. Then the Nationalist infantry moved in. On 14 December they captured Boadilla del Monte, a village 20 miles to the west of Madrid dominated by a small monastery. A counter-attack led by Russian T26 tanks forced the Nationalists to withdraw, but, after reforming, they attacked once more.

Opposing them were the German volunteers of the Thaelmann Battalion, including the remnants of the British section which had fought with them at Madrid. Esmond Romilly detailed the fighting that ensued:

> It started with two men falling dead from close-range bullets in a dug-out nearby. Then the real hailstorm of lead came at us. I was lying flat on my stomach. We shoved in clip after clip of cartridges until the breeches and barrels of our guns were red hot. I never took aim. I never looked up to see what I was firing at. I never heard the order to open fire. I never saw the enemy – never knew for certain where they were... My head was in a whirl – I was almost drunk with the smell of powder. I remember a young Spaniard next to me, wondering what he was doing and how he got there; but there was no time to work it all out. It was a mad scramble – pressing my elbows into the earth, bruising them on the stones, to get my rifle to my shoulder, rasping back the bolt, then shoving it home, then onto my elbows again.[10]

By the time the fighting had finished, the Nationalists had only managed to advance five miles. The Corunna road had been held, but at a terrible price. Hundreds of Republicans had fallen and, of the ten British volunteers who had survived the battle of Madrid while fighting with the German volunteers, eight had died. Only Romilly and one other had lived to tell the tale.[11]

Meanwhile, 150 miles to the south at the town of Lopera, in an attempt to take some pressure off the beleaguered Madrid front, the Republicans were about to launch an offensive of their own. Having travelled by train from Madrid, the newly formed XIV International Brigade was to spearhead the advance. Amongst the troops was a detachment of 145 British volunteers under the command of George Nathan, a Great War veteran who would serve on the Brigade staff at Jarama. Most of the others were new arrivals, but some had fought at Madrid.

Casualties at Lopera were heavy. As soon as the men alighted from the train on the 28th, enemy planes dived out of the cloudless blue sky to strafe them. Nathan Segal, a Jew from Walthamstow, took cover with the rest, but was killed when an explosive bullet 'entered his back and tore open his chest'.[12]

Advancing overland to Lopera the battalion had to capture a 400ft fortified hill. They took the feature twice, but were repulsed on both occasions by furious counter-attacks. John Tunnah recalled the fighting: '[As we got closer to the village] the resistance stiffened ... at times I could see ... [buildings] just coming out of the trees ... [and] it seemed as if every point of it was spouting fire'.[13] In the first two days of the fighting, fifteen of the British Company were killed and twenty-eight wounded. On 30 December, the brigade was ordered to retreat. Machine guns raked their lines and Nationalist artillery caused further losses. That afternoon the British halted and dug in along a series of lightly wooded hills, here they received a visit from Dave Springhall, the battalion's senior political commissar. Jumping into a slit trench dug behind a tree, he found himself face-to-face with several men who would go on to fight at Jarama. Maurice Davidovitch, a Jewish communist who would take charge of the stretcher bearers, was 'as perky as ever' and Ken Stalker, a Scottish communist who was always to be found with a lit pipe clenched between his teeth, had just had a lucky escape. Earlier in the fighting a bullet had hit his helmet. Passing straight through, it struck him on the forehead, momentarily stunning him, but otherwise doing no lasting harm.[14]

After their withdrawal from the front, André Marty, the chief political commissar of the Internationals, hailed the men of the British 1st Company as the best fighters in the brigade. George Nathan, ably supported by his section commanders, Kit Conway and Jock Cunningham, had particularly distinguished himself. Leading from the front, the Englishman had shown bravery and discipline, and the British company had been the only one to withdraw in good order from the field. Colonel Delasalle, the French commander of the XIV Brigade, paid dearly for the defeat. Looking for a scapegoat, Marty had him arrested on trumped up charges of colluding with the enemy.[15] He was court-martialled and shot the next day. Nathan was promoted in his place.[16]

The XIV Brigade was then transferred to Las Rozas, the new front line to the north-west of Madrid following the Nationalists' minor gains at Boadilla. After a few days' rest in the capital, the British company were back in action. 10 January saw them climbing onto lorries and being driven into the

Guadarrama mountains. One veteran remembers how 'cold, wet and tired' they were as they formed up in thick woods and marched to the front through 'swirling mists [that] made it impossible to see more than a few yards ahead'. On reaching the outskirts of Las Rozas, the fighting began. 'Deadly sniper fire came from the church tower. Then, bang on target our artillery scored a direct hit.'[17] The Nationalists made repeated attacks over the next five days until a heavy snowfall finally brought their offensive to a standstill on the 15th. Despite suffering heavy casualties, the Nationalists had achieved their aim. The road to Corunna had fallen and Madrid's supply lines were now teetering on the verge of collapse. British losses had also been significant. Jock Cunningham was amongst the wounded and by the time the unit returned to their base at Madrigueras, just sixty-seven of the 145 who had set out on Christmas Eve remained.[18]

By January 1937 the only major road in Republican hands leading to Madrid was the Valencia highway. Heading south-west from the capital to the Republicans' main port on the Mediterranean coast, the road carried vital supplies, arms and ammunition to Madrid's besieged defenders. If it were cut, the capital would surely fall and the Republic's international credibility would suffer a blow from which it would be impossible to recover. Although originally planned for mid-January, the Nationalist offensive to take the road began on 6 February when the late winter rains had finally ceased. General Luis Orgaz Yoldi, the commander of the front, and Colonel José Varela, the senior officer in the field, had five brigades, each of between four and six infantry battalions, at their disposal. With artillery, anti-tank, armoured car and cavalry support, and a further four battalions in reserve, they commanded a total of 25,000 men. The shock troops spearheading the attack included eleven Moroccan *tabores* (battalions) and five *tercios* from the elite Foreign Legion. There were also two German heavy machine-gun battalions, 100 Mark I Panzer Tanks and a battery of 88mm guns under the command of Colonel von Thoma, whilst the planes of Mussolini's Legionary Air Force (*Aviacion Legionara*) and Hitler's Condor Legion soared overhead.[19]

Initially the Nationalist advance went well. Each brigade moved forward independently along a 10-mile front running due south from Madrid. Colonels

Overview of Jarama

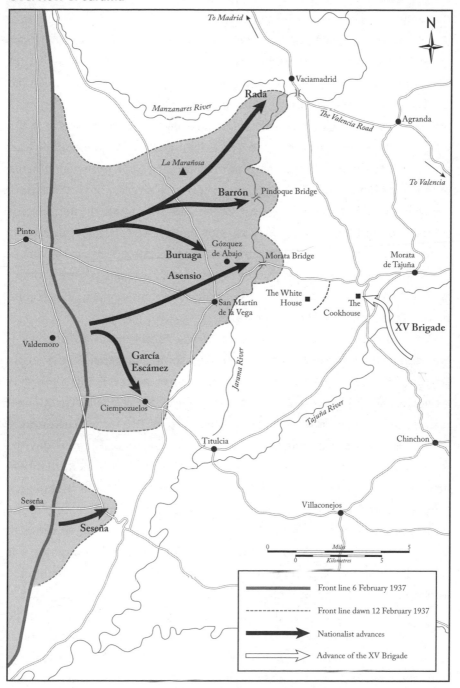

Rada, Barrón and Buruaga started at the town of Pinto, whilst colonels Asensio Cabanillas and García Escámez began at Valdemoro, three miles to the south. Caught by surprise and faced with overwhelming odds, the government troops stood little chance. On the first day, Rada's brigade assaulted the hill of La Marañosa. Two Republican battalions, dug in on the summit, defended stubbornly, but were driven back with heavy casualties. To the south, Buruaga's brigade captured the hamlet of Gózquez de Abajo, Asensio's troops took the village of San Martín de la Vega and García Escámez, on the far left of the line, captured Ciempozuelos. By the morning of 8 February, when fresh rainfall again put the operation on hold, the Nationalists were within a few hundred yards of the western bank of the Jarama River. Grateful for the respite, the Republicans reorganized and the Spanish Lister Division and the XII International Brigade were rushed to the front.[20] High command also reinforced the north bank of the Manzanares, towards which they believed the Nationalists were about to switch their attack. At dawn on 11 February, the rains stopped. The second phase of the battle was about to begin.

Bypassing the Republican build up, Orgaz continued to advance east, concentrating his forces on the two crossings over the Jarama. To the north, Barrón's brigade launched a successful pre-dawn assault on Pindoque Bridge. As the rest of the brigade enlarged the bridgehead, the Garibaldi Battalion of Italian anti-fascists counter-attacked, supported by T26 tanks. Their efforts were repelled, however, and the bridgehead was secured. The next day the Republicans lost the San Martín Bridge to the south in a near-identical attack.[21] At 4.00am the 3rd *Tabor* of Tetuán from Asensio's 4th Brigade fell upon the sentries before they could react, then crawled up the plain to the east of the river. Moving behind the government trenches dug on the high ground, they hurled grenades amongst the defenders. The slaughter was prodigious. After the wounded were finished off with triangular bladed knives, the rest of the brigade crossed and formed up on the far bank.[22] By 11.00am on 12 February the 4th Brigade was ready to advance. Asensio Cabanillas, a forty-one year-old career officer who had joined the rebellion at the outset, ordered one of his two regiments, the 7th, to attack to the north of the Morata road. This would bring it into contact with the XI International

Brigade and the Franco-Belgian and Dimitrov battalions (the latter a unit of Balkan volunteers) of the XV.[23] The 8th Regiment, meanwhile, was sent to the south. Within the hour it was to have a fateful encounter with the XV Brigade's final component: the British Battalion.

Following the battle of Las Rozas in January, the survivors of George Nathan's company had been ordered to return to the village of Madrigueras. Awaiting them were over 300 new recruits. Together they went on to form the first British Battalion. Assigned to the XV Brigade, along with the Dimitrovs and Franco-Belgians and two Spanish units, by the time the British battalion left Madrigueras on 6 February 1937, it was over 500 strong. With orders to join the Reserve Brigade on the Jarama front, the men travelled by train to Albacete, headquarters of the International Brigades, then by lorry to Chinchon, a village 10 miles from the River Jarama.[24] On the afternoon of the 11th, little realizing that the Nationalists would soon cross the river and penetrate the Republicans' first line, Captain Tom Wintringham and his scouts moved out to occupy an old villa close to the front designated Battalion Headquarters (HQ). The rest of the men were woken before dawn on the 12th, herded aboard lorries and driven to join them. Although most had never fired a rifle in anger in their lives, they were about to be thrown into the bloodiest encounter of the conflict so far, the like of which had not been seen in Europe since the Great War. This book focuses on their first three days under fire.

DRAMATIS PERSONAE

Aitken, George – Battalion Commissar, British Battalion (b. *c*.1895, Glasgow)
A 'rugged Scots Commissar' and Great War veteran, who had been wounded at the battle of Loos, Aitken was 'strong in his communist convictions, but by no means uncritical. If he thought that the leadership was wrong he did not hesitate to say so'.[1]

Asensio Cabanillas, Carlos – Colonel, Commander 4th Brigade (b.1896, Madrid)
A career soldier loyal to the military uprising from the start, Asensio had earned the respect of his men during Spain's final colonial wars against the Rif rebels of Spanish Morocco.

Azaña, Manuel – President of the Spanish Republic (b.1880, Alcalá de Henares)
An accomplished writer and translator who was reluctantly drawn into public life, Azaña was an admirer of Cromwell and regarded 'politics as an art, with the people as the palette'.[2]

Ball, William – Private, 2nd Company, British Battalion (b.1916, Reading)
A twenty-one year-old graduate of Reading public school, Ball had served in the military cadets and was a fine marksman having passed his rifle shooting qualification with an 'A' grade.

Beckett, Clem – Section Leader, 4th Company, British Battalion (b.1900, Oldham)

'Never tidily dressed', Beckett was a communist and ex-speedway champion, who 'looked as if he had come [straight] out of the garage. When not on parade he always had a little stub of a cigar in his mouth.'[3]

Blum, Léon – Prime Minister of France (b.1872, Paris)
Jewish socialist and head of France's left-leaning Popular Front from 1936.

Bowler, Kitty – Journalist (b.1908, Plymouth, Massachusetts)
Champagne socialist who visited the Soviet Union, Italy and France before travelling to Barcelona to report on the Civil War. There she met and fell in love with Tom Wintringham, who went on to become the commander of the British Battalion from early February 1937.

Briskey, Bill – 3rd Company Commander, British Battalion (b. *c*.1890, London)
A sergeant in the Great War who went on to become a London bus driver and leading figure in the Transport Trade Union, Briskey was 'a quiet ... gentle man, a most unmilitary type to look at but ... most dedicated to the fight against fascism'.[4]

Charlesworth, Albert – Private, 4th Company, British Battalion (b.1915, Oldham)
A metal polisher and engineer's apprentice from Oldham, Charlesworth was a member of the local Socialist League. Always one to back those he saw as the underdogs, he left for Spain in late 1936.

Conway, 'Kit' – 1st Company Commander (Acting), British Battalion (b.1897, nr Burncourt, County Tipperary)
A 'self taught' orphan, who was 'highly intelligent ... articulate [and] humorous ... with a generous capacity for friendship', Conway fought on both sides in the Irish Civil War before joining the Irish Republican Army (IRA) in 1920. He was later jailed by the British and chose to live in the USA after his release. On his return to Ireland in the early 1930s, he joined the Communist Party and became one of its 'most effective proselytisers'.[5]

Copeman, Fred – 'Spare Officer', 1st Company, British Battalion (b.1907, Suffolk)
Born into poverty, Copeman grew up in an orphanage before joining the Royal Navy at the age of fourteen. When Ramsay MacDonald's government

announced a cut in sailors' pay in 1931, Copeman helped organize the Invergordon Mutiny and was dismissed from the service as a result. 'An exceedingly large and brutish man' prone to flights of fancy, Copeman was 'a colourful bluffer' who resorted to violence to get his way and was loved and hated by his comrades in equal measure.[6]

Crook, David – Private, 1st Company, British Battalion (b.1910, London)
A Cheltenham College alumnus, 'university graduate ... [and] profound Marxist' from an 'impoverished middle class' background, Crook fought Oswald Mosley's Black Shirts at the battle of Cable Street before leaving for Spain.[7]

Cunningham, Jock – 1st Company Commander, British Battalion (b.1903, Coatbridge, nr Glasgow)
One of the first British volunteers to reach Spain, Cunningham was a veteran of the Argyll and Sutherland Highlanders who mutinied over pay and conditions whilst serving in Jamaica. Once in Spain he fought at the battles of Madrid, Lopera and Las Rozas before joining the British Battalion in January 1937. 'Handsome and ... loveable, [and as] tough as they come', Cunningham was a natural leader and adored by the men.[8]

Davidovitch, Maurice – Commander of the First Aid Section, British Battalion (b.1914, Bethnal Green)
A member of the Youth Communist League (YCL) and Communist Party of Great Britain (CPGB), before leaving for Spain Davidovitch had been a merchant sailor. '[His] life had been a hard one, spent in the forecastle of many a tramp steamer.' Nicknamed 'sailor boy', his 'particular blend of Jewish and Cockney humour ... [gave] him a capacity for clowning around and getting a laugh out of everyone'. One of the earlier volunteers, Davidovitch fought under George Nathan at Lopera and became a close friend of Jock Cunningham's.[9]

Diamant, André – Private, 1st Company, British Battalion (b.1900, Cairo, Egypt)
Formerly a student based in Paris, Diamant volunteered for service in Spain in late 1936 and fought at Lopera. Wintringham thought him 'the maddest, most mysterious little Levantine I have ever come across; but ... a natural born leader'.[10]

Dickenson, Ted – Second-in-Command, 2nd Company, British Battalion (b. *c.*1900, Australia)

With his 'overcoat top-boots ... smartly clipped moustache, legs apart and back straight as a poker', Dickenson was 'every inch a soldier'. Blessed with a 'calm courage', the Australian had emigrated to England in the 1930s and 'had been very active in the Jewish Ex-Serviceman's Movement for Peace in East London'.[11]

Economides, Michael – Private, XV Brigade Guard (b.1910, Nicosia, Cyprus)
The son of a wheat merchant, Economides emigrated to London in 1929 where he worked as a waiter before joining the Communist Party in 1932. He went to Spain in December 1936 and fought at Lopera.[12]

Franco, Francisco – Commander in Chief of Nationalist Forces (b.1892, Ferrol, Galicia)
Before the outbreak of the Civil War, Franco served in the Army of Africa. He built a reputation as a cruel and ruthlessly efficient disciplinarian during the Rif War in the 1920s and was renowned for his bravery under fire.

Fry, Harry – 2nd Company Commander, British Battalion (b.1907, Edinburgh)
Formerly a 'corporal in his Majesty's Brigade of Guards', Fry had served in India and China in the 1930s before returning to Edinburgh where he worked as a shoe maker. 'A tall ... good-looking man ... he had ... very little formal education, but had a natural genius for organization and ... was an exceedingly pleasant man to talk to.'[13]

Gálicz, János, 'Gal' – Colonel, XV Brigade (b. c.1890, Hungary)
A naturalized Russian of Austro-Hungarian birth, Gal 'had distinguished himself in the revolution' in Hungary and had joined the Red Army in 1919. Sent to Spain in 1936 by order of Stalin, he had acquired the nickname Gal and a reputation of being a man who had 'an easy, pleasant manner ... [but also] ... a passion for orders of an arbitrary kind'.[14]

Garber, Joseph – Private, 2nd Company, British Battalion (b.1911, Bethnal Green)
One of several London Jews with the battalion, Garber won a Royal Humane Society Medal when he was fourteen for saving a man who fell into the Thames. He later went on to join the Merchant Navy before volunteering for service in Spain.

Gregory, Walter – Runner, 3rd Company, British Battalion (b. *c*.1915, Nottingham)
A brewery worker and member of the Communist Party, Gregory had fought Mosley's Black Shirts at fascist rallies in Nottingham. He was delighted when he was approached by the local Party organizer and asked to volunteer for Spain.

Gurney, Jason – Battalion Scout, British Battalion (b.1910, Sheringham, Norfolk)
Raised in South Africa, after leaving school Gurney found work on a Norwegian steamer and returned to Europe. In Paris he studied art at the Académie Colarossi before moving back to the country of his birth, where he worked as a sculptor out of a Kings Road garret in Chelsea before volunteering for service in Spain.

Hilliard, Robert – Private, 1st Company, British Battalion (b.1904, Moyeightragh, nr Killarney)
A Trinity College graduate, Olympic boxer, father of three and parish priest, the 'Boxing Parson' was 'one of the most amusing characters' in the battalion. Gurney, a friend of Hilliard's who served alongside him, remembered him as 'a great drinker' who was well liked for 'his sense of humour and consistently cheerful attitude'.[15]

Hyndman, Tony – Private, Company Unknown, British Battalion (b. *c*.1915, Cardiff)
An ex-Welsh Guardsman, Hyndman was formerly the secretary and lover of Stephen Spender, whom the poet referred to in his memoirs as 'Jimmy Younger'. He was not cut out for service in Spain and hated it from the start.

Jones, John 'Bosco' – Private, 4th Company, British Battalion (b. *c*.1917, London)
A veteran of the battle of Cable Street, Jones left for Spain after leaving a note for his sister. He carried a single suitcase and wore a 'nice, neat overcoat'. 'I looked a bit like a tourist,' he later confessed.[16]

Leeson, George – Lieutenant, 2nd Company, British Battalion (b.1907, County Cork)
Born into a 'comfortable middle class ... devout Roman Catholic [family]', Leeson joined the Royal Navy and served as a riverboat gunner in China. Later

he became a London Underground worker and Transport Union member before volunteering for service in Spain.[17]

Levy, Bert 'Yank' – NCO, 2nd Company, British Battalion (b.1897, Hamilton, Ontario)
'One of Fry's best men', Levy had already had an adventurous life before travelling to Spain. A chauffeur and printer by trade, he first saw action in the Great War, serving as a machine gunner in the Jewish Legion in the Jordan Valley in 1918. Two years later he was fighting alongside anti-government rebels in Mexico and later worked as a 'fund raiser' for Nicaraguan revolutionaries, a role which saw him imprisoned in the US for six years for armed robbery.[18]

Macartney, Wilfred – Battalion Commander, British Battalion (b.1899, Malta)
A veteran of the Great War, Macartney was arrested for spying for the Soviet Union in 1927. Upon his release from prison in 1936, the publication of his memoirs gained him respect amongst the far left and he was later appointed as the first commander of the British Battalion in Spain. His time in the role was short lived, however. He was replaced by Wintringham in early February 1937.

Maley, James – Private, 2nd Company, British Battalion (b.1908, Glasgow)
A lifelong Celtic fan, Maley left his native Glasgow for Cleveland, Ohio in 1929 to work in a car factory, but returned to Scotland after just one year. He later served in the Territorial Army and worked for the Communist Party as a soapbox orator before volunteering for Spain in late 1936.[19]

Marty, André – Base Commander of International Brigade Headquarters (HQ), Albacete (b.1886, Perpignan, France)
Having risen to prominence for his part in the French fleet's Black Sea mutiny of 1919, Marty was appointed to a leading role in the International Brigades by Stalin. 'Both a sinister and ridiculous figure', Marty's paranoia deepened as the war progressed.[20]

McDade, Alex – Sergeant Major, British Battalion (b.1905, Glasgow)
'A prodigious liar and a natural clown', part 'orderly officer', part 'jester', and part 'mascot', wee McDade 'was the most popular man in the battalion and the only one who could get discipline'.[21]

Meredith, Bill – Private, 2nd Company, British Battalion (b. *c.*1910, Bellingham, Northumberland)
A member of the Northumberland Labour Party, Meredith was well-liked by his comrades and would perform well under fire.

Nathan, George – Assistant Chief of Staff (b.1895, London)
A veteran of the Great War who also fought with the Black and Tans in Ireland, Nathan commanded the British 1st Company at Lopera and Las Rozas. He was 'a lean figure with a pipe and walking stick ... [whose] accent was sometimes too gentlemanly to be real. He swanked ... but ... proved himself a first rate soldier.'[22]

Overton, Bert – 4th Company Commander, British Battalion (b.1905, Stockton-on-Tees)
One of the battalion's few apoliticals, Overton was an ex-Welsh Guard who performed well in training and 'still looked the part', but was later revealed to be 'a fool, a romantic, [and] a bluffer'. He 'wanted to be courageous, but had lived too easily, too softly'.[23]

Pollitt, Harry – Head of the Communist Party of Great Britain (CPGB) (b.1890, Droylsden, Lancashire)
'A smallish, balding individual, with small dark eyes which looked as though he had never smiled in his life', Pollitt was a deeply serious man and utterly committed to the communist cause.[24] He oversaw the running of the battalion from his offices in London's King Street and his work would take him to Spain on three occasions during the war.

Prendergast, Jim – Private, 1st Company, British Battalion (b.1914, Dublin)
Born of working class parents, Prendergast had worked from the age of fourteen as a machinist in a mineral water factory in Dublin, before leaving for Spain. He saw action at Lopera and Las Rozas before joining the battalion.

Romilly, Giles – Private, Company Unknown, British Battalion (b.1916, London)
A nephew of Winston Churchill and Oxford undergraduate, Romilly was 'a very pleasant and unpretentious character ... who had come to Spain out of a spirit of bravado rather than from any deep political conviction'.[25]

Ryan, Frank – Assistant Commissar, XV Brigade (b.1902, County Limerick).
An IRA activist and 'ardent catholic' who was 'experienced in leading banned demonstrations in Ireland'.[26]

Sexton, Cyril – Private, 2nd Company, British Battalion (b.1914)
A self-confessed 'non-political', Sexton left school aged sixteen to work as a junior clerk and shop assistant, but his true passion was for all things military. In 1936 he toured the battlefields of northern Europe, and was visiting Waterloo when he learnt of the outbreak of war in Spain.

Sprigg (Caudwell), Christopher – Private, 3rd Company, British Battalion (b.1907, London)
A prolific writer, Sprigg had published several novels, volumes of poetry and Marxist cultural and scientific studies including his best known work, *Illusion and Reality*, before volunteering for Spain. Known to his friends as 'Spriggy', he was 'an exceedingly modest, pleasant man' and a close friend of Clem Beckett.[27]

Thomas, Frank – Sergeant, 6th *Bandera* Foreign Legion (b.1914, Pontypridd)
Born into a middle class family, Frank Thomas was one of just a dozen Britons who fought for Franco. A conservative who was convinced that communism posed a grave threat to civilization, Thomas joined the Nationalists due to his disgust with the apparent anarchy of the government forces in Spain.

Watters, George – Private, 2nd Company, British Battalion (b.1904, Prestonpans, East Lothian)
A former miner who was barred from the pit following an active role in the General Strike of 1926, Watters was arrested for challenging Oswald Mosley at a British Union of Fascists rally at Edinburgh's Usher Hall.

Wild, Sam – Battalion Armourer, 1st Company, British Battalion (b. *c*.1910, Manchester)
'A quick-witted, devil may care' Mancunian with Irish roots, Wild had started work as a labourer at the age of ten to support his family. Later he joined the Royal Navy before volunteering for service in Spain.[28]

Wintringham, Tom – Captain, British Battalion (b.1898, Grimsby, Lincolnshire)

The product of 'a well known liberal family' and a veteran of the Great War, Wintringham 'was cool, quick in deciding who did what' and had a 'wry sense of humour'. He was 'invariably pleasant, informal and unpretentious' with the men, but his steel-framed spectacles ... high domed bald head and ... academic stoop' gave him more of the air of a kindly schoolmaster than a soldier. After a brief period of service as a machine-gun instructor and unofficial second-in-command, Wintringham took over the leadership of the British Battalion in early February 1937.[29]

PART ONE
'A CROWD OF BOY SCOUTS'

*No man is an island entire of itself; every man is a piece
of the continent, a part of the main; if a clod be washed
away by the sea, Europe is the less, as well as if a
promontory were, as well as any manner of thy friends
or of thine own were; any man's death diminishes me,
because I am involved in mankind. And therefore never
send to know for whom the bell tolls; it tolls for thee.*

JOHN DONNE, 'DEVOTIONS UPON EMERGENT OCCASIONS', 1624

*My first battle was the bloodiest of the whole war,
at Jarama, near Madrid. Oh, it was horrible.*

JOE GARBER, 2ND COMPANY, BRITISH BATTALION, XV INTERNATIONAL BRIGADE

CHAPTER 1
FIRST BLOOD
(5.30–10.00AM, 12 FEBRUARY 1937)

We should have known it all already from those bitter books about the First World War which we had read with such envious avidity. But because Siegfried Sassoon and Wilfred Owen, Remarque and Barbusse, had not convinced us that war is dull and dispiriting: still less could they have persuaded us that our own war might disillusion us. In fact it seems to me now that our picture of war was as falsely romantic, in its different way, as anything which had stirred the minds of Edwardian boys, brought up on Henty and the heroics of minor imperial campaigns. The desolate No-Man's-Land pictures of Paul Nash; Bernard Partridge cartoons of the Kaiser; songs from Cavalcade and the compassionate poems of Wilfred Owen had made a powerful, complex and stimulating impression on us, so that we felt less pity than envy of a generation which had experienced so much. Even in the Anti-War campaigns of the early thirties we were half in love with the horrors which we cried out against, and, as a boy, I can remember murmuring the name 'Passchendaele' in an ecstasy of excitement and regret.[1]

Colonel Gal was in a foul mood. The XV Brigade's British Battalion should have been in position by now, but as he drove up to the Cookhouse in the pre-dawn light only Captain Tom Wintringham and a handful of scouts were visible. 'Where are your men?' the Hungarian demanded. 'All round us,' Wintringham replied. On closer inspection Gal could make out several knots of volunteers

The British Battalion's Area of Operations: 5.30am, 12 February 1937

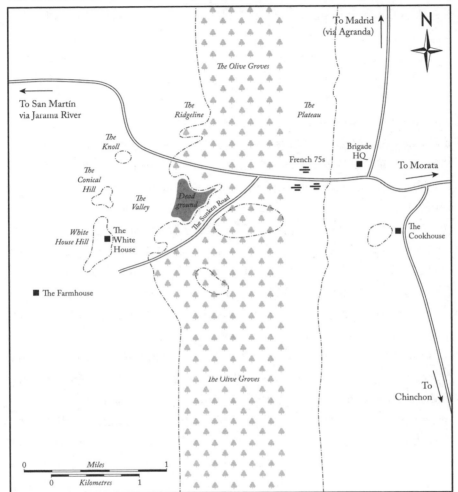

sheltering under the olive trees to the west of the track.[2] Exhausted following their drive from Chinchon, some had fallen asleep without bothering to remove their boots. Others, wrapped in blankets to escape the cold, nursed mugs of scalding hot coffee or tore into hunks of brown bread handed out by the hulking figure of the chef, 'Tiny' Silverman. Grunting his satisfaction, Gal barked a command to his driver and the staff car sped off to the north. Wintringham smiled to himself: so far everything was going according to plan. Calling for his scouts to board a lorry and follow him, the Balliol graduate climbed onto the back of his motorcycle. Before the battalion moved out, he would need to take a look at the ground they had to hold. Revving his engine, his driver headed west towards the sound of heavy guns.[3]

The Cookhouse was a sprawling old villa commandeered as Battalion HQ. Twin doors, wide enough to permit a wagon to enter, led into a shady courtyard overlooked by a row of balconies. Jason Gurney, a twenty-seven year-old South African sculptor who had arrived with Wintringham the day before, thought it a fascinating building. Before the war, it had been the country retreat of Borgaria, a liberal cartoonist who worked for the Madrid-based daily *El Sol* and his satirical paintings still covered the walls. 'The majority were anti-clerical, all rather bawdy and extremely funny,' Gurney recalled. In the grounds were a number of outhouses, including a vast *bodega* lined with forty ceramic vats, complete with cavernous wine cellars cut into the hillside. As the scouts and cooks of the British Battalion had been in residence for a little over twelve hours, the villa was in 'the filthiest and most bedraggled' state. Anything not nailed down had been looted, the murals had been defaced and the dry, white, chalky soil of the groves had been trodden through its halls.[4]

Beyond the walls of the villa was a cluster of volunteers from the heavy machine-gun company. Hassbrook, the battalion's sole Dutchman, was deep in conversation with Bill Meredith, a well-liked young man from Bellingham in Northumberland who by virtue of a few words of French and German was the only man in the section able to understand him. Hassbrook was demonstrating how a sundial could be constructed from a couple of sticks stuck in the dry ground.[5] As Meredith looked on, he was distracted by a dull hum. At first it barely registered over the rumble of lorries bringing men to the front, but then it steadily built into an ear-splitting roar. High overhead a lone Nationalist bomber came into sight. For most of the British volunteers dispersed round the Cookhouse it was the first time they had seen the enemy. Although they had had little time for training, their commanders had at least managed to instil a healthy respect for the power of aviation. Scattering throughout the groves, the men took cover.

Kit Conway, the commander of the 1st Company, was amused by his comrades' panicked response. Unlike those cowering around him, it was not the first time that the forty year-old had been under aerial attack. On the first morning of the battle of Lopera three months before, Conway had seen Nathan Segal, a young Jew from Walthamstow, killed when an enemy biplane had strafed their position. Lopera had been terrifying, but, as Conway realized, the lone bomber at Jarama posed no such threat. The pilot was far too high to spot them and, besides, his mission was to destroy the government's supply dumps at Morata de Tajuña, not worry about a few hundred infantry several miles behind the lines.[6] 'Highly intelligent, articulate and humorous', Conway was popular with his men.[7] Like several of his compatriots in the battalion, he had learned his trade with the Irish Republican Army (IRA). After a jail term for his role in the Irish conflict of 1918–23 and a period of self-imposed exile in the United States, Conway had returned to Dublin, found work as a builder and joined the Communist Party. He was a dedicated adherent and soon became one of its 'most effective proselytisers'.[8] Upon learning of the Nationalist uprising in Spain, Conway had immediately known where his destiny lay.[9]

Beside Conway were two of his countrymen, Jim Prendergast and Paddy Duff. Prendergast had believed that the battalion was about to take part in the Republic's first large offensive, but, as Conway now explained, the Nationalists had already pre-empted the move. For the last six days, four columns of infantry had been advancing from the west. Initially all opposition had scattered before them, but on 9 February, when they had reached the western bank of the Jarama, Republican militia, backed by the XI and XII International Brigades, had managed to hold them. This, as far as Conway was aware, was the current situation. If the bridges over the river were captured, however, only a few miles of rising land would stand between the Nationalists and Madrid's final uncut lifeline, the Valencia road. The British Battalion and the other reinforcements that had been rushed up to the front were to prevent this happening at all costs.[10]

As Conway explained the situation a group of Brigade staff officers passed by. Prendergast, a Dubliner who had worked as a machinist in a mineral water factory, noticed his friend Frank Ryan amongst them. A tall, heavily built man, whose small head 'sunk into his shoulders', the thirty-four year-old was sporting a steel helmet for the first time since he had arrived in Spain.[11] Having despaired of ever finding one small enough to fit him, Ryan had resorted to sitting on a spare until he had crushed it into shape. 'We'll need them boys,' he said. 'It's hell up there, and we're in for a tough fight.'[12] As Ryan continued up the road, the Irishmen were joined by three more of their compatriots, Ted Bourne, Dick O'Neill and Dan Boyle. The latter, a boy from Belfast, was in a buoyant mood. John Tunnah, the battalion postmaster, had just done his rounds and Boyle had received a packet of Woodbines from home. If there was one thing the volunteers missed it was British cigarettes. The only smokes in Spain were made of loosely packed bone-dry leaves. Known as 'anti-tanks', they induced a coughing fit in anyone desperate enough to try them. As Boyle handed round the Woodbines, cheerily telling his comrades to smoke up as he might be dead before he could finish them, he read aloud from a newspaper from home which had prematurely printed his obituary. Boyle and the others thought it a great joke, but before the day was out, three of them would be wounded and one would be killed.[13]

Two miles to the west, Captain Wintringham and his scouts were standing on a ridgeline overlooking the Jarama valley. Although the early morning air was cold, the brilliant sunshine and the climb up from the road had warmed them. Jason Gurney, the South African sculptor, was busy drawing sketches of the landscape spread out beneath him. Beyond the ridge, the land fell sharply to a grassy valley, dominated by two small hills. The one to the left was wooded and capped by a white farmhouse. The other, named the Conical Hill, was covered in light scrub. To the west of the hills the ground sloped unevenly two miles down to the river. To the north was the road they had followed from the Cookhouse, beyond which lay the olive groves where the Franco-Belgians and Dimitrovs, two of the other battalions of the XV Brigade, would soon take up position. Around 15 miles away on the north-west horizon, framed by the snow-capped peaks of the Sierra de Guadarrama, the buildings of central Madrid sparkled through the early morning haze.[14]

Aside from the scouting party, the landscape was deserted. The local peasants had long since moved out and the Nationalists were still consolidating their position by the river. Occasionally lone bullets whipped overhead and the crump of three French 75s positioned halfway up the road to the Cookhouse could be heard, but Gurney and Archibald Francis, a fellow scout and

Communist Party member from Hackney, barely looked up from their work. Wintringham was also unmoved. It was not the first time the thirty-nine year-old had been under fire. Half a lifetime before, on his eighteenth birthday, he had joined the Royal Flying Corps. Although his poor eyesight prevented him from becoming a pilot, he had served as a mechanic and despatch rider attached to the Balloon Corps and seen action during the First World War at Vimy Ridge in April 1917. The following year, whilst at Balliol College, Wintringham had discovered communism, a passion which led to a career as a journalist with the Party's London-based newssheet, *The Daily Worker*. In August 1936 he was despatched to Barcelona as a war correspondent, but grew frustrated with the job as it kept him far from the front line. In December he resigned and joined the International Brigades. With his 'round, steel-framed spectacles ... bald head and ... academic stoop', Gurney thought his captain resembled the scholar he had once been more than the soldier he had since become.[15] The observation was a valid one. Inside, Wintringham was plagued by self-doubt.[16]

Looking back to the road, Wintringham noticed Colonel Gal and his aides walking towards him. Tall, well-built and dressed in a peaked cap and creaking leather coat, Gal was an imposing figure who had served as a lieutenant in the Austro-Hungarian Army during the Great War. In 1916 he had been taken prisoner by the Russians on the eastern front, later became a communist in captivity and then joined the revolution.[17] After graduating from the Frunze Military Academy, Gal had been ordered to travel to Spain. 'Gruff' and 'grim-faced', the forty-eight year-old veteran had no time for courtesies. 'You will advance at once in this direction,' he commanded Wintringham, indicating a 'heavy blue pencil line' scrawled on a map unburdened by scale or accuracy.[18] Two other lines, drawn to the north, showed where the Franco-Belgians would hold Wintringham's right flank, whilst the Balkan volunteers of the Dimitrov Battalion would remain in reserve.

As Gurney and Francis watched the improvised conference, the latter was struck by a stray bullet. 'God! I've been hit!' he cried, grasping his shattered left arm as blood poured down his coat. Veterans of the Great War, the officers soon turned back to their maps. Gurney, on the other hand, was fascinated by his comrade's misfortune. He had never seen anyone shot before and thought the whole thing 'faintly improper'. There they were, in perfect isolation on a glorious spring morning, when all of a sudden their polite little gathering had been interrupted by an anonymous soldier several miles away. After patching him up with a temporary splint and field dressing, Gurney sent Francis to the rear with a passing despatch rider. From that moment on, things would move quickly. The South African would never see his friend again.[19]

Having concluded his conference with Gal, Wintringham raced back to the Cookhouse to brief his company commanders. Lieutenants Bill Briskey, a Great War veteran, London bus-driver and trade union man, and Bert Overton, a thirty-two year-old ex-Welsh Guards officer from Stockton, were to lead the advance. The former, in charge of the 3rd Company, would hold the open left flank whilst the latter, heading the 4th, was to take up position in the centre. Both were ordered to halt and form line when they reached the ridge where Francis had been hit. Lieutenant Conway's 1st Company, at 143 strong the largest of the four, was to take the right flank, but keep 500 yards behind the first line. The Irishman's disgust was clear when told that his men would act as a reserve. Nevertheless, he nodded his assent. Commanding the 2nd, or Machine-gun Company, Lieutenant Harry Fry, a tall, handsome Scot, whose career in His Majesty's Brigade of Guards had taken him to India and China, was told to give the others a ten-minute head start before following. Having received their orders, the company commanders bellowed at their men to fall in. The shout was taken up by the section and group leaders and the volunteers scrambled to their feet.[20]

Within minutes, 500 men were lined up on the road. They were an incongruous group. The youngest, Ronnie Burgess, was just seventeen, whilst the eldest, George Bright, was fifty-six. Most were single, but a few, such as Francis Casey, a Glaswegian father of seven, had left wives and children to travel to Spain. The vast majority were city bred. Large contingents came from Dublin, Belfast, Glasgow, Liverpool, Newcastle and Manchester. Others were from London, with a bias towards King's Cross and the Jewish East End. Amongst the Scots, Irish and English were thirty Welshmen, including George Fretwell, an unemployed quarryman, Willie Lloyd and Bob Condon, best friends from the village of Aberaman, and Tony Hyndman, a former Guardsman from Cardiff. Fifty were Irish and 100 were Scots. Most of the rest were English, although there was also a smattering of other nationalities. As well as Gurney, the South African scout, there were a dozen London-based Cypriots led by Panayiotis Katsaranos, a forty year-old 'veteran of the Greco-Turkish War and four revolutions'; Hassbrook, the Dutchman from the 2nd Company; his Australian section commanders, Ted Dickenson and Ron 'Aussie' Hurd; 'Yank' Levy, a forty year-old Canadian machine gunner who had served time in the US for armed robbery; two New Zealanders from Hawke's Bay; André Diamant, an Egyptian Jew who had been studying in Cairo; a boy from Jamaica; and 'great hump-shouldered Manuel', a Cuban sailor who had inexplicably been assigned to the battalion back at the International Brigade headquarters (HQ) in Albacete.[21]

Ninety per cent of the battalion were working class. Many had been miners, labourers, sailors or dock workers. Others had mastered trades, such as Sidney Silvert, a twenty-two year-old tailor, and Basil Abrahams, a baker from Hackney.[22] The rest were from more privileged backgrounds. Amongst them were a novelist, a poet, an artist, a priest, a cartoonist and an actor. United by their cause, the two groups got on well. In Briskey's 3rd Company were Clem Beckett, a thirty-six year-old former speedway champion from Oldham, and his good friend Christopher Saint John Sprigg. Whilst Beckett's background was working class, Sprigg was a university-educated academic and the author of *Illusion and Reality*, 'a super-technical … frightfully fundamental, very revolutionary and disgustingly erudite' piece of literary criticism.[23] Another of Beckett's friends was Noel Carrit, the son of an Oxford don. After attending the Dragon Public School, Carrit had studied at Oriel College where he had set up the October Club, the university's first communist society.[24]

Clem Beckett was not the only British sportsman of merit. Also present were Bobby Quail of South Hylton, a weight lifting champion, and Clifford Lawther, 'a well-known North East amateur boxer'.[25]

Whilst most of those outside of the 1st Company had little military experience, a few had served with the British armed forces in the inter-war years. Leonard Bibby, a twenty-five year-old with the 2nd Company, had been a corporal in the Territorials and John Cameron, a heavy drinker of bourgeois extraction, had served as an officer in the regulars for several years. Others were Great War veterans, including Wintringham, Alex McDade, the battalion sergeant major, George Aitken, the political commissar, Bill Briskey, the commander of the 3rd Company, and Harold King, a stretcher bearer who had fought at the second battle of Ypres twenty-two years before.

Whilst most were highly political, there were a few exceptions. Cyril Sexton and Charley Hart, a reservist in the Royal Sussex Regiment, were adventurers and apoliticals who had become 'muckers' after mutually confessing their lack of zeal during the train ride through France.[26] Of equally dubious motivation was Alfred Chowney, a thirty-five year-old veteran of the Great War who had fallen on hard times. Unable to find work as a bricklayer, by late 1936 Chowney had been reduced to pawning his old war medals and sleeping in Salvation Army shelters. When he heard that men with military experience would be paid to serve in Spain he had volunteered without hesitation. Another apolitical was Lieutenant Bert Overton, the commander of the 4th Company. After a chance meeting at the Communist Party's recruiting offices in London in late 1936, where both had gone to volunteer, Tony Hyndman, an old comrade from Overton's British Army days, had come to doubt his friend's political credentials. That afternoon in Lyons, 'a huge anonymous acre of tearoom' in Marble Arch, Hyndman's suspicions had been confirmed.[27] What he had no way of realizing, however, was that Overton was a coward, unfit for front line service. As he lined his men up on the road at Jarama, his nerves had already begun to fray. Over the next three days, the decision to entrust him with a company would end in disaster.

Aside from these few exceptions, the vast majority of the volunteers were highly politicized and utterly committed to the cause. Over half were members of the Communist Party of Great Britain (CPGB). Others were liberals, socialists, Marxists, trade union members, anarchists and Trotskyites. All were anti-fascists, convinced that if their enemies were not stopped in Spain, Britain and the rest of free Europe would be next. Disgusted by their government's policy of Non-Intervention, many had crossed the line from political protest to direct action long before travelling to Spain. The most obvious target had been

Oswald Mosley's British Union of Fascists (BUF). Walter Gregory, a runner from Briskey's 3rd Company, had had his nose broken after barracking a Black Shirt meeting in his home town of Nottingham; Jack Coward, a tall, lean Scouse docker known as 'Snowy' for his prematurely grey hair, had made a dash for Mosley at a rally in Liverpool in October 1936; and Donald Renton, the 2nd Company's political commissar, had begun singing the *Internationale* at a meeting in Edinburgh as soon as the fascist leader took the stage.[28]

Others, like David Crook, a former member of the Officer Training Corps (OTC) who had studied at Cheltenham College, John 'Bosco' Jones, a Londoner from the 4th Company, and Tom Spiller, one of the battalion's two New Zealanders, had been at Mosley's biggest defeat – the battle of Cable Street – when 300,000 anti-fascists had kept the BUF from marching through the East End. Ordered to clear the route, mounted police had charged the 'Reds' and the protest had degenerated into a brawl. 'This cop came at me,' Spiller recalled, 'murder in his eye and a baton up in the air. I let him have a straight bloody left right in the mush.'[29] Unfortunately for Spiller, the 'cop' was a divisional inspector. The New Zealander was convicted of inciting a riot and assaulting a police officer, but by January 1937 had been released and was on his way to Spain. Others had been arrested for their role in the General Strike of 1926 or the Jarrow Hunger March a decade later. As one volunteer would later write, 'you have to believe in something, in a cause that will make the world a better place, or you have wasted your life'.[30] The men of the British Battalion knew what they were fighting for – to strike a blow against international fascism, to free Spain and to pave the way for a free Europe – and they were willing to lay down their lives to achieve it.

CHAPTER 2

DEPARTURES
(NOVEMBER–DECEMBER 1936)

It is easy to see now that the Spanish Civil War was, from the very beginning, the tragic, drawn-out death-agony of a political epoch. Once the Generals had made their revolt, they would eventually win it: once they had won it, a world war would be fought against fascist aggression, but not for anything which we had hoped for in 1936. And even at that time there was some sense that this was a last chance for the politics of Attempting the Good, as opposed to the subsequent politics of Avoiding the Worse. The political optimists were never more united in England, or more enthusiastic.[1]

For most of the volunteers, the journey to Spain had begun in the offices of the CPGB. Harry Pollitt, the deeply serious General Secretary, ran an efficient organization, but had little public backing or political clout. Ordered by the Comintern to organize recruitment for the International Brigades, Pollitt set about the task with typically authoritarian zeal. Initially, his selectors had not been fussy, but by November 1936, they started to refine their search. Led by 'Robbie' Robson, a veteran of the Great War, they favoured single men, preferably over the age of twenty-one and with military experience, and fellow party members were selected above all others. In Manchester, Maurice Levine was told he lacked the training. The refusal was particularly bitter as the same day another man was accepted. Levine recognized him immediately.

Clem Beckett was a champion speedway rider whose photo regularly appeared in the press.[2]

Another volunteer snapped up by the recruiters was William H. Ball, a twenty-one year-old receptionist who seemed tailor-made for service in the International Brigades. Having volunteered for the Officer Training Corps (OTC) whilst at Reading College, Ball had some military experience and was also a fine marksman: he had passed his rifle shooting qualification with an 'A' grade 'and was recognised as one of the best shots [to have emerged from] ... the school for a number of years'. Ball had also studied medicine at Middlesex hospital and spoke fluent French and Spanish. 'His father [Henry], seeing his mind was made up put no obstacle in his way and gave him all the help he could before he left for Spain.'[3]

In some areas, the Communist Party actively recruited. In November 1936 Walter Gregory, the runner from Briskey's 3rd Company who had tackled Mosley's thugs in Nottingham, was approached by the local party organizer. 'Wild with excitement', Gregory leapt at the chance. 'Here was somebody really asking *me* to do something important. I was over the moon, I thought it was absolutely marvellous.' His mother did not. 'She was astounded at what she considered my stupidity at going to fight in another nation's war, but having struggled unsuccessfully against my political involvement for so long, she came to accept ... [it] surprisingly quickly.'[4]

George Leeson's wife was less accommodating. 'You've got a good job,' she told the London Underground worker, 'Why give it up?' Leeson's parents, whom he would later describe as 'comfortable middle class types' and 'devout Roman Catholics', were equally adamant. 'You're ... wrong in taking part in other people's wars,' his father had warned him. 'None of you will ever come back alive.' But after Leeson had seen a newsreel of a Nationalist bombing raid on the outskirts of Madrid, there was no going back: '[I was] absolutely determined to go.'[5] Others were more worried about their family's reactions. Albert Charlesworth's mother had no idea her son was off to war until the day before his departure. Otherwise, he admitted, 'she'd have tried to stop me'.[6] In the valleys of Aberaman, Willie Lloyd's mother cried for days after he left, whilst the Londoner John 'Bosco' Jones didn't tell his parents about his intentions at all. Instead, he sent a note to his sister, packed a single bag and made his way to Victoria railway station. It was the opening scene of an adventure of a lifetime that he would never forget.[7]

Whilst some volunteers admitted to knowing virtually nothing about the situation in Spain, others were better informed. Tony Hyndman, the former Guardsman from Cardiff, was close friends with Giles Romilly, an Oxford undergraduate and nephew of Winston Churchill, whose brother, Esmond, the husband of Jessica Mitford, had fought with the XII Brigade during the defence of Madrid.[8] Looking for something more meaningful than student life, Romilly was determined to follow in his sibling's footsteps, whilst Hyndman, having recently split up with his boyfriend, the poet Stephen Spender, went along for the ride. The day they applied, 'the party recruiting office [in Kings Street, London] was crowded' with would-be volunteers, but as Hyndman had served in the Welsh Guards and Romilly claimed to have been in the OTC they were both accepted straight away. After being given the money for the journey to Paris they were told to report to Victoria Station later that month. Romilly's parents took the news in their stride. His father, a retired colonel who had served in the Great War, suggested that they 'go to the Army and Navy [stores]' and 'get ... well kitted out with the best boots they have, besides a good supply of their warmest underwear', whilst Romilly's mother presented Hyndman with 'the longest scarf' he had ever seen. 'I knitted it myself,' she informed him. 'It is to be worn next to your skin, around your stomach, to keep you warm.' On the day they left, Hyndman's former lover turned up at Victoria to wave goodbye. Just before the train pulled out, 'Stephen handed me thirty one-pound notes, in case ... I changed my mind and wanted to get back home'. Then the whistle blew and, with a cry of '*Viva España!*', their odyssey began.[9]

Jason Gurney, Wintringham's South African scout, had also set off from Victoria. After tea with his mother and a farewell drink with friends, he boarded the train with fifteen others. In contrast to Romilly and Hyndman's departure, the atmosphere had been subdued: it was a miserable morning, cold and drizzling and no-one had come to see them off. 'We had ... been brought up on horror stories of the 1914–18 war and none of us felt too happy about our prospects,' Gurney explained.[10]

The departure of the Glaswegians who would form the basis of Harry Fry's machine-gun company, on the other hand, had been distinctly more upbeat. Early one morning in December 1936, three double-decker buses drew up in George Square. Amongst those who climbed on board was James Maley, a twenty-nine year-old former soap box orator, dedicated communist and football fanatic. Peering out of the window, he waved at the cheering crowds. Maley was having a great time. 'It was like a Celtic supporters' outing,' he recalled.[11]

After reaching the south coast, the volunteers took the ferry to France. The tickets, which had been paid for by the Communist Party, cost 'ten bob'. Although serving in Spain was not to be outlawed until late January 1937 when Prime Minister Baldwin rushed a bill through parliament, the men still had to be wary of the police. Several were questioned and Hector Crake, an unemployed man from Houghton-le-Spring who had walked and hitch-hiked his way from London to the south coast, was turned back: 'When [I was] about to go on the boat, I was stopped by Scotland Yard officers, who told me that as I had not sufficient money to maintain myself, I would not be allowed to land at Boulogne.' The boat carrying Crake's eleven companions left without him. After waiting for six hours, he attempted to board the next ferry only to be turned back once again.[12]

For those who had served in the Great War, the Channel crossing brought back painful memories. The last time they had left England, many of those travelling with them had not returned. As the coastline slipped out of view, they wondered if they would ever see home again.[13] However, for several of the younger volunteers, the journey was hopelessly exciting and offered an opportunity to get drunk. Having been put in charge of the group he was travelling with, Gurney felt it was his responsibility to make sure matters did not get out of hand. 'I tried to keep them all in the same bar so that, drunk or sober, I knew where they all were.' The men were less than grateful for his efforts. 'They thought that I was being pompous and officious, but finally I got them all onto the train [to Paris] where they collapsed.'[14]

From the Gare du Nord, the volunteers took taxis to the Bureau des Syndicats, the French Communist Party's headquarters in Montmartre, where they would stay for a few days before travelling to Perpignan in southern

France. The taxi drivers realized who they were immediately. They 'were all Red enthusiasts,' Gurney recalled. Refusing to take the volunteers' money, they dropped them at the Bureau, wished them luck and waved goodbye. Inside 'was a scene of feverish activity and a babble of different languages.' It was the assembly point for volunteers from all across Europe and gave the British a taste of what awaited them in Spain.[15]

Whilst in Paris the volunteers were given a medical examination, a test of political affiliation and a lecture on the perils they were about to face. They were then given an opportunity to turn back. One of those to embrace it was in George Leeson's group. The Londoner thought that the man in question was 'a bit of a braggart': on the ferry to Dieppe he had pulled a Great War trench periscope out of his coat pocket, boasting that it would 'come in useful when we get out there'. Once in Paris his bravado had failed him. On the day they were due to depart for the south, the men had arranged to meet at the station. The 'braggart' never arrived and the group left without him. Leeson didn't bear a grudge: it was too serious an undertaking for hard feelings.[16] Following the speech at the Communist Party headquarters, Tom Spiller, one of the battalion's two New Zealanders, also got cold feet. 'I was 26 and [thought that] soon I was going to be dead.' Nevertheless, he believed that he had already gone too far to turn back. 'He said he didn't have the courage to drop out,' a friend later recalled; 'he'd cut his ties with home and [had] told his parents he was off to war.'[17]

On their first night in Paris, Cyril Sexton's group shared double beds in a cheap hotel. 'That night,' Sexton recalled, '[William] Ball [the crack shot from Reading] taught me the tune and words of the *Internationale*'. Sexton would come to know the anthem well in the next few months.[18]

For Jason Gurney, Paris presented an opportunity for 'one last touch with the world in which I had lived'. After a bath and a shave, he rang friends who lived in the city and went out for the night. Having studied sculpture at the Académie Colarossi, the South African knew Paris well and was happy to be back in town. The next afternoon, after a meal and several rounds of drinks, his group left for Perpignan from Gare Austerlitz. Two hundred volunteers of thirty nationalities were there. 'The departure of the "Red Train" had become one of the sights of Paris,' Gurney explained; 'there was no secrecy and crowds with banners came to wave us off.'[19] Exhausted after all the excitement, David Crook, the Cheltenham graduate later assigned to the 1st Company, fell asleep on the overhead luggage rack.[20]

For most of the men, the journey was tremendously exciting as very few had ever left Britain before. Cyril Sexton, however, was an exception. In the summer of 1936, he had toured the battlefields of France and Belgium, visiting Ypres, Vimy Ridge, Arras and Waterloo.[21]

Several hours after leaving Paris, the men arrived at the border town of Perpignan, where Walter Gregory was delighted to receive a hot meal for the first time in days. The Nottinghamshire man was unimpressed with French cuisine. '[The] food was much too oily and far too heavily flavoured with garlic for a palate accustomed ... to simple English fare.'[22] Some of the volunteers inscribed their names into the trunk of a giant palm which stood in the grounds of the local hospital. The bark was lacerated with dozens of signatures of the volunteers who had passed through before.[23]

From Perpignan, the British continued their journey by bus to Figueras in Spain. Although later volunteers would have to sneak across the Pyrenees by goat trails under cover of darkness, the pioneers had an easier ride. The French Popular Front government, headed by Léon Blum, tacitly supported the Spanish Republic and many gendarmes turned a blind eye until Non-Intervention forced them to tighten up controls in February 1937. George Watters, one of the Glaswegian contingent, remembered just how simple the border crossing had been. Although all travellers were supposed to have valid passports, the policemen who boarded his bus were satisfied with a quick look at just one man's documents and then waved the vehicle on. 'They were obviously all sympathetic and knew what was happening,' Watters recalled.[24] Jason Gurney remembered a much more distressing event. Whilst the gendarmes were inspecting the papers of the men on the bus in front, one of his party stood up and started screaming 'I don't want to go! I don't want to go!' Worried about unwanted attention, Gurney 'hit him on the point of the jaw and he dropped'. The man cried a lot that night, but to the South African's relief, he 'seemed to be quite content thereafter and never held it against me'.[25]

Once in Figueras, the volunteers were quartered in the Castell de Sant Ferran, 'a magnificent ... [Napoleonic] fortress which had served as an army base for many years'.[26] On his first morning, Walter Gregory was taken on a tour by the Spanish troops stationed there. 'They proudly showed us ... the dungeon in which their own officers, who had thrown in their lot with Franco, had been cornered and killed ... [by a] well directed hand-grenade.' Their 'blood ... had left dark stains on the ... walls'.[27]

The volunteers were dazzled by the array of nationalities at Figueras. Amongst others, there were Frenchmen, Belgians, North Americans, Serbians and Czechs, Italians, Germans, Japanese, Chinese, Cubans and Colombians. John Henderson, a twenty-five year-old cabinet maker from Gateshead, decided that the occasion warranted a souvenir. 'I had a Spanish fan [with] ... twenty-four blades, each of which I had signed by a volunteer from a different country. Twenty-four nationalities and I swear one of them was Icelandic!'[28] Although some of the Germans and French spoke English, communication between the different nationalities was limited. Apart from the marksman, William Ball, Sam Wild, 'a quick-witted, devil may care Manchester Irish merchant seaman', was one of the few able to speak any Spanish at all.[29] Having learnt a little during his navy days in South America, Wild was amused to be considered 'a linguist of some distinction' by his peers.[30]

The morning after Jason Gurney's arrival at Figueras was Christmas Day. The weather was cold and crisp and there were beautiful views across the Pyrenees. 'Far away ... we could see the white capped mountains standing clear against the intense blue of the sky. It was a scene before which we could only stand silent and awed.'[31] After a parade, the men were dismissed. As the communists who ran the base 'neither recognized, nor approved of Christmas', Gurney decided to walk into town. In the plaza locals were selling 'long, thin, murderous-looking knives'. Gurney bought one before moving onto an 'evil smelling brothel... We all thought that it might be our last chance and it would be a pity to miss it,' he explained. 'The whores were ... amiable and motherly ... They fed us and patted us and told us we were fine brave kids.' The men were then taken upstairs. The whole episode left Gurney feeling distinctly unsatisfied. It 'was more reminiscent of the sick-room of a spoilt child being fussed over by Mummy ... than a sexual extravaganza as a prelude to war'.[32]

From Figueras, the volunteers travelled to Barcelona, 70 miles to the south-west. 'We were on ... [a] ramshackle train, clattering along at a snail's pace,' recalled David Crook. 'Everyone was in high spirits, singing and whistling revolutionary songs, including the *Internationale*.' When the men in his group started singing the hallowed hymn in the toilet, however, Crook decided that even youthful exuberance should have its limits. 'This struck me as out of place and I made it clear.'[33]

On arrival at Barcelona the volunteers were paraded through the city preceded by a military band. The Catalans spilled out onto the streets to receive them. 'There must have been half a million bloody people there.'[34] As they marched down *La Rambla* four abreast, the Reverend Robert Hilliard was struck by a face in the crowd. 'She was about four feet in height ... wore a brown shawl ... [and] carried a basket on her left arm,' he recalled. 'Her hand [was] clenched in the anti-fascist salute... She stood to attention as we passed ... her mouth was moving rapidly up and down, [and she was struggling to hold] ... back the tears.'[35] The Reverend Robert Hilliard was an extraordinary character. A communist, Trinity College graduate, Evangelical Christian, Olympic bantam weight boxer and family man whose daughter adored his bedtime stories softly voiced amidst aromas of 'tobacco and tweed', the Irishman had crammed several lifetimes of experience into his thirty-three years.[36] Jason Gurney thought he was 'one of the most amusing characters' in the battalion. Hilliard 'had developed the most startlingly irreverent manner', the South African explained. 'When in wine he would put on his parsonical voice and make a benediction ... in the name of Marx.'[37]

The volunteers found Barcelona 'deliriously' exciting. 'Everybody that I met was kind and helpful,' Gurney remembered. 'I ate and drank and made hundreds of undying friendships with people that I have never met since.'[38] Walter Gregory was even more enthusiastic. 'What a city!' he recalled. 'It was just like a volcano, erupting in all directions at the same time. [It was a] ... breathtaking awe-inspiring and heart-warming spectacle of noise, bustle, enthusiasm and gaiety. A revolutionary city in full flood of ... zest and zeal; an unforgettable sight.'[39]

The volunteers were not the only Britons enjoying Barcelona in January 1937. In the Lenin Barracks on the other side of town were thirty Independent Labour Party (ILP) members who had joined the POUM (Marxist Workers Party) militia. Amongst them was Eric Blair, a lanky, mop-haired individual who stood head and shoulders above his comrades. Although the ILP's military contribution in Spain would prove minimal, Blair, or George Orwell as he would come to be known, wrote a memoir, *Homage to Catalonia*, which would become one of the defining literary pieces of the war.[40]

Two days after arriving in Barcelona, Gurney's group boarded a train which took them 250 miles south-west to Albacete, the headquarters of the International Brigades. It was 'a delightful journey': the tracks hugged the coastline, with each twist and turn offering up marvellous views across the Mediterranean. The first night they slept on the wooden floor of a third class cabin and awoke on the outskirts of Valencia, which had been the seat of the Republican government ever since Largo Caballero had been persuaded to abandon a besieged Madrid in November 1936. The volunteers disembarked and once more were paraded through the city. In contrast to Barcelona, the local population seemed to lack revolutionary zeal. 'I began to feel that we were being used for a propaganda stunt,' Gurney recalled. 'There was little response in the streets and the whole affair was pretty much ... a flop.'[41]

The next stop was Albacete, where the volunteers were billeted in 'a large and gloomy barracks ... previously ... occupied by the Guardia Civil', a para-military police organization which had almost universally sided with Franco.[42] Again Walter Gregory was given a tour by grinning local militiamen of the scene of their oppressors' last stand, a bloodstained room reminiscent of the cellars at Figueras.[43] Afterwards the volunteers were paraded in the bullring and sorted into national groups. Gurney took an immediate dislike to the communist administrators who conducted the process. 'They lived in the guardhouse where they loafed around like a bunch of gangsters ... without any pretence at military discipline or any serious attempt to see that the barracks were properly maintained.'[44] In charge was 'a tall, proud, white-haired old man'.[45] This was André Marty, one of the most sinister figures of the Spanish Civil War. Having made his name as a leader of a naval mutiny, which had prevented the French from supplying the White Russians at a crucial stage in their struggle with the Bolsheviks nearly two decades before, Marty was a celebrated figure in communist circles. With Stalin's backing, he had risen to prominence in the Comintern and had been appointed Chief Political Commissar of the International Brigades. Like his omnipotent benefactor, Marty was paranoid, ruthless and insane. Influenced by the Moscow show trials then decimating Russia's high command at the height of the Terror, the Frenchman would become infamous for ruthlessly purging any Brigaders his fevered mind suspected of Trotskyist or fascist leanings.[46]

During the sorting process in the bullring, the volunteers were asked if they had any particular skills. Artillery men, cavalry, telephonists, electricians and motor mechanics were asked to step forward. Gurney thought his group's response was typically British. 'After a hurried colloquy, we decided that we would all sooner go into the poor bloody infantry, rather than get mixed up with a lot of foreigners,' he recalled. By way of farewell, André Marty delivered a speech in French, which the vast majority were unable to understand. The British then set out on the last leg of their journey to Madrigueras, a small village 20 miles to the north. After an hour traversing 'the bare featureless plain of Murcia', they arrived.[47] Stepping down from the back of their lorry, Tony Hyndman and Giles Romilly were approached by a tall young man, who took down their details in a notebook. This was John Lepper, 'a liberal anti-fascist' who was the product of public school and the OTC. With the formalities taken care of, he took the Welshman and his English friend to one side. With a conspiratorial nod, he uttered a memorable opening line: 'Welcome to the biggest shambles in Europe,' he said.[48]

CHAPTER 3

TRAINING

(MID-DECEMBER 1936–8 FEBRUARY 1937)

Madrigueras, the village where the battalion underwent its training, lay 170 miles south-east of Madrid. When Gurney had arrived in early January he had been far from impressed. 'It had never been much of a village,' the South African recalled.[1] Standing 'out in the middle of the bare, featureless, plain of Murcia', Madrigueras had just one main street intersected by numerous passageways running between the dwellings of the poor.[2] A light rain fell most days, the skies were dull and low grey clouds hung overhead. Many volunteers felt cheated by the weather. 'They had all seen the [pre-war tourism] posters,' one observer explained, and 'had the impression they were going to Sunny Spain'.[3] In the central plaza stood the ruins of a fire-gutted church. 'It was a very large building,' Gurney remembered, 'with a tower that could be seen for miles across the plain.' Inside were signs of the desecration that had been so widespread across Republican territory in the first weeks of the war. 'The sculptures had all been defaced' and shreds of tattered paintings hung on the walls.[4] Outside, by the village water trough, David Crook, the Cheltenham graduate and former OTC man who described his background as 'impoverished middle class', found a line of bullet holes which bore testimony to the fighting that had followed the generals' coup. 'With the connivance of the priest, local landlords had hidden machine guns in the church,' the young Londoner learnt. 'Next morning as people flocked to the village square ... they were fired at from the ... tower. How many casualties there were [and] how the doors were forced and the gunners dealt with I never found out.'[5]

On arrival at Madrigueras, new recruits were met by battalion headquarters staff. They were issued with 'strong boots, rough khaki uniforms, a tin hat and two coarse woollen blankets' and shown to their quarters.[6] Frank Graham, a classics student from Sunderland who had given up a three-year scholarship at King's College, London to fight in Spain, reached Madrigueras on New Year's Day. He and his friends Tommy Dolan, an unemployed labourer, and Eddie Wilkinson, a nineteen year-old bus conductor, were billeted in 'an old disused theatre with a stage and balcony' where they slept 'on the floor on straw mattresses'.[7] Nine days after they had arrived, Cyril Sexton, Charley Hart, Leonard Bibby and William Ball reached Madrigueras and were given spaces beside them.[8] As the theatre filled up, later arrivals commandeered abandoned houses, whilst others were billeted with local villagers.

In total, some 300 indentured peasants called Madrigueras home. Although freeing them from the immediate tyranny of the Guardia Civil, Spain's pro-nationalist police organisation, the war had failed to improve their economic situation. Although the lands they worked were now their own, they still produced little more than subsistence rations. The poverty was unlike anything the volunteers had ever seen. Compared to them, Walter Gregory explained, 'the unemployed of Nottinghamshire were affluent'.[9] Some of the volunteers and villagers became friendly over time. David Crook grew close to a thirty-five year-old named Maria who was 'lean and worn with work'.[10] When he was billeted in her house, she took the young Londoner under her wing, whilst her daughter, Antonia, helped him learn Spanish. Andrew Flanagan, a twenty-five year-old Irish bricklayer of ordinary education who claimed to have served in the IRA, flirted with the daughter of another family. The attraction proved mutual and by the time the battalion left for the front the unlikely couple had fallen in love.[11]

Rations in Madrigueras were poor. 'Without going into great detail I think ... [they] could be accurately described as awful,' Walter Gregory recalled.[12] Rice and beans, occasionally supplemented with mule meat, were ever present, but it was the Mexican lentils known as Doctor Azaña's miracle pills that the volunteers despised the most. Whilst most of the men ate in the ruined church, each night several were invited into the houses of the locals for a home cooked meal. Despite their poverty, the peasants were generous hosts, on several occasions they went hungry so their guests could eat.

Although the war had caused severe food shortages, there was an abundance of wine. Often the peasants would simply give it away, refusing the volunteers' offers of payment and when they did accept money it was sold at ridiculously low prices. Bob Condon, the twenty-three year-old Welshman from Aberaman, remembered the difficulties he had in getting used to the Spanish way of drinking. The ubiquitous wine skins, known as *porrons*, fired a jet of the liquid under high pressure and were hard to control. 'I wet many a shirt before I learnt the trick,' Condon admitted.[13] 'Getting all the drinkers back to their billets after an evening out was a problem on occasions,' according to Walter Gregory.[14] Drunken men staggering the streets in the small hours singing '*Bandera Rosa*' became a common sight. One English volunteer named Fred Copeman, who was always ready to apportion blame, thought that the Irish contingent was most at fault. He recalled that they 'drank like bloody fish'.[15]

Discipline proved a major problem at Madrigueras. By mid-January the situation had gotten so serious that Wilfred Macartney, the battalion commander, decided to compile a battalion blacklist. The entries are illuminating. John Parr, a volunteer with the 3rd Company, was considered 'a parade dodger'; Stewart Wallasey had been sent back from Paris to England for disorderly conduct only to appear at Madrigueras in the following week's contingent; Philip Boyle of Donegal City, another who frequented the improvised cells in the village guardroom, stated in his defence that he had only come to Spain on holiday; John Murray from Glamorgan had a 'tendency to drunkenness and indiscipline'; Robert Davidson from Liverpool was listed for 'fighting on parade'; and Charles Dempsey, a thirty-seven year-old from Bristol who had arrived at the village on 10 December 1936, had 'deliberately missed the train' to Lopera to 'escape ... being drafted' when the rest of the volunteers had gone off to fight on the Cordoba front.[16]

Not long after arriving at Madrigueras, the men found out that they would be paid. Walter Gregory was as surprised as the rest. 'No one had ever suggested pay to us and I had not even thought about it,' he admitted. It amounted to seven pesetas a day, compared to the ten pesetas that the regular Republican soldiers were given. As a peseta was worth one British sixpence, this was 'a paltry sum'. Nevertheless, it was not a cause of resentment. 'Surprisingly it proved virtually impossible to spend even this meagre amount,' Gregory explained. 'With wine costing but a few centimos a glass we found that we quickly accumulated quite a stack of money in our pockets which we gave to collections for orphans, comforts for the Madrid Fund and other causes connected with the Republic's war effort.'[17]

For the first five weeks of the battalion's existence, Wilfred Macartney was in charge. A journalist and author of the Left Book Club's bestseller *Walls Have Mouths*, Macartney had just been granted early release from a ten-year prison sentence at Parkhurst served for spying for the Soviet Union. As well as having proved his political credibility beyond doubt, Macartney also had solid military experience. At the age of sixteen, he had served as a staff officer in the Great War and had gained a reputation as an expert in night raids. On one occasion he had been captured, but had later managed to escape from a prisoner of war camp and make his way back through the lines. Despite such credentials, Gurney was unconvinced of his commitment to the cause. 'He was a well-educated man, a great drinker and bon viveur,' the South African explained, 'and I find it difficult to believe he was ever a very dedicated Communist.'[18] George Leeson, the former British Navy man who had served in China, agreed. 'I thought [he was] a complete poseur ... [who] never should have been put in charge of the battalion with his 1914 ideas.' Leeson was particularly aggrieved by Macartney's sense of superiority. 'He had a little villa in Madrigueras,' he recalled, 'where he ate and was attended by servants.'[19]

Wintringham held Macartney in far higher esteem. 'He had a quick eye and a quicker tongue' and 'knew his onions in the field'. As well as organizing parade ground drill, led by his fearsome Scottish adjutant, Alex McDade, Macartney tried to prepare the volunteers for the realities of warfare in Spain. 'He brought more realism into our practice manoeuvres than I had known elsewhere,' Wintringham explained. 'We used large wooden rattles to simulate machine-gun fire, [and] made men scatter and lie still at unexpected moments at the sound of imaginary aircraft'. In this way, 'Macartney and I tried to get the ideas of cover, approach from the flanks, cross-fire, and accurate fire control into the heads of our sections and group leaders.'[20] To supplement the training, visiting lecturers provided expert advice. Instructors taught the use of hand grenades and a variety of automatic weapons and on 1 January, after a football match which the British lost 2–1 to a local team, Professor J.B.S. Haldane, an eccentric thirty-eight year-old scientist, gave a speech on gas warfare.[21]

Initially the training was severely hampered by the lack of guns. According to Donald Renton, the machine-gun company's political commissar, those they did have 'were completely obsolete ... [and] liable to explode in your face if actually used'.[22] As well as the antiques, some of which dated from 1888, wooden 'rifles' and sticks were used on manoeuvre. In the evenings, Macartney indulged his passion for night-time raids. Whilst he remained in his villa, the men would fumble their way across the sodden fields seeking check points in the dark. The marches often ended in farce. On one occasion Churchill's nephew, Giles Romilly, confidently led his group on a looping march. Hours later, as Patrick Curry recalled, they ended up in 'exactly the same place ... [they had] started from'.[23] On other evenings, the men concentrated on building up their knowledge of the few weapons available. 'In every barrack room, late into the night, groups of men could be seen with a rifle or machine-gun, pulling it to pieces and putting it back together again.'[24]

When they weren't tramping through the dark, knocking back cheap red wine or undergoing weapons' training, the men were expected to attend evening lectures given by the political commissars. Subjects included the role of the commissars in the Brigades, an overview of Spanish history and the reasons for the failings of the Republican militia in the opening stages of the war.[25] The commissars, whom the volunteers jokingly referred to as 'political comic stars', first appeared in the Red Army during the Russian Revolution and had a variety of functions in the Brigades.[26] Whilst the officers were concerned with military matters, the commissars were in charge of morale. At their best, they were intermediaries between the men and their commanders, who would fight the formers' corner in any dispute over conditions, pay and discipline. At their worst, they were petty, pistol-wielding tyrants with little understanding of battlefield conditions. In other battalions, summary executions took place for cowardice in the face of the enemy. The British volunteers were more fortunate in their commanders' choice of commissars, however. At Jarama they would perform well.

Many volunteers made close friendships in their time at Madrigueras. Gurney grew fond of the 'Boxing Parson' Robert Hilliard and Frank Graham and William Clifford, the scholar and amateur boxer from Sunderland, also bonded, but perhaps the most endearing friendship was the one forged between Clem Beckett and Christopher Saint John Sprigg. The two men made a mismatched couple. Sprigg was a twenty-nine year-old middle class Marxist intellectual who had published several books on aviation, eight detective stories and a novel entitled *This, my Hand*. He was well-dressed and softly spoken and was well liked by his comrades, the majority of whom were unaware of his literary talents. Clem Beckett, by contrast, was a scruffy, working class communist with an oft broken 'square' nose, who was prone to fits of temper and rarely seen without a cigar stub clamped between his teeth. Despite his humble origins in Oldham, 'Daredevil' Beckett had led an extraordinary life. His enduring passion for all things mechanical had led him to take up dirt-bike racing at an early age. His career had been phenomenally successful. By the end of his first year, he held twenty-eight track records, had defeated the famous American rider 'Sprouts Elder' and had forged a reputation as a specialist at broadsliding. The years that followed saw him travel the world, winning titles in France, the Balkans, Russia and Turkey and breaking the record for the flying mile at White City. It had not all been plain sailing, however. Whilst racing in Germany he had broken his thigh and when performing on the gravity-defying Wall of Death for the King and Queen of Denmark in June 1931 his arm was broken. When he heard of the uprising in Spain, Beckett had not hesitated. Bidding his Danish wife Leda a tearful farewell with the words 'so long kid, don't worry', he set out in October 1936. At first both Beckett and Sprigg worked as ambulance drivers for a project organized by the CPGB. Frustrated with these back line posts, they demanded a transfer to the infantry and joined the British Battalion in January 1937.

Not long after Sprigg and Beckett's arrival, an argument began that led to a major split in the battalion. Many of the Irish volunteers, having fought against the British Army in the course of their country's struggles for independence, resented being grouped together with their former enemies. After they heard that Wilfred Macartney and another of the battalion's officers had been involved in the British Army's notorious covert snatch squads that had operated during the conflict, the situation got out of hand. With both the English and Irish parties drinking to excess, a brawl developed.[27] The next day a meeting was called at which the Irish proposed joining the Abraham Lincoln Brigade, a newly formed American unit which had its base in nearby Villanueva de la Jara. Several dissenters spoke against the proposal, arguing that a distinction must be made between the anti-fascist working class Britons and the Imperialist elite. Nevertheless, the vote went against them twenty-six to eleven and the dissenters joined the Americans. Two similar incidents occurred later, one of which ended with André Marty insisting that 'mutineers' be shot. The British commissars managed to calm him and the incident was later forgotten. From that point on new Irish arrivals would remain with the British Battalion. Following Marty's outburst, there were no more national divisions and each group would go on to earn the other's respect.[28]

On 18 January the battalion received a boost when the 1st Company returned to Madrigueras. Made up of some of the first British volunteers to arrive in the country, the unit had left the base on Christmas Eve to take part in the offensive at Lopera and had then fought at Las Rozas to the north-west of Madrid. Both battles had been bloody and by the time they reached Madrigueras, just sixty-seven of the 145 who had set out remained. When they arrived, they were given a grand welcome by their countrymen, who lined both sides of the main street applauding. At the veterans' head came George Nathan looking as if he had just stepped out of Sandhurst: 'his riding boots [were] shining like a new pin, every button [was] polished, [his] hat [was] at the right angle and [his] riding crop [was] in [his] hand.'[29] Amongst those marching behind was Willie Lloyd. 'Short, squarely built, with … deep brown eyes and a shock of dark brown hair', the twenty-three year-old Welshman had left the valleys of Aberdare just six weeks before.[30] Although Lloyd and some of the others still looked like boys, the newcomers regarded him and the other veterans with awe. Fred Copeman thought them an 'inspiring sight': they 'gave

... [us] a wonderful boost ... [just as] our enthusiasm ... was ... beginning to flag'.[31] Even Jason Gurney was caught up in the moment. 'We all turned out, wild with excitement, to welcome these almost mythical figures,' the South African recalled. The good feeling 'soon turned sour', however. Stories of communication mix ups, bad leadership from Brigade HQ, unreliable weapons and insufficient supplies circulated through camp. Gurney was particularly depressed by the fate of Delasalle. 'He may have been a coward,' the South African conceded, '[and] he was certainly ... pretentious with an exaggerated idea of his military capacities, but it was manifestly absurd to maintain that he was in the pay of Franco.'[32]

In early February, shortly after the return of the 1st Company, a bizarre incident occurred that would have a profound effect on the battalion. As a condition of his early release from Parkhurst, Wilfred Macartney was required to report to the British authorities on a regular basis. On the eve of one such trip to London, a farewell supper was held at Albacete. At the end of the evening, Macartney and Peter Kerrigan, the base commissar, who was also due to return to England, took a taxi to the station. During the ride they decided to exchange pistols. Whilst they were cleaning them prior to the swap, one of the guns went off and the bullet hit Macartney in the arm. He was sent back to England as planned, but his wound would prevent him returning and Wintringham was promoted in his place. The details of this story have been debated over the years. Many of the volunteers believed that the shooting was a result of a direct order from the Communist Party hierarchy as they had realized that Macartney was not up to the job. Others argued that if this had indeed been the case, they could easily have prevented his return once he had arrived in England without recourse to such dramatic tactics. Whatever the truth behind the story, Fred Copeman raised a pertinent question: 'What would a bloke be doing cleaning a bloody revolver in a taxi ... [when] he's got all day and night?'[33]

Three days after the incident, the battalion's new rifles arrived. As the wooden crates were unpacked, the sense of excitement was palpable. Even Gurney was caught up in the moment: 'one by one we signed our names in an old exercise book and were issued with a rifle and bayonet and several packages of ammunition. [We then] ... filed out in silence, each ... holding his new-found manhood to his chest. This was the real thing,' the South African recalled. 'All the degrading pretence of the "training" was over and the reality of what we had come to do was now upon us.'[34] After firing a few rounds down a hastily constructed range with whitewashed stones as targets, the men were ordered to pack. They would leave for the front the next morning.

Everything seemed to happen so quickly. 'Suddenly there were rumours,' Tony Hyndman recalled. 'There was a big push near Madrid. The fascists had to be stopped.' After leaving his civilian clothing near his billet, the Welshman said goodbye to the family with whom he had stayed for the last few weeks. It was an emotional moment.[35] With the volunteers formed up in the main square, a representative of the local workers' committee gave a farewell speech. '[He] praised [our] work ... in the previous engagements,' Willie Lloyd remembered, 'and expressed the hope that [we] ... would keep it up.' Having gathered to see the volunteers off, the villagers gave out gifts of 'eggs and sandwiches and goats' milk'.[36] The volunteers then clambered onboard a line of waiting lorries and were driven out of town in a cloud of dust. The local children chased after the trucks, offering the clenched fist communist salute. Meanwhile, the women wept, reminded of previous farewells with lost brothers, fathers, husbands and sons.

CHAPTER 4
THE ADVANCE
(10.00–11.00AM, 12 FEBRUARY 1937)

At 10.00am the three rifle companies moved out from the Cookhouse. Immediately to the west was a steep slope leading to the plateau where Wintringham, Francis and Gurney had been an hour before. The columns wound their way upwards in single file, using gullies cut through the hillside by winter rains. Each man carried a brand-new Mosin-Nagant Russian rifle with an effective range of 500m (547 yards), a fixed bayonet and 150 bullets in five-round clips. The officers also had pistols, holstered in 'Sam Browne' belts. The rifles had arrived at Madrigueras only a few days before the battalion had left for the front. Opinion on their quality was divided. Wintringham thought they were 'good plain bread-and-butter rifles, of no very delicate accuracy', but built to last.[1] Walter Gregory's reaction to holding it for the first time had been purely emotional; 'I can still remember the sense of pride and power I felt.' 'I was going to conquer the world ... nothing and no one was going to stand in my way.'[2] Others complained that they were too light or that the kick was too severe, but it was the bayonets that caused the most grumbling. The rifles had a tendency to overshoot if they were removed, but when left on they invariably got snagged in the undergrowth as they advanced.[3] Every seventh volunteer carried parts for the rifle companies' light machine guns. One man carried the gun, either an ancient American Colt or a more modern but equally unreliable French Chauchat. A second took the stand and a third carried ammunition.

As well as his personal weapons, each volunteer was equipped with a water bottle, often filled with wine, anis or brandy, a Czechoslovakian gasmask and a paper-thin steel helmet from France. Rolled blankets were slung across their chests and overcoats, spare clothes, hard rations, cigarettes, books and letters from wives, sisters, mothers and friends were stuffed into their packs. David Crook, a group leader in the 3rd Section of the 1st Company, had several tangerines, a gift from Maria, with whom he had been billeted at Madrigueras. The Cheltenham College graduate also had a leather-bound volume of Shakespeare's *Tragedies* and a copy of Hitler's *Mein Kampf*, both of which he would soon come to regret lugging round Spain.[4] Crook was not the only one who was overloaded. To the amazement of his comrades, Tom Clarke, a stretcher bearer from Dundee, carried a mandolin into battle.[5]

The volunteers' uniforms varied considerably. Some had short buttoned jackets with elasticated waistbands and cuffs. Others had long coats and many wore baggy trousers with large pockets on the thighs, which were elasticated beneath the knee, giving them the appearance of plus fours. John 'Bosco' Jones, the young Londoner who had become a runner in Overton's company, thought they looked ridiculous. '[They] would have been nice for a ballet or if I was going on stage,' he complained.[6] Some of the men wore berets. Others had caps. George Bright, the eldest member of the battalion, had sewn an ASW (Alliance of Socialist Workers) badge to the front of his. 'When I leave for the front,' he explained in a letter home, 'I shall be known by all ... members'.[7] Amongst the Irish contingent there was a smattering of green headgear and scarves and Cyril Sexton, the self-confessed 'apolitical', wore a Royal Navy Volunteer pullover under his jacket.[8]

As they ascended the slope, the men were in excellent spirits. After the chill of the early morning, the day was now warm and the smell of wild thyme and sage, crushed underfoot amidst the gorse bushes, perfumed the air. The atmosphere was informal. At this stage in the war there were few airs and graces in the British Battalion. Men of diverse rank often called each other by their first names and no military salutes were given. Many of the volunteers talked or joked as they climbed. Ken Stalker, a quiet Scot in the 1st Company who had fought in the Great War as well as at Lopera, puffed away contentedly at his

The Advance: 10.00–12.30am, 12 February 1937

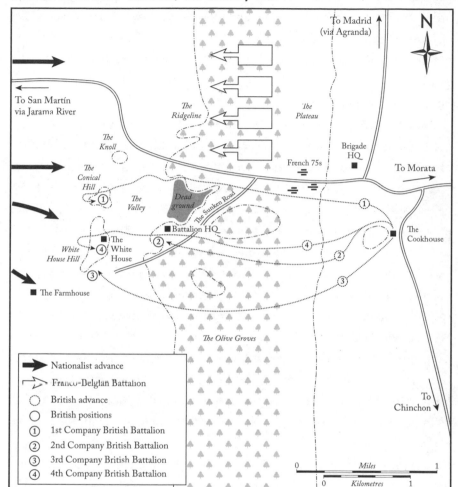

ever-present pipe whilst those with cigarettes smoked them. Others sang. On the right, Ralph Campeau, the 1st Company's political commissar, began a rendition of the *Internationale*. A 16-stone giant and former secretary of the London branch of the Youth Communist League (YCL), Campeau's voice carried clearly and the song was taken up by his men. One of the best singers in the 1st Company was William Benson, a twenty-six year-old who had spent much of the last five years unemployed in his native Manchester. Benson, a veteran of Lopera and Las Rozas, was a 'sympathetic character' and popular with the men.[9]

For Patrick Curry, a middle class communist from Southport with the 3rd Company, the whole scene had an innocent air. 'It was just like a crowd of boy scouts really,' he recalled, 'we had no idea what … [combat] was [going to be] like.'[10] Fred Copeman, an Englishman not known for understatement who would play a crucial role at Jarama, went even further. The advance 'looked like a bloody summer's outing', he thought.[11]

Born in 1907 at the Wangford Union, a workhouse near Beccles in Suffolk, Fred Copeman had endured a miserable childhood. Exposed to the bullying of his peers, he learned to defend himself with his fists and grew into a giant of a man, square-jawed and muscular. After joining the Royal Navy in 1929, he established a reputation as a heavy-weight boxer of some merit and later played a leading role in the half-hearted Invergordon Mutiny of 1931. As a result, Copeman was dismissed from the service and later joined the CPGB. By 1936 he was back in London. His days were spent organizing party meetings and taking part in protests. On one march, from Norwich to London, the police tried to disperse Copeman's group. In the struggle that followed, Fred ended up biting an officer on the bottom. 'I got bloody six months for that,' he recalled. At the weekends he watched Arsenal at Highbury or spent time with his girlfriend Kitty, a 'good looking' Scottish student of seventeen with 'lovely skin' and flame red hair, who was also dedicated to the cause. 'Why don't you go to Spain?' she had asked Copeman one night. Fred signed up the next day.[12]

In Madrigueras Copeman had been appointed commander of the battalion's anti-aircraft section, a small squad equipped with British Lewis guns from the Great War precariously mounted on improvised stands. He was pleased with the role but the unit was disbanded just before going into action. Wintringham then reassigned him to the 1st Company as a 'spare officer'.[13] Short-tempered and paranoid, Copeman had his fair share of detractors. Gurney thought him 'brutish'. Michael Economides, one of the battalion's Cypriot recruits, described him as a 'small time bully' and Tom Clarke, the mandolin-playing stretcher bearer from Dundee, believed he was insane.[14] Some of the other volunteers, on the other hand, admired him. For David Crook he was 'a good military technician' who 'works hard' and 'gets results' and the postman John Tunnah admitted to feeling safer when the big man was around.[15] Whatever their opinion, Wintringham recalled, '[Copeman] was ... a tornado of energy and swore grand'.[16]

––––––––––––––––

Ten minutes after setting off from the Cookhouse, Harry Fry, the commander of the 2nd Company, realized the machine-gun ammunition he had been given was of the wrong calibre. The Russian Maxims he had received just one day before were Great War models and could not take the rifle bullets supplied. With the other three companies disappearing up the slope ahead of him, Fry decided to send fifteen men under Sergeant Charles West back to find the right belts. He then set off up the hill. The sun had now risen higher and the slope proved hard going. As well as their standard equipment, the seventy-two men of the 2nd Company also had to carry their eight machine guns. With an effective range of 700m (766 yards) and able to fire 500 rounds per minute, the Maxims were the battalion's most effective weapon. Their weight and tendency to overheat, however, were major drawbacks. Each gun weighed close to 140lb and although they had been broken down into three parts, the barrel, the wheeled base and the thick metal shield, the men hauling them up the hillside were soon exhausted. To make matters worse, the guns were extremely cumbersome: the only way to carry them was by slinging them over the back with the two wheels bouncing uncomfortably against the kidneys. Before they had even gone 100 yards Fry had little option but to give his men a break. As soon as the order was given, the men began emptying their packs of extra weight. Overcoats, blankets, back copies of the *Daily Worker* and earnest communist literature soon littered the hillside. When he discovered what his men were doing, Dickenson, Fry's second-in-command, was furious. Although the days were warm, the temperature on the high Castilian plains plummeted after sunset and he knew his men would sorely miss their blankets that night. As Fry had already moved off, however, Dickenson had little choice but to follow him.[17]

Whilst Fry's men were still struggling up the hillside, the three rifle companies had already reached the top of the rise. Beyond was an open plateau, where

Conway, Overton and Briskey called a halt. The men fell out and were ordered to pile their belongings on the rocky ground. Looking to the north-west, the volunteers could make out the buildings of Madrid. At that distance, Jim Prendergast recalled, the city somehow seemed less real. 'That's how it must look ... to Franco,' he thought.[18] Suddenly, out of the west, a dull hum was heard approaching. Conway called for silence and panned his binoculars across the sky. Two squadrons of Nationalist planes were approaching at high altitude. Twelve German biplanes, Heinkel 51s, were escorting a mixed flight of bombers, Italian Romeos and mono-wing German Junkers 52s, on a mission to destroy the Republican supply dumps at Morata de Tajuña.

The foreign aircraft were proof of the inadequacy of the policy of Non-Intervention. Since the late summer of 1936, whilst assuring the governments of France, America and Britain that they remained neutral, Hitler and Mussolini had been supplying the Nationalists with men and arms. 'Il Duce' saw the conflict as a chance to win personal glory, raise the profile of fascist Italy and instil a martial spirit in his countrymen. For the Führer, Spain provided training for selected soldiers and aircrew and a testing ground for his tanks and planes. Initially the German machines would prove inadequate, but, as the war rumbled on, the manufacturers remodelled their hardware and the officers formulated the tactics that would be unleashed with devastating effect in 1939.[19]

With the planes approaching, the British riflemen spread out amongst the boulders covering the plateau. The raw recruits rolled onto their backs, raised their rifles skywards and opened fire. Conway's veterans, on the other hand, remembering 'the sickening aerial attacks' at Lopera, pressed their bodies into the ground and waited for the bombs to burst about them.[20] By now the roar overhead was deafening, but still nothing happened. Wondering what was going on, Conway stole a glance skywards. Seven Russian Polikarpov I-16 fighters, known as Moscas or 'flies' because of their squat superstructure and stubby wings, were approaching from the east to intercept the Nationalist planes. 'They're our boys!' the Irishman roared in delight.[21]

Glimpsing the Russians approaching, the Nationalist bombers and seven of their escorts returned to base. The remaining five German fighters dived to attack. It was a brave decision. With a maximum speed of 224mph, the He 51s were far slower than their mono-wing opponents, who could also out-turn and out-climb them with ease. Soon the air was alive with the crackle of machine-gun fire. The planes swooped about, dog-fighting in pairs, all semblance of squadron formation quickly forgotten. For the men on the ground, the spectacle was enormously exciting. When the planes dived low they could hear the wind whistling through their struts and make out the pilots leaning forward over the controls in their cockpits. Jason Gurney thought the whole thing seemed 'rather unreal – a bit like watching a film'. The South African found it impossible to comprehend that a few hundred yards above his head men were actually trying to kill one another.[22] Half way up the hill, the men of the 2nd Company were also enjoying the show. Lying flat on his back, Bill Meredith was reminded of Great War newsreels he had seen at the pictures as a child. After a few minutes a German biplane spun away from the fight trailing smoke, its tail wreathed in flames. Later a second, then a third machine plummeted earthwards. No parachutes were seen.[23] Each plane dived out of sight and crashed into the ground, engulfed in a fireball. The explosions were greeted by roars of approval from the British troops, who were unaware that one of them had signalled the demise of a Russian plane.[24]

After losing their second fighter, the Germans realized they were outclassed and headed for home. As their planes disappeared into the morning haze, the men of the three rifle companies continued their advance. They were now in even higher spirits. It was the first time any had seen the Nationalist air force driven off by Republican planes. Inspired, the commissar of the 1st Company, Ralph Campeau, began singing *The Ploughboy*. The song was taken up and soon reverberated across the plain. After crossing half a mile of open ground, the riflemen descended into gently shelving olive groves. The trees had been planted in neat rows, 25ft apart. They were 10ft high and 8in wide, each casting a pleasant, dappled shade. Maurice Davidovitch, a 'tubby' twenty-three year-old YCL leader from Bethnal Green who was in charge of the battalion's stretcher bearers, was one of those relieved to be out of the sun.[25]

Nicknamed 'Sailor Boy' for the years he had 'spent in the forecastle[s] of … tramp steamer[s]', Davidovitch was liked throughout the battalion for his 'particular blend of Cockney and Jewish humour' and his ability to get 'a laugh out of everyone'.[26] His current popularity, however, was a far cry from the reception he had first received on joining the Brigades back in October 1936. Prior to going into action at Lopera, Davidovitch had been deeply disliked by his comrades. In Paris 'his impudent conduct' (brazenly flaunting his 'YCL badge' and wearing 'semi-military clothes') had caused one of his travelling companions to be detained by gendarmes. Davidovitch had later got drunk and cheated two others out of some money and to cap it all he 'behaved indecently' in a café once they had reached Albacete. A report written in November 1936 stated that he was so 'thoroughly disliked by all the English comrades' that 'some of them [had] ... threatened that if he goes into the line they will shoot him', an act that the anonymous archivist noted wryly was 'an old English custom'. This was all written before the volunteers had seen action, however. After Davidovitch's selfless bravery at Lopera and Las Rozas, where he repeatedly risked his life to drag wounded comrades out of the firing line, their opinion of the cheeky young Londoner had undergone a radical transformation. By the time they reached Jarama, he was one of the most popular figures in the battalion.[27]

Turning to Tom Clarke, a fellow stretcher bearer from Dundee, Davidovitch joked that so far the advance seemed 'just like manoeuvres'. The young Cockney had spoken too soon. His Scottish companion was still chuckling when the roar of an approaching shell sent both men diving to the ground.[28] Although the majority were exploding some way ahead of the British troops, the sound alone was terrifying. Jim Prendergast noticed an 'old Scotch Communist' methodically going down on his hands and knees with each shot. The Irish veteran was trying to reassure him when a high pitched screech drowned out his words. The shell exploded just 30 yards away, uprooting an olive tree and hurling it through the air.[29]

Shortly before midday, the 1st Company passed through some Spanish infantry in reserve. Having been in position for two days, they had grown accustomed to the shellfire and, to the novices of the company, they seemed unnaturally calm. Some were playing the guitar. Others sang revolutionary songs or sad flamencos. When Conway called a halt, they gave the British chocolate and wine then shouted '*Viva las Brigadas Internacionales*!' when they moved on once more.[30] Half a mile to the south where the 4th Company was advancing, another unit of Spaniards was less composed. Tom Spiller, known to his comrades as 'Kiwi' for his origins in Hawke's Bay, Napier, saw them flying past in full retreat with 'a look of ... horror on their faces'.[31]

After the Spaniards had gone, Albert Charlesworth, the metal polisher from Oldham, also with the 4th Company, noticed a strange whistling sound. Having never heard machine-gun fire before, he put it down to birdsong.[32] Just over a mile to the right, Fred Copeman saw leaves dropping from the olive trees and realized they were under indirect fire. The new recruits in the 1st Company, however, were as confused about the noise as Charlesworth had been. Happy in their naivety they marched on unconcerned. One individual even put the noise down to the abundance of crickets in Spain.[33]

On a sharp rise on the edge of the plateau, level with the leading sections, Wintringham and his staff had a panoramic view over the groves. So far the 'English Captain' was pleased with the advance. His company commanders had followed his instructions to the letter. 'Briskey on the left hand had his three sections wide apart', Overton's men were similarly positioned in the centre and 'Conway was off to the right'. Wintringham's only concern was that Fry's men were still lagging behind. After dispatching a runner to find out about their progress, the English Captain's thoughts strayed.[34] As a boy he had been fascinated by Wellington's Peninsular campaigns and had spent many hours learning the names of his engagements whilst studying at Gresham's, a small public school near the Norfolk coast. Turning to Gurney he remarked 'that there had not been a better-looking body of troops in Spain since Wellington's day'. Perhaps still mulling over Francis' untimely departure, the South African failed to respond.[35]

By the time Wintringham's runner reached them, the 2nd Company had finally hauled their Maxims onto the plateau. Exhausted, they collapsed on the ridgeline just as the retreating Spanish troops Spiller had seen came past. James Maley, the twenty-nine year-old Celtic fan, thought they seemed reasonably composed now they were out of the artillery fire. Nearby, Bill Meredith had begun to notice the bullets passing overhead. Like Charlesworth, at first he thought the noise was nothing more than birdsong, but his comrades soon put him right. To his surprise, the realization actually pleased him. Ever since he had left his home town of Bellingham in Northumberland, Meredith had been worried how he would react under fire.[36] But now he experienced 'a certain indifference, as if … [he] were not in the war at all'.[37] Moments later, one of the men Fry had ordered to bring up the ammunition returned empty-handed. The armoury truck had gone missing. Cursing his luck, Fry ordered the men to leave the Maxims behind on the plateau. After nominating a section under Basil Abrahams to guard them, he led the rest of his men towards the groves.[38]

Half a mile to the west, Wintringham spotted the XV Brigade's assistant chief of staff approaching his position. A lean figure, 'immaculately clean and well turned out', smoking a pipe and swinging a cane, George Nathan was the embodiment of the British Army Officer. 'Your Battalion's a bit late Tom,' he said when he reached his position. Wintringham smiled. He thought Nathan's tone 'as matter-of-fact as if he had been going to some parade or tattoo'. 'I've told Conway to hurry on and swing left a bit,' the staff officer continued, 'and I've sent a message through him to Overton. Get them over to the left,' he said pointing at the men, 'but be ready to turn the whole Battalion half-right. The battle seems to be mainly up north from us, over there' – he waved his stick towards the groves on the far side of the road where the Franco-Belgians were heavily engaged. With that Nathan returned to his motorcycle, parked near the French 75s on the Morata road, and roared off to the rear.[39]

For Wintringham everything had suddenly changed. Previously, he had believed that the San Martín Bridge was still in Republican hands. From Nathan's comments and the ever-increasing fire whistling overhead, however, it was obvious that the Nationalists had already crossed the river. The offensive he had been preparing for had turned into a holding action against an unknown foe. Somewhere to the west they were advancing. They would be upon him soon.[40]

The troops advancing towards the British were the 8th Regiment of Asensio Cabanillas's 4th Division. The regiment was divided into three battalions: the 7th *Tabor* of Melilla, a Moroccan unit, was 598 men strong and led by a Spanish officer, Captain León. Founded on New Year's Day 1937, the unit had only reached the mainland on 17 January and had immediately been rushed to the front. Each soldier was armed with a 7mm Mauser rifle, two Lafitte hand grenades and a 1913 model machete. The 7th *Tabor* also had a heavy machine-gun company equipped with 8 Hotchkiss M1914s and 8 Valero mortars. When they closed with the British, the extra firepower would prove decisive.[41]

As well as the Moors there were two *banderas* of the Foreign Legion: the 6th, whose 729 men were commanded by Fernandez Cuevas, and the 8th, 647 strong and led by Captain Regalado.[42] Originally raised to fight in the Rif War against Moroccan separatists, the legionnaires, 90 per cent of whom were actually Spanish born, were fanatics whose motto '*Viva la Muerte!*', or 'Long live Death!', reflected their no-holds-barred approach to combat. One of their number, who had fought through the early campaigns on the approach to Madrid, believed that his comrades could be divided into five categories. The first was the 'philosophical, religious crusader'. The second was the 'impecunious criminal without hope, taking to the Legion for shelter and obscurity'; the third was 'the adventurer', the fourth 'the fascist' and the fifth 'the patriotic type'.[43]

Since the *banderas* had left Seville in August, hundreds had been killed or wounded, but a handful of veterans had survived the siege of Badajoz, the relief of Toledo and the bloodbath at the Clinical Hospital in Madrid's University City. By a curious twist of fate, one of them was British. Born into a middle class family in Pontypridd in 1914, Frank Thomas was one of just a dozen Britons who fought for Franco in the Spanish Civil War. A conservative who was convinced that communism posed a grave threat to civilization, Thomas joined the Nationalists due to his disgust with the apparent anarchy of the government forces in Spain which he had witnessed on pro-Franco newsreels shown in his local cinema. In the assault on Madrid in late 1936, Thomas had seen most of his comrades in the 6th *Bandera* killed or wounded and had since been given a rear echelon role in deference to his time under fire. During the battle of Jarama, he was to spend most of his time in the relative safety of San Martín de la Vega, but would visit the front on several occasions, during one of which he became aware that his unit was facing his countrymen. Thomas's experiences had been intense. He had seen the brutality of the war first hand and witnessed summary executions, yet his faith in Franco's cause remained unshakeable.[44]

Whilst the Foreign Legion was considered the elite of Franco's army, the troops most feared by the Republicans were the Moors, 78,000 of whom would fight for the Nationalists in the course of the Civil War. Whilst some stories suggest that a handful had joined up to take revenge on the Spanish for the decades of war they had brought to their country, most had baser motivations. A few had signed up 'in the spirit of adventure', but the vast majority were drawn by the lure of regular pay. Each recruit was given five pesetas a day with a further six pesetas as a signing-on fee and their families in Morocco were given bonuses of food and oil. Tribal leaders were also bribed to encourage their men to join up. Rifles, hand grenades and even anti-aircraft guns were supplied to those who persuaded the largest numbers. The Moroccans were also attracted by the regular opportunities for looting. Tobacco, alcohol, clothes, paintings, jewellery, books, religious icons and family photographs had all been stolen during the advance on Madrid and sold to their Spanish comrades at impromptu markets set up by the roadside. Much of the profit was sent home to subsidize struggling families.[45] Other Moroccans had been tricked into joining up. One, 'a lonely looking Moor ... from the village of Maedamra on the River Duarga' had been told he was going to Spain to work and had no idea that he would be pushed into the front line. 'I am afraid,' he admitted, 'especially of aeroplanes – and I want to go home.'[46]

Republican propaganda, unafraid of manipulating the widespread racism of the period, depicted the Moroccans as 'bestial Africans', 'barbarians' and 'savages' and equated their presence in Spain to a 'Mussulman invasion'. Tales of their propensity for the rape and murder of civilians, the slaughter of prisoners and the mutilation of enemy corpses abounded. The British troops advancing towards them on the morning of the 12th were well aware of their fearsome reputation. Whilst only a handful had previously encountered them on the battlefields of the University City, Lopera and Las Rozas, all feared and loathed them in equal measure.[47] 'The worst blokes we ever came across were the Moors,' one veteran explained. 'God they were vicious... They'd put the fear of God into you. They were death or glory blokes ... [who] thought they'd be going to heaven as soon as they were shot.'[48] Fred Copeman also had a begrudging respect for the Moroccans. '[They] didn't sit around doing nothing,' he recalled. 'If they're in the line, they're in the line and they're always looking to kill someone.'[49] Tom Patten, a fervent Catholic from County Mayo, told another story.

> It was out in University City ... we were holding a very rough line ... when one of
> our French comrades was separated from us in an advanced position. It was ...
> quiet ... and he slept like the rest of us, except for those on guard. In the night
> Moors crept forward, found him ... and ... gouged out his eyes as he lay there
> helpless. We heard his screams ... [but by the time] we found him they had killed
> him and fled.[50]

By midday on the 12th 600 Moors supported by over a thousand legionnaires were closing in on the British line at Jarama. Wintringham's men were outnumbered three to one.

CHAPTER 5

WHITE HOUSE HILL
(11.00AM–1.00PM, 12 FEBRUARY 1937)

At midday Overton's 4th Company reached the ridge where Francis had been hit three hours earlier. Although Wintringham had instructed the former guardsman to halt at that point, Nathan had since countermanded the order, so Overton led his men down the slope to the long grass of the valley floor. Directly ahead were two low hills, neither more than 32ft high. The one to the left was flat topped, thickly wooded with low thorn trees and capped by a small whitewashed farmhouse. The other, conical in shape, was smaller, steeper and sparsely covered with grass, low gorse bushes and wild thyme. Half a mile to the right was a third rise. Isolated and perfectly symmetrical, it came to be known as the Knoll. Once down in the valley, Overton advanced towards White House Hill. Half a mile to his left, Bill Briskey's 3rd Company had also reached the ridgeline. From their position the ground sloped evenly down towards the Jarama affording his men a marvellous view. Although still two miles distant, Walter Gregory, one of Briskey's runners, could clearly see the San Martín Bridge in the crisp morning light. The sight set his pulse racing. The Nationalists were streaming across the river in their hundreds.[1]

Meanwhile, the 1st Company was still in the olive groves. With the bullets singing high overhead, Jim Prendergast fell in with 'the old Scotch Communist' he had noticed taking cover from the artillery on the advance. 'I don't like these kind of birds,' he remarked after pulling on his pipe. Emerging from the groves, Kit Conway called a meeting of his section commanders. Indicating the valley, he pointed out the Knoll to the right where he intended to take up position.[2] Before they could reach their destination, a Brigade runner intercepted them on the valley floor and handed Conway a message. It was from Brigade HQ and ordered the Irishman to realign his advance to keep in closer contact with Overton's men to his left. Turning 45 degrees to the south-east, Conway headed for the Conical Hill.[3]

The 1st and 4th Companies reached the reserve slopes at 12.30. Conway and Overton ordered their men to spread out and a half-mile long line was formed.[4] Advancing at walking pace, the volunteers picked their way up the steep slopes. Thorn bushes caught at their clothing and their feet sank into the sandy soil. Once on the summits, the troops passed down the far side into the rolling scrubland beyond. Although still over half a mile away, the lead units of Asensio's brigade could be seen advancing in skirmish formation up the slope from their bridgehead. John Tunnah, a Scot from the 1st Company, thought it 'a terrific sight'.[5] Whilst their uniforms were largely non-descript, the insides of the Moors' cloaks were bright red. As they moved over the hills and through the wooded gulleys, flashes of colour caught Tunnah's eye.

Silhouetted against the skyline as they crested the hills, the British riflemen made an easy target for the German heavy machine-gun teams supporting the Moors' advance. As they walked through the hip high bushes on the western slopes, several men were hit by the raking fire. William Benson, the veteran of Lopera with the best singing voice in the battalion, was amongst the first, when a bullet grazed his arm. Wishing his comrades luck, Benson made his way to the rear to have the wound dressed.[6]

With the 4th Company, advancing beyond White House Hill, John 'Bosco' Jones thought it all seemed rather surreal. 'It hit us before you knew what was happening ... you just walked on and people sort of fell down,' he recalled. Although amazed and upset to see his comrades dying, Jones didn't yet feel afraid. Instead, the adrenaline kicked in, revealing his baser instincts. Anger overtook him and he began firing wildly ahead. Overton, meanwhile, had disappeared and no one seemed willing to take command. Beside Jones a Scottish sergeant 'was crying his eyes out'. 'Get them off the skyline!' he shouted to no one in particular between sobs.[7] All around, men continued to slump to the ground, hit in the legs, chest, stomach or head. Some cried out and were dragged back over the hills by their comrades. Others crumpled silently into the bushes and were left where they lay.

As well as the machine guns sweeping their lines, the British also came under rifle fire from the infantry of Asensio's 7th Regiment. As they advanced, the Nationalists appeared to be swallowed up by the ripples in the ground. Jones could now see nothing more than small puffs of white smoke where the advancing units had been.[8] The Moors were experts at finding cover in open ground and within seconds their entire skirmish line had disappeared. Meanwhile the majority of the 4th Company plodded on, seemingly oblivious to the hail of Mauser and Hotchkiss fire whipping past them. To Jones' right, the veterans of the 1st Company were faring somewhat better. Although also taking casualties, Conway had taken charge of the situation. Running from group to group, he directed their fire, calling out ranges and pointing to targets with his cane.[9] Initially several of his men had taken cover, but the thick bushes studding the forward slope of the hillside obscured their view, rendering their fire next to useless. 'Don't lie down!' Conway bellowed when he saw them. 'Stand up and show you're not afraid of the Fascist bastards!'[10]

Alongside Conway on the slopes of the Conical Hill, Fred Copeman thought the ex-IRA man looked faintly ridiculous. He was 'like a bloody sergeant major', Copeman explained, 'striding through the undergrowth with a walking stick'.[11] Nevertheless, the men leapt to their feet as ordered. As they crept closer, the Moors occasionally broke cover and briefly offered a target. '[The] brown, ferocious bundles dashed forward a few yards, before disappearing back into the ground.'[12] Standing and firing, Prendergast could see for miles. The slope ahead of him fell away across rolling ground to the distant river. To his left front there was a farmhouse which the Nationalists seemed to be using as a base and to the right a white road along which enemy 'cars and lorries were travelling … [at] a tremendous speed'.[13] Alongside the Dubliner were Peter Daly, Leo Greene, Paddy Smith and Sean Goff. All four were seeking targets ahead of them. Adjusting their sights to the ranges called out by Conway, they blazed away with five-round clips until their rifle barrels were burning hot. Then Daly shouted a warning: 'They're advancing on our left!'[14] Sure enough several

Moors had risen from the ground and were picking their way forward. They were only 500 yards from the British line.

Holding the low ground on the far left, the majority of Briskey's 3rd Company were safe from the fire that was killing and maiming their comrades. The only group in particular danger was a thirty-strong section under Sergeant Watson, whom Briskey had ordered to take up position to the left front in case the Moors tried to outflank the line. Similarly fortunate were a section from Overton's company. Amongst them was Albert Charlesworth, the metal polisher from Oldham. Assigned a position on the saddle between the two hills in the middle of the British position, his section had also escaped the maelstrom of fire.[15]

Watching proceedings from the ridge with Wintringham's staff a few hundred yards to the rear, Jason Gurney couldn't help but admire the professionalism of the enemy advance. The South African thought their ability 'to exploit the slightest fold in the ground ... amazingly skilful. Bobbing up and down, running and disappearing again', they came on 'while all the time maintaining a continuous and accurate fire'. The feat was made even more impressive as 'they had to travel more than two thousand yards ... with no apparent cover'. Gurney thought them formidable opponents and feared for his comrades, 'a group of city bred young men [most of whom had] ... no experience of war, no idea of how to find cover on an open hillside, and no competence as marksmen'. He held out little hope for their survival. 'We were frightened by the sheer din of the battle,' he recalled. It was 'far louder than anything [I] had previously experienced ... [and] so intense as to seem to have an inescapably destructive force of its own'. Nevertheless, like Jones, Gurney felt oddly removed from the chaos going on around him. 'The horror of seeing close friends and comrades being killed and broken did not really penetrate my mind until later. It was all too fantastic for immediate realization, like something seen in a nightmare,' he explained.[16]

Amongst those that Gurney saw killed was the volunteer who had panicked at the Spanish border crossing two months before. He had wanted to turn back, but when he had become hysterical, Gurney had knocked him unconscious to avoid an awkward incident with the French police. Looking at his body amongst the bushes, Gurney was suddenly wracked with guilt. 'I felt like a murderer,' he admitted. 'It was all very well trying to be a good soldier but it needed a kind of ruthlessness which was not in my nature. I could do the things which it was necessary to do at the time but I always had to pay the price in retrospect.'[17]

Alongside the South African, Captain Tom Wintringham reacted to the chaotic scenes with anger. Just a few moments before, everything had been going according to plan. The men of the 3rd and 4th companies had been advancing as ordered, well spread out and maintaining discipline, with the 1st and 2nd companies held back in reserve. But as the lead units had reached the ridge, everything had suddenly changed. His orders to halt had been countermanded by runners from Brigade HQ and the plan he had devised that morning had been torn to shreds. His men were now exposed on the far side of the hills and Wintringham had lost control of the situation. To make matters worse, a 'voluble officer of engineers, [who was] almost hysterical in his excitement [was stood by his side], pouring out floods of Russian'. The officer, who was from Brigade staff, had brought a telephone from the Morata road where the staff had gathered earlier that morning. Whilst his men were trying to get the contraption to work, the officer was wildly gesticulating to the gap between the Conical Hill and the Knoll where a group of Nationalist troops was now advancing. The engineer insisted that Wintringham had to counter the threat. 'Angry that his orders had been overruled and uneasy in a position where neither flank seemed safe', Wintringham pretended not to understand. Then the telephone rang. The Brigade staff officer grabbed the receiver. From the few words of Russian he understood, Wintringham gathered that he was informing Colonel Gal that the British were allowing the Nationalists to advance unhindered. Just then a burst of fire cut through their ridge top position. By the time Wintringham had turned round to assess the damage, to his relief the officer had fled the scene.[18]

Freed from his tormentor, Wintringham took a few moments to assess the situation. Beyond the hills, his men were under heavy fire, but as yet he had little idea of just how much they were suffering. Indeed, his main concerns were his flanks. To the left, beyond Briskey's position, were a mass of olive groves and scrubland, currently unoccupied by either side. If the enemy realized that his flank was so exposed, they could easily overrun his position.

The situation to the right was equally worrying. From the groves on the far side of the Morata road, the 'guttural, often stopping' Colt light machine guns of the Franco-Belgian Battalion could be heard. So far they appeared to be holding their position, but as a group was currently retreating across the valley towards him, how long they could hold out was a matter of speculation. The Franco-Belgians also had a company positioned on the top and sides of the Knoll that Conway had been heading for, from where the 'slow, rather woolly noise' of a Chauchat machine rifle was carrying across the valley.[19]

As Wintringham moved to his left to get a better view of the position, the telephone rang again. It was yet another staff officer, this time speaking in French, a language that the Balliol graduate had no problem understanding. 'Can you hold your position?' the staff officer asked him anxiously. 'Yes,' Wintringham replied, 'if there is support on my flanks. What has happened with the Franco-Belges?' He heard a muttered consultation before the voice returned. 'The cavalry will come up on your left; watch that side very carefully. There is a gap on your right; half the Dimitrov Battalion will come there to give you direct support. But watch the left, the left!' Then there was static. Far from reassuring, the phone call had merely confirmed Wintringham's worst fears. His battalion was 'in the air', stuck out in front with no security on either side.[20]

By 12.30 Kit Conway's position beyond the Conical Hill was becoming untenable. The Moors were closing and their fire was becoming increasingly accurate. Exposed on the forward slope, the British made easy targets. 'A young English chap' standing next to Jim Prendergast was shot and crumpled into the bushes. Above the din of rifle fire someone yelled for stretcher bearers. Maurice Davidovitch and his men were outstanding. Doubled up as if running into the wind, they moved ceaselessly around the hillside, lifting the wounded and carrying them to the rear. On the forward slope, Prendergast saw Sean Goff tumble over with his hand pressed to his head. Seconds later he rose again, his face white with shock, but otherwise unhurt. The bullet had merely grazed his helmet. Moments later Prendergast noticed a Spaniard who had joined them during the advance. Suddenly, the bush he had just left was riddled with machine-gun fire. Looking up, the Dubliner caught his eye and both men began laughing uncontrollably.[21]

Elsewhere on the slope, Tommy Fanning, a six-year veteran of the British Army, was having problems with his rifle. Used to the Lee Enfield, which required a double squeeze of the trigger, the Mancunian was firing off rounds before he had taken the time to aim. Nevertheless, he continued to blaze away at half caught glimpses of shuffling Moors, provoking a comrade, cowering behind a bush, to berate him. 'Don't fire,' he yelled, 'you're giving the position away.' Disgusted, Fanning loaded another clip and turned back to the enemy advance.[22] A few yards further back, David Crook was fascinated by the sounds of the bullets whizzing overhead. A veteran taking cover beside him saw his concern. 'Don't mind them,' he quipped, 'it's the ones you don't hear that get you.'[23] Elsewhere, John Daly spotted a knot of Moors breaking cover 500 yards away and called out a warning. Several men swung their rifles to meet them and the company's light machine guns were brought into action. 'Don't waste your fire boys!' Kit Conway warned as the Colts and Chauchats rattled into life. Firing 200 rounds a minute from a 20-round magazine, the Chauchats added considerable firepower. They were inaccurate over 200 yards and hopelessly prone to jamming, however, and Conway could see that the Moors were still gaining ground. As he looked around he saw 'men lifting their heads to fire ... shot through the face'.[24] Realizing his position would soon be overwhelmed, he ordered his men to fall back. Firing from the hip as they went, they retreated to the top of the Conical Hill.[25]

Wintringham, meanwhile, was following a worrying development on the battalion's right flank. The French troops who had occupied the isolated Knoll by the Morata road were falling back. First the Chauchat fire ceased. Then a rearguard scrambled down the slope and ran across the valley. Hot on their heels was a company of grey-clad Moors. Taking up the Frenchmen's abandoned position on the hilltop, the Africans set up a machine gun of their own. From there they could enfilade the entire British line. Within minutes of the French retreat, machine-gun fire was raking Wintringham's position and the 'English Captain' had little choice but to pull back. Moving in pairs, Battalion HQ withdrew to the safety of the Sunken Road, an ancient cart track which over the centuries had cut a five yard-wide rut waist-deep into the dusty white soil of the groves. On reaching the position, a hundred yards back from the ridgeline, Wintringham found the French section that had been holding the Knoll had got there before him. Wild eyed with panic, their young commander blurted out his battalion's story, whilst Wintringham caught his breath.[26]

Under pressure from the Moors and legionnaires of Asensio's 8th Regiment, the Franco-Belgians had been retreating for the last hour and had soon lost cohesion. The section commander who was talking to Wintringham, having been assigned the role of protecting his battalion's left flank, had become separated from the rest. He had lost all his machine rifles in the retreat and now had no idea where his comrades were. When the Frenchman finally stopped babbling, Wintringham took command. 'Put your men along the terrace twenty metres [twenty two yards] ahead of us here,' he ordered. 'On your left you are quite safe ... there are three English companies on the ridge up there, well ahead of you. Make sure your men do not fire at them!' The Frenchman eyed Wintringham incredulously. 'Then you are not retreating?' he asked. 'No,' replied the Englishman. 'We hold.' Bolstered by Wintringham's conviction, the Frenchman slowly regained his composure. '*A vos ordres, mon capitaine,*' he replied and led his men to the ridgeline.[27]

At 1.00pm, an hour after the rifle companies had advanced into the valley, Harry Fry's machine gunners reached the ridgeline that Wintringham had just abandoned and took up position behind a dry stone wall. Although just 18in high, it commanded an excellent field of fire. From there they could dominate the entire valley. Nevertheless, there were two distinct disadvantages. The position was too small to accommodate all of Fry's men and, more importantly, to the right front the ridgeline dropped so steeply that there was an area of dead ground which would later prove their undoing. For the moment, however, such worries were academic. The commander of the 2nd Company had more pressing concerns. The twenty men who could not fit into the position were sent a few hundred yards to the left. As they dashed along the ridgeline, passing some of the casualties already dragged back from the hills, a burst of fire from the Knoll cut through them. Two men fell. One had his face slashed open by a passing bullet. The other, George McKeown, a cheerful Scouser popular with the men, was shot through the head. He was dead before he hit the ground.[28] The rest kept running and took up position on the edge of the olive groves. Cyril Sexton, the number three man on the first of the two Maxims, thought it 'an ideal spot… On rising ground, [with] good background cover', the men could see the two hills held by their comrades and the Jarama River beyond.[29]

Both sections of the 2nd Company began to dig in. As the handful of entrenching tools the battalion had been issued with had been left behind at the Cookhouse, they clawed at the thin white soil with their helmets, gas mask covers, bayonets and bare hands.[30] With desperation driving them on, they soon had well sighted, if shallow, gun pits. Shortly after they had finished, a runner arrived from Wintringham ordering Fry to report to the Sunken Road. On arrival, the Battalion Commander gave him the same instructions he had given the French section moments before: concentrate your fire on the Knoll on the right and don't let the Moors advance any further. Rushing back to his trench, Fry spread the word and soon rifle fire was crackling up and down the line.[31]

George Leeson, the London Underground worker whose wife had been adamant that he should remain in England, was one of the few men with the 2nd Company who had any experience of battle. Before becoming a transport worker, he had served with the British Navy in China as a gunner on river boat patrols during the Kuomintang War. Noticing that the men in his section seemed to be firing wildly, Leeson decided to check that they knew how to use their guns.[32] 'What have you set your sights to?' he asked the first rifleman he came across. The man stared back at him blankly. Leeson grabbed the rifle from his hands to find that the sights had been set at zero. The Knoll was 700 yards away. Although well within range, the distance had to be taken into account by elevating the rear sight. The man's bullets must have been ploughing into the ground just 50 yards in front of his position. To his disgust, Leeson soon discovered that the majority of the men had no idea of what they were doing.[33] Most had only fired five rounds in their entire lives, and that had been just a week before, at an improvised range in the training base at Madrigueras. Hopelessly outclassed by their enemies, the battalion's situation was already critical and was about to take a turn for the worse.

PART TWO
DEATH STALKED THE OLIVE GROVES

The sun warmed the valley
But no birds sang
The sky was rent with shrapnel
And metallic clang

Men torn by shell shards
Still on the ground
The living sought shelter
Not to be found

Holding their hot rifles
Flushed with the fight
Sweat-streaked survivors
Willed for the night

JOHN LEPPER, BRITISH BATTALION, XV INTERNATIONAL BRIGADE

CHAPTER 6

'THE BODIES WERE ROLLING DOWN THE HILL'

(1.00–3.30PM, 12 FEBRUARY 1937)

On Conway's command the men of the 1st Company withdrew to the summit of the Conical Hill. They were being slaughtered out in the open and although the hill offered little in the way of cover at least its height would afford a slight advantage. Firing their rifles from the hip, the men walked backwards up the slope. Halfway up, Paddy Duff was hit in the leg. He stumbled then dragged himself on. Once on the hilltop, the men sought cover. There was precious little to be found. In places the thin, white soil was bare. Elsewhere it was covered by grass or weeds only ¼in high. Pressing their bodies into the contours of the earth, the men tried to shelter from the hail of bullets coming from their front. On the right hand side of the hill were David Crook and Sam Wild. Whilst Crook aimed and fired at the puffs of white smoke that signalled the extent of the Moors' advance, Wild, the Royal Navy veteran from Manchester, clawed at the soil with his bare hands to build a parapet. Wild was used to hard graft. When he was ten his mother had died and he had started work as a labourer to support his family. Meanwhile the commander of the 1st Company was pacing around the hilltop. Seemingly oblivious to the hail of bullets, Kit Conway was firing his rifle and yelling commands to his men.

When the Moors on the Knoll to their right opened up, the enfilading fire caught the British by surprise. Patrick Curry, the middle class communist who had thought the whole thing was like a boy scouts' outing just three hours before, was one of the first to be hit. Entering at the left kidney and exiting near his right shoulder, the bullet broke his right arm as it drilled through his body. Curry was convinced he was dying. 'I sort of got drowsy,' he recalled, 'and ... lay there and expected to go.'[1] Elsewhere on the Conical Hill, Fred Copeman was talking to George Bright. A sixty year-old carpenter and the oldest man in the battalion, Bright was well known to Copeman from the unemployment rallies both had attended in London. Due to his age, he had been told to remain at the rear, but had made his way up to the front line regardless. 'What are you doing here?' Copeman yelled above the firing. 'I wanted to see some of the action,' Bright replied. 'You're bloody well seeing it now,' Copeman cursed. Before Bright could respond a bullet struck him, leaving 'a small red hole in the centre of his forehead'.[2] He was dead before he hit the ground. As his union card fluttered away on the breeze, Copeman was left wondering where the bullet had come from. Looking round, he suddenly felt a burning sensation in his right hand. A bullet had burrowed through his sleeve, smashed his watch and buried itself in his thumb. Gritting his teeth, Copeman wrapped the wound in a field dressing and continued his search. Panning his binoculars to the right, he spotted the Moors on the Knoll slightly to his rear. Copeman immediately realized the significance of his find: the Moors had outflanked them. The British riflemen were caught in a cross-fire and could surely not hold out for long.[3]

Two hundred yards to the south, the 4th Company had also withdrawn and had now taken up position on the summit of White House Hill. The walled yard at the back of the farmhouse was filled with wounded waiting to be taken to the rear. Several had already died. Their twisted, purple bodies were slowly bloating in the sun. The rest of the company were spread out across the hill top, taking cover behind the rocks and trees. The twenty-seven year-old Kiwi, Tom Spiller, and nine others had set up their Colt light machine gun inside the farmhouse. With frequent blockages, the American gun was hopelessly ineffective. On a practice range several weeks before, it had taken Wintringham, an expert in automatic weaponry, five minutes to fire a mere 25 rounds. To make matters worse, its distinctive, coughing bark drew the enemies' attention. By now the Moors had worked their way to within a few hundred yards of the hill and their fire was pouring into the house. Combined with the heavy machine guns of the German support battalions further to the rear, the hilltop was a death zone. Men were frantically digging into the earth with their bayonets and helmets to escape the fusillade. Despite their efforts the casualties were mounting with every passing minute. Things were already bad, but they were about to get a lot worse.[4]

Seeing the Moors' advance slowed by the determined resistance on the two shallow hills to their front, Lieutenant Colonel Asensio ordered his artillery to lay down a barrage across the enemy position. At 1.00pm they opened fire. The White House made an excellent target. Through their binoculars the gunnery officers saw the first shell fall short. Adjusting their range a second salvo was sent over, exploding just beyond the target. The third scored a direct hit. Roof tiles and hunks of whitewashed wattle and daub flew through the air. Soon shells were peppering the hill and obscuring the summit with dust.

With the artillery zeroing in, the 4th Company panicked. As the only solid cover available, the White House drew the men like a magnet and soon the building and its yard were packed. They needed firm leadership, but Bert Overton was unable to cope. After disappearing for some time during the advance, he briefly rejoined his men at 1.30pm. Comrade Roe, the company's second-in-command, saw him approaching through the dust. With the shells exploding around him, Overton snapped once more. 'God damn it!' he yelled. 'It's too bloody hot here. I'm getting out of it!' With that he took off again, leaving Roe dumbfounded.[5] Hiding himself on the rear slope with a few of his men, Overton left the rest to their fate. When the first shells hit the White House, pounding into its roof and walls, they caused carnage. The men of the 2nd Company, safe on the ridgeline, saw body parts raining down onto the rear slopes. Inside the building, Spiller's machine-gun group were slaughtered. When the New Zealander came to, blood was seeping from his ears and his eyes and mouth were clogged with dust. Looking round him, he saw the walls of the farmhouse had been splattered with gore. Eight of his ten-man light machine-gun team had been killed.[6]

Further south, Briskey's 3rd Company were also coming under pressure. The odd stray shell aimed at the White House burst near them and the machine-gun fire playing havoc with Conway and Overton's men was also beginning to take its toll. Sergeant Watson's section, which had taken up position on the left flank, had also come under heavy fire. After toughing it out for an hour, they had been forced to rejoin the rest of the company.[7] Frank Graham, the scholar from Sunderland, was feeling the pressure: 'I could hardly hold ... [my] gun, couldn't shoot straight and was as nervous as a mouse.'[8] Nevertheless, Briskey still felt his men were largely playing the role of passive observers. Determined to serve the battalion well, he sent Walter Gregory, the company runner, to Wintringham to ask if his men were needed to reinforce White House Hill. What Briskey did not realize was that he would soon need all the men he had. Twenty minutes earlier a group of Moors had begun to work their way towards them. Crawling forward through the undergrowth from the farm that Prendergast had spotted from the Conical Hill, they had advanced unseen and were now closing on Briskey's position. If the Nationalists broke through, they could push on towards the Valencia road unmolested.[9]

From his position on the ridgeline, Wintringham could see the pounding his front line was taking. The Nationalist gunners had now spread their fire and shells were also bursting around Conway's men on the Conical Hill. Nevertheless, Wintringham still believed things were under control. As far as the English Captain could make out through his binoculars, Conway was unconcerned. Strolling around the hilltop, the Irishman appeared to be casually pointing out enemy concentrations with his stick. Detachments of the 1st and 4th companies, meanwhile, were visible on the rear slopes, seemingly acting as a reserve, and although a few wounded were limping back across the valley, or being dragged or carried to the rear by their comrades, the volume of casualties that Wintringham could see did not seem to be extreme. 'They were doing well,' the English Captain recalled; 'they needed ... no direct support, only a guarding of their flanks.'[10] What Wintringham did not know was that the riflemen were close to panic, the majority of the wounded were coming back from the line through a thin belt of olive trees which hid them from his view and Conway was taking extreme risks by exposing himself to heavy fire. Wintringham's ignorance was compounded by the lack of information coming in from his company commanders. Whilst he had not expected to hear much from Conway, who as a veteran of Lopera and Las Rozas considered Wintringham's interference superfluous, Briskey and Overton were a different matter. The lack of information gnawed at him and doubts began to enter his mind. His left flank remained badly exposed and he had heard nothing from the men of the 3rd Company since they had advanced over an hour before. Taking a pencil stub from his jacket, he scribbled down a note ordering Briskey to deploy a section to his left front to prevent the Moors outflanking them. Wintringham sent his runner, Ronnie Burgess, a long-legged seventeen year-old whose now-blank eyes had once sparkled with amusement, to carry the note to the forward line. If Briskey was already dead or could not be found, Burgess was to deliver the note to Overton and inform him to pass on the message to whoever was in command of the men on the left flank.[11]

Head down, Burgess set off at a sprint. He ran south down the Sunken Road until it curved round and petered out near Briskey's position. With stray bullets whipping overhead, he then turned north-east, cutting through the olive groves to the rear slopes of White House Hill. The scene on the hilltop was appalling. The dead and wounded were everywhere. Bodies were rolling down the slope and severed limbs, heads and shattered torsos lay scattered about. Heading upwards, Burgess found Overton in a hollow just below the summit. The former guardsman was in a state of shock. Babbling incoherently he rattled out a series of demands for reinforcements, food, water, barbed wire, entrenching tools and artillery support. His men, meanwhile, had been left to fare for themselves. Two section commanders had been wounded and Overton himself was clearly unable to command. Some of his men were attempting to fight back, shooting wildly with blazing hot rifles or loosing off a few rounds with their light machine guns before they jammed. Others were digging into the earth, scraping shallow trenches to hide themselves from the worst of the enemy fire. Some had even formed low barricades from the bodies of their dead comrades, which seemed to shiver each time a bullet or chunk of shrapnel bit home.[12]

A dozen feet to the rear, screaming to make himself heard above the thunder of the guns, Burgess passed on Wintringham's message to protect the left flank. As Overton had no report to give in return, the runner set off down the hill, heading back through the olive groves to Wintringham's position. Rather than passing on the message to Briskey, who remained in the dark as to his commander's requirements, Overton decided to act on the information himself. As Wintringham would later remark, the former Welsh Guardsman 'wanted to be courageous, but had lived too easily, too softly'.[13] Nevertheless, over the course of the next few days, he would occasionally master his baser instincts and show himself capable of momentary valour. Gathering a section of his men, Overton ordered them to advance south-east and protect the left flank. They moved forward in short rushes. Running down the slope, they hurled themselves to the ground to fire off a few rounds before advancing once more. In this section of the front, the gradient was shallower, and as there was a little more cover, the section initially made good progress. Little did they realize, however, that the Moors advancing from the farmhouse were well hidden just a few dozen yards to their left. When the enemy commander gave the order his men opened up and the British section was caught in a cross-fire. Unable to find cover from both the Moors to their front and those to their left, the section was annihilated in minutes. Only a handful made it back. Nevertheless, the sortie achieved its objective. Startled by the sudden charge, the Moors were discouraged from making further encroachments on the British flank. Instead they pulled back to the farmhouse to prepare for a frontal assault.[14]

Seeing the remains of the shattered section staggering back up the hillside towards him, Overton lost the last vestiges of self control. Wide eyed with panic he deserted his men. John 'Bosco' Jones saw him go. '[He] came over to me,' the Londoner recalled, 'and said "I've forgotten my binoculars".' 'I'll go back for them,' Jones offered, but Overton insisted he should go himself. 'You can't go and leave us,' Jones called after him, but his pleas were ignored. Running down the slope, Overton cut through the long grass of the valley floor and climbed up the ridge to the heavy machine-gun position. 'What are you doing here?' Fry demanded as he leapt over the low stone wall, 'Get back and find your company!' 'Leave me [to] catch my breath first and then I'll go!' Overton replied.[15] After resting for twenty minutes, he reluctantly returned to White House Hill. He was later seen lying on the lee slope, his head in his hands, weeping uncontrollably.

On the Conical Hill the 1st Company were faring little better. The machine-gun fire from their front and right flank was literally eating the summit of the hill away. Adding to the chaos were the artillery and mortar rounds and occasional strafing runs made by Nationalist planes. A veteran of the Great War later said it was 'worse than the Somme'.[16] Casualties were steadily mounting. With blood pouring from wounds to his head and arm, Paddy Smith spent several minutes crying out for help, before finally losing consciousness. Goff and Daly had fallen and been dragged to the rear and the Spaniard who had shared a wry smile with Prendergast had been killed. George Gowans, a Scottish veteran of the fighting in Madrid's University City, had been wounded in the head and his entire six-man light machine-gun team had been wiped out by strafing planes and mortar fire. Despite the losses, which amounted to one third of the company, the men were still fighting back. A young Scot was firing bursts from his light machine gun and Fred Copeman had taken charge of a section of the men. Having ascertained the source of the enfilading machine-gun fire coming from the Knoll to their right, he pulled them round into cover on the south-eastern slope of the hill. Kit Conway, meanwhile, still refused to go to ground. His stubborn defiance would prove his undoing. At 2.30pm, whilst he was standing to fire his rifle, three machine-gun bullets ripped open his groin. His weapon spun from his hand and Conway crumpled to the ground. Prendergast saw him fall and immediately realized the wound was fatal. By the time he reached him, Conway's face had already drained of colour. His flesh drawn taut in agony, with his last words he urged his men to do their best and hold on. Tears glistening in his eyes, Prendergast watched as his friend was loaded onto a stretcher and carried to the rear.[17]

Prendergast had precious little time to mourn. Moments later, he noticed a line of Nationalist tanks backed by an infantry battalion moving up the Morata road to their right. The vehicles were captured Russian T26s armed with 45mm cannon. Spotting the British on the hills to their left, the tanks paused and opened fire. The first blast lifted Prendergast off his feet. Badly winded and bleeding from several shrapnel wounds down one side of his body, he had landed several feet away. After being bandaged up, he too was carried to the rear by Davidovitch's men. Meanwhile, the tanks had also spotted Albert Charlesworth's group from the 4th Company who up until then had been relatively safe in their position between the two hills. Within seconds the cannon shells were bursting amongst them. Charlesworth and the rest were forced to withdraw and took up new positions on White House Hill. Finding cover on the rear slopes amongst a group of stretcher bearers, Charlesworth realized he still had some Woodbines left. Reaching into his jacket pocket he shared them round. Encrusted with dust, blood and sweat, his comrades' faces cracked into smiles as they accepted them.[18]

Minutes later, Ralph Campeau, the 1st Company's singing commissar, was badly wounded. Whilst belting out the *Young Guardsman* over the roar of exploding shells, a volley of machine-gun fire ripped open his stomach. Tom Clarke, a stretcher bearer from Dundee, had the unenviable task of carrying the 16-stone giant from the field. Whilst he and his partner were struggling down the slope into the valley, a burst of fire from the Moors on the Knoll cut through them. Clarke and his companion were unhurt, but Campeau was hit for a second time and died shortly afterwards. Back on the hilltop, Ken Stalker, the Scot who had served in the Great War, had taken command of Conway's Company.[19] Aided by André Diamant, the Egyptian student who Wintringham thought 'the maddest, most mysterious Levantine I have ever come across', Stalker ordered the remains of his company to join Copeman's men on the south side of the hill.[20] Leaving Wild, Crook and a few others on the hilltop to watch for an enemy advance, the rest moved into their new position, grateful for the respite.[21]

In the momentary lull, Copeman decided to see what had happened to Fry's machine-gun company. Throughout the afternoon, he had been getting increasingly irate at the lack of covering fire from the ridge and the Englishman was now furious. After picking his way across the valley floor, he climbed the ridge and launched into a fusillade of foul language as soon as he caught sight of Fry. 'What the bloody hell happened to you?' he demanded. Fry tried to explain, but Copeman was in no mood to listen. 'You're responsible for all this slaughter,' he roared. 'If your guns were working we could have stopped this bloody bunch.'[22] Just then Copeman was hit in the side of the head by a stray bullet. 'It was a curious feeling,' he later recalled, 'rather like receiving morphia. Everything went warm and I felt sleepy.' The blood pouring from his scalp began running into his eyes. 'All that I looked at had a red tinge about it, and yet I could still see to move round.' On the positive side, he no longer felt the pain from the bullet lodged in his thumb. Like a man possessed, Copeman ignored his wounds and stormed back to the Sunken Road to berate Wintringham. Whatever happened, the former mutineer was determined to get the Maxims into action.[23]

By 3.00pm Wintringham was starting to realize the precariousness of his situation. Behind him, the Sunken Road was filling up with casualties from the forward positions and the volume of fire directed at the hills ahead was overwhelming. He also knew that to order the rifle companies to withdraw without significant fire support from the ridgeline would be suicide. With the Maxim heavy machine guns still out of action, the Moors could follow any retreat and overwhelm their second line. As if to add to his woes, a burst of bullets crackled through the foliage overhead. The fire seemed to be coming from the rear. Beside him, a man panicked, yelling that Nationalist tanks had broken through their lines. Wintringham soon calmed him and turned his attention back to the fire coming from behind them. The noise had convinced him it was Maxims, which could only mean one thing – reinforcements had been sent up to join them! Alex McDade, his ever-reliable adjutant, agreed.[24]

At 5ft 2in, McDade was the shortest man in the battalion and also one of the most remarkable. 'A prodigious liar', he claimed to have been a hero of the Easter Rising, a former member of the French Foreign Legion and an Irish Guard who had served in India and seen action at the Somme.[25] While not everyone believed his claims, the punctilious drill major was well liked for his sense of humour and respected for his discipline and 'trim efficiency'.[26]

Turning away from the Nationalist line, Wintringham and McDade yelled in vain at their unseen assailants to cease fire. Their pleas lost in the cacophony of screaming metal, they slipped out of the trench and crawled on their bellies towards the Sunken Road. Minutes later they encountered a terrified Spanish officer who had been inadvertently directing his company's fire onto the British forward positions on the hills. The officer was shoved to the ground by McDade. In the scuffle that followed the Spaniard's revolver went off, the round going straight through his foot. Wintringham later surmised that the wound had been self inflicted, an attempt to get himself out of harm's way, but in the confusion the English Captain could not be sure.[27] As their commander limped to the rear, Wintringham pointed out Conway's and Overton's positions to the Spaniards and ordered them to stay where they were and hold their fire until he told them otherwise. He then went to examine their guns. The company had eight Maxims, newer weapons than Fry's, which could take rifle ammunition. Remarkably, the rear sights had been set to zero. The Spaniards had been firing at nothing in particular, merely blazing away in panic to their front, their bullets cutting a swathe through the earth some 50 yards ahead. Poorly led and in a state of panic, Wintringham thought the Maxims wasted on the Spaniards. Fry's company, on the other hand, could make great use of the guns. As Wintringham returned to the Sunken Road, a plan to commandeer them began forming in his mind. By the time he reached the position, however, the idea was redundant. Fry's Maxims had arrived.

CHAPTER 7

RETREAT!

After berating Harry Fry for failing to provide covering fire for the rifle companies, Fred Copeman set off through the olive groves. Back at the Cookhouse, he met George Aitken, the battalion's political commissar. A rugged Scots communist, Aitken was a veteran of the British Army and was already well acquainted with the horrors of war. In a single afternoon in 1915 during the battle of Loos, his brother and five best friends had been killed by shell fragments and Aitken had been badly wounded.[1] 'If [the splinter] ... had gone in another five centimetres [two inches] to the right,' he later explained, 'I wouldn't be here today.'[2] Following his experiences in the Great War, Aitken had travelled to Moscow to study at the Marx-Engels Institute, where he later became a lecturer, before returning to Britain to work as the Communist Party's chief organizer in the north-east.[3] Having left his wife and young son in tears as he departed for Spain, Aitken was willing to put personal commitments in second place and was utterly dedicated to the cause.

Whilst having his wounds attended to, Copeman informed Aitken of the mix up with the Maxim ammunition. Together they then set out for the front. Whilst still three miles from the Sunken Road, they chanced across Sergeant Hornsby's abandoned ammunition truck. Earlier that morning, the sergeant, a thirty-seven year-old father of one notorious for his drinking, had had several brandies after loading up in Morata. Whilst navigating the winding tracks leading to the battalion's forward position, he had rolled the truck on a corner, killing his

The Retreat: 5.00pm, 12 February 1937

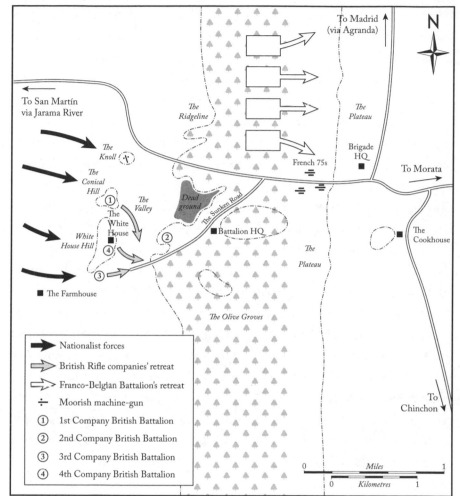

To Madrid
(via Agranda)

N

To San Martín
via Jarama River

The Ridgeline

The Plateau

The Knoll

Brigade
HQ

To Morata

French 75s

The Conical Hill

The Valley

Dead ground

The Sunken Road

The White House

■ Battalion HQ

The Cookhouse

White House Hill

The Plateau

■ The Farmhouse

The Olive Groves

To
Chinchon

Nationalist forces

British Rifle companies' retreat

Franco-Belgian Battalion's retreat

Moorish machine-gun

① 1st Company British Battalion

② 2nd Company British Battalion

③ 3rd Company British Battalion

④ 4th Company British Battalion

Miles   1

Kilometres   1

assistant, and spilling the ammunition across the road. By the time Copeman and Aitken came along, Hornsby had long since fled the scene.[4]

Grabbing a box of cartridges each, Copeman and Aitken dragged them through the groves, crossing an open ploughed field shortly before reaching the ridgeline. Years later, Copeman would admit that it was only then that he realized the danger of the situation. As the bullets whipped overhead, he had become gripped by a fear that he would be hit in the guts. Clasping the box firmly to his stomach, he set off on a sprint across the field, only realizing the irony of protecting himself with a box of ammunition after he had reached the safety of the groves.[5] Wintringham was delighted to see them. Smiling up at Copeman, he asked if there was more ammunition. 'Yes, of course there's fucking, blinding, sodding ammo; but we'll have to fill the belts,' Copeman replied.[6] Wintringham did not need telling twice: with the machine guns up and running, the rifle companies could be withdrawn from the ridgeline under covering fire. Immediately he began organizing his men. One group was assigned the painstaking task of hand filling the belts bullet by bullet. Another was sent to bring up the Maxims from the olive groves where Fry had left them.

Amongst those who volunteered was Tony Hyndman, Overton's former comrade in the Guards. A prominent member of the battalion's 'middle class intellectuals', the 'sandy-haired' Welshman had gained notoriety with the British press as the former secretary and sometime lover of Stephen Spender, the pre-eminent Marxist poet of the age.[7] In his memoirs, Spender would confess that he felt himself partly responsible for Hyndman's decision to travel to Spain as the couple had split up shortly before the Welshman had left.[8] Such thoughts were far from Hyndman's mind on the afternoon of the 12th. It had been a frustrating day for the twenty-one year-old: his rifle had not been properly greased and had proved next to useless. Keen to contribute, he set off to collect the Maxims with a dozen others, running bent double down a pathway through the groves. The fire overhead was increasing in intensity and as they crossed the open field a patrol of Nationalist fighter planes swooped down to strafe them. Several were gunned down as they ran. Hyndman and the rest made it to the far side where they split up into pairs to drag the Maxims back to the front. Grabbing the gun with one hand and a box of ammunition in the other, the Welshman and his partner re-crossed the field as the planes dived for a second pass. The roar of the approaching aero-engines filled their ears as they struggled over the uneven ground. As the fighters got closer, they could hear the wind whistling through the struts on their wings; then the Nationalist pilots opened fire. A volley of bullets stitched a line down Hyndman's partner's back. Heaving the body to one side, the Welshman dragged the gun across the last few yards then dashed back for the ammunition as the planes returned for a final pass. Curling into a ball, he covered his crotch with the ammo boxes and awaited the inevitable. It was Hyndman's lucky day. The bullets missed him entirely.[9]

As the machine guns were hauled into position, George Nathan appeared with news of what was happening on the battalion's flanks. The Franco-Belgians had been driven back five times by determined Nationalist charges led by the tanks that Prendergast and Charlesworth had seen earlier. Each time the volunteers had counter-attacked and had now established a line to the right rear of the British position. Spanish troops were with them and the German Thaelmann Battalion was about to join the fight. After receiving the news, Wintringham pointed out the whereabouts of his rifle companies. Nathan was pleased the hills were still being held, but remained concerned about the battalion's open left flank. The Spanish cavalry that had been ordered to fill the gap were nowhere to be seen. 'I'm going back to Brigade [HQ] now and will insist that the cavalry report to you,' he told Wintringham. 'And I'll ask Gal to make you sector commander, so that you take over this Spanish Battalion that you say is near here. Get down to the telephone – it's half-way down this sunken road – in an hour's time and ask for me.'[10]

Just then the bright red cab of the battalion's second ammunition truck came into view. Charles West, the former assistant secretary of the Mitcham Divisional Labour Party, was behind the wheel. The twenty-four year-old, whom Wintringham had previously dismissed as a 'useless, harmless little pip-squeak', had defied his orders to remain behind the lines after hearing of Sergeant Hornsby's crash. The Studebaker, packed with bullets for the Colts, Chauchats and Maxims as well as boxes of rifle ammunition, was cheered as it made its way up the Sunken Road. Wintringham had to admire the youngster's courage. He had a ton of bullets and high explosives packed behind him that any stray round could have touched off. As if to echo his thoughts, a rolling wave of heavy machine-gun fire made the men scatter. The Nationalists' German allies had spotted the truck. Nathan ordered the driver to back up 'ten yards into cover' and then 'hurried away with a wave of his gloves'.[11]

Moving south down the Sunken Road to where a gap in the olive groves afforded a view of his forward positions, Wintringham saw a steady trail of walking wounded and stretcher bearers coming back from the hills.

Davidovitch's men had been so busy that their supply of stretchers had long since been exhausted and they were now reduced to using folded blankets to carry the wounded from the field.[12] The sight caught Wintringham by surprise. It was only then that he realized the full extent of casualties that his rifle companies had suffered. As he pondered the development, he was approached by Fred Killick, 'a solid, useful corporal' barely out of his teens, who had previously been a bank manager's son from Stockport.[13] Having just come from White House Hill, Killick reported that the situation was getting desperate: Conway had been hit and Overton hadn't been seen for the last hour. '[They] want definite orders about retiring,' he said. Reaching for his pencil stub, Wintringham wrote out instructions to withdraw if they felt they were about to be outflanked or that their position was untenable.[14]

By the time Killick reached André Diamant and Ken Stalker on White House Hill, the late winter sun was already low in the sky. Wintringham's ambiguity caused them several moments of doubt. Should they hold or retire? If they withdrew with no machine-gun support, the retreat could turn into a massacre, but if they remained in position it was only a matter of time before they were overrun. Killick was sent back to ask Wintringham for confirmation, but before he could return the decision was suddenly taken out of Diamant's and Stalker's hands. One of the scouts left on the hilltop came running towards them with urgent news. The Moors were attacking! Climbing upwards Diamant and Stalker saw the advance with their own eyes. A horde of enemy troops, the entire 7th *Tabor* of Melilla, were preparing to sweep up from the farmhouse to their left front. Knowing they could not hold out, Diamant and Stalker gave the order to retire.[15]

Safe behind their parapet on the far side of the Conical Hill, Sam Wild and David Crook failed to hear the order. Whilst their comrades pulled back with the wounded, the two companions remained oblivious. Crook, who had earlier complained to Wild that he had not had a decent target to fire at all afternoon, was now presented with a better shot as the Moors broke cover and moved in on their position.[16]

Concentrating on the advancing enemy, he and Wild failed to realize they were alone until the first Moors had reached the western slopes of the hill.

Looking around them, they saw the hillside was empty apart from the crumpled corpses of their comrades. The dead looked nothing like the Cheltenham graduate had imagined. Some had 'a curious muffled look, like a dead bird'. Others had holes torn into them the size of a man's fist.[17] Realizing their predicament, Crook decided 'it was time to get off that bloody hill'. Picking up several discarded rifles and a box of ammunition, they began the descent, but soon dumped the lot after struggling through the thorn bushes. By now they could hear the Moors moving into their old positions above them. Knowing that anything that would delay them had to be abandoned, Crook reluctantly discarded his haversack to further lighten the load. Inside were the last of the tangerines Maria had given him back in Madrigueras and his copy of Shakespeare's *Tragedies*. Since his arrival in Spain two months before he had not had time to read a word.[18]

A few hundred yards to the south, John Henderson had also been caught out by the speed of the Moors' attack. As he sheltered in the hollow on the rear slope of White House Hill where Overton had hidden earlier that afternoon, the Nationalist troops came flying over the top of him. 'I fired some shots,' he recalled, 'and then I did what everyone else was doing. I beat it.'[19]

Back at the Sunken Road, Wintringham sent out two runners. One went to Fry's machine gunners on the ridgeline, 'ordering him to hold his fire, if the Moors came over ... until he got a nice target'.[20] A second, who spoke fluent French, set off northwards to telephone Brigade HQ. His message read: 'I shall hold the main ridge, which I believe is considerably farther forward than the troops on my right. There is a gap of a thousand metres [1,094 yards] between my position and these troops. Can you fill this gap? No sign of our cavalry on my left. Please send up filled Maxim belts, hand-grenades, and barbed wire.'[21] As the runners set off, a company of Spaniards jumped down into the Sunken Road to Wintringham's left. The men seemed exhausted. After setting up two Colt light machine guns on the bank of the road, several fell asleep, whilst their comrades kept a nervous watch on the olive groves to the west. Through an interpreter Wintringham learnt that they were all that remained of the Spanish battalion that had been sent to reinforce him. The rest, including their commander, were still somewhere to the east, well behind the front line.

Wintringham was informing them of the positions of his forward companies, when a staff officer arrived. Although the staffer 'talked very bad French', when asked to wait for an interpreter he refused. After telling the officer about the weight of machine-gun fire his men were under, estimating that some fifty guns were trained on their positions, Wintringham informed him that he had given his forward companies an order to withdraw. The officer was appalled. 'To retire?' he screamed. 'You have not the right! It is Colonel Gal's order that you hold at all costs. The Colonel shall hear of this.' With that he stormed off up the Sunken Road in search of the telephone.[22]

Down on the valley floor, the remnants of the 1st and 4th companies were retreating. Running southwards through a narrow belt of olive trees, they headed for the dead ground to the south east of White House Hill. Although safe from the fire to their front, they were fully exposed to the Moors' Hotchkiss machine guns set up on the Knoll a few hundred yards to the north. Dozens were gunned down. Ken Stalker, the Scottish Great War veteran whose helmet had saved him at Lopera, was 'shot through the head and killed' and Maurice Davidovitch, the young Jewish cockney in charge of the stretcher bearers, was also hit.[23] Watching from the ridgeline with the machine gunners, Fred Copeman saw him fall: 'Just as he opened his mouth to say something ... a burst of machine-rifle fire ripped out his stomach. [Then] his ... guts fell out ... [but] he just picked [them] ... up in his hands and stuffed [them] ... all back again ... [with] blood pouring down his ... legs.'[24] Davidovitch instructed his comrades to leave him there and 'attend to men whose lives might be saved'. Ignoring his protests, they dragged him back towards the Sunken Road.[25]

In charge of the remnants of the 1st Company following Stalker's death, André Diamant was one of the few men not to panic. After organizing a group to escort Davidovitch and the rest of the wounded, the thirty-seven year-old Egyptian asked for volunteers to fight a rearguard action. Thirty men stepped forward. They would remain in the valley for half an hour as their comrades drew back. Firing at any Moors who appeared on the hilltops they had abandoned, they bought enough time for the majority to escape.[26] Dan Gibbons, the secretary of the Saint Pancras Communist Party, was amongst those who agreed to stay behind. At about 5.00pm, Gibbons later remembered, a group of Moors suddenly appeared just 20 yards away from them. 'It was impossible to miss them. We just had to stand up [and fire].'[27] After finishing his clip, Gibbons turned to retreat, but was shot in the back. With a bullet lodged in his right shoulder blade, he feared the worst, but was helped clear by Londoner Tony Yates.[28]

Meanwhile, Sam Wild and David Crook were just reaching the valley floor. Pausing beside an olive tree, they turned and fired on the Moors gathering above them. As he spun back, the Hotchkiss on the Knoll riddled Wild's left side with machine-gun bullets. At first the former sailor thought he was dead. 'One [bullet] had ... rolled around the back of my spine and paralysed me,' he explained.[29] Crook was not fooled, however. Heaving Wild onto his shoulder, he set off after Diamant's rearguard, which was now disappearing southwards down the valley. Staggering under the weight of his comrade, Crook was hit by yet another burst of machine-gun fire. Two bullets caught him in the thigh, 'another ... landed in the heel of my right boot and one went through my water bottle'. Promising not to abandon each other, the companions huddled under cover, wishing that 'the bastards would leave [them] ... alone'. As the last of the red wine he had kept in his water bottle soaked into the chalky soil, Crook prayed for nightfall so they could make their escape.[30]

Half a mile to the south, the 3rd Company was also retreating. Although largely unexposed to the fire that had decimated their comrades in the opening stages of the battle, since mid-afternoon they had been under severe pressure. First artillery shells had peppered their position, then the planes that had killed Hyndman's comrade in the ploughed field had strafed them, and finally the Moors had set up three machine guns to rake their lines. By 2.00pm Briskey had deployed all his reserves and from then on matters had deteriorated even further. Having heard nothing from Battalion Headquarters and increasingly worried about his open left flank, the former Dalston busman had finally decided to withdraw at the same time as Diamant and Stalker. With the Moors hot on their heels, they pulled back towards the valley floor. As they ran, the Moors opened fire. Eddie Wilkinson, the nineteen year-old bus conductor from Sunderland, was killed instantly. His close friend, Frank Graham, saw him fall. 'In the heat of battle, I didn't fully appreciate how much

Eddie's death meant to me,' he later admitted.[31] At the same time Noel Carrit, the founder of the October Club, Oriel College's first communist society, was wounded. The 'bullet hit the barrel of his rifle and broke his wrist'.[32] As he was helped from the field, Clem Beckett and Christopher Saint John Sprigg decided to buy their comrades some time. Ignoring the order to retire, they set up their Chauchat light machine gun, 'a queer blunderbuss-looking thing' which they had been employing to great effect all afternoon.[33] Soon the first enemy troops appeared. Pausing to see what would become of them, Frank Graham saw Beckett and Sprigg open fire. Several Moors fell but then the gun jammed.[34] As Graham watched, they desperately tried to clear the blockage, but the enemy charged. Hurling grenades, they closed in, then finished them off with bayonets and machetes.[35]

By now the rest of the 3rd Company had reached the valley floor. As company commander Bill Briskey was running across, he looked up to see Walter Gregory, the messenger whom he had dispatched to ask Wintringham for instructions several hours before. Gregory had had an eventful afternoon. Dodging artillery shells, he had made it to Wintringham's position only to find out the withdrawal had already begun. As Briskey and Gregory stood staring at each other across the valley floor, the Nationalists' heavy guns fell silent. Confused by the sudden calm, the British didn't know what to expect. Then hundreds of Moors came boiling over the crest of White House Hill. 'Howling' a bloodcurdling war cry, they fired machine guns and Mauser rifles from the hip as they ran.[36] To his horror, Gregory found himself caught up in their advance. With Moors ahead, behind and to both sides of him he ran towards his comrades a few hundred yards to the south. Seeing him surrounded by the enemy, Briskey sprinted towards him, but was hit before he had run more than a few dozen yards. 'As I approached,' Gregory recalled, 'I could see that he was staggering, holding his stomach and groaning ... by the time I was a few yards away, [he] ... collapsed.'[37]

Gregory had no time to mourn his commander. As he stood over the former bus driver's prostrate form, he heard footsteps behind him. Turning round, he beheld the biggest Moor he had ever seen. Although just a few yards away, the African had somehow failed to notice him. Raising his rifle to his shoulder,

Gregory aimed at the Moor's armpit and fired. At first he thought that the shot had missed. 'With a mounting feeling of panic', he reloaded and aimed a second time. Before he could pull the trigger, the Moor's 'legs sagged and he ... collapsed. [He now] looked pathetic ... like a heap of dirty old clothes waiting for wash-day.'[38] A shout interrupted Gregory's contemplation. Another huge Moroccan was bearing down on him at speed. Angered by Briskey's death, Gregory lost his composure. Rather than firing his rifle he charged with his bayonet. With no thoughts of taking on the crazed Englishman in hand-to-hand combat, the Moor calmly took aim and fired. The bullet hit the metal work of Gregory's rifle, ricocheted down the barrel and tore off the thumb knuckle of his right hand. The impact spun him 'round like a kiddie's top' and he 'fell to the ground in a dead faint'. Luckily, the Moor was too busy to check if he was dead.[39]

Whilst Gregory was lying unconscious on the valley floor, the last stragglers of the 1st, 3rd and 4th companies were still retreating through the olive groves to the south of the British line. Diamant's band had already passed through on their way to the rear and, with Briskey dead, no-one was in command. The Moors were in hot pursuit and those who remained were close to panic. Amongst them was Tommy Fanning, a rifleman from the 1st Company who had left the Conical Hill minutes earlier with a group of his comrades. Five of them were carrying a sixth who had been wounded. When they reached the southern end of the Sunken Road, a group of Moors appeared through the trees, still several yards behind but well within rifle range. Seeing them, one man fled, Fanning and two others threw themselves to the ground, and the other two stood frozen to the spot. A burst of fire from the Moors killed them both. Crouching down behind the bank of the road, Fanning and the wounded man were left alone with one other, Alec Armstrong, a twenty-six year-old plumber from Hulme. Unable to carry the casualty on his own, Fanning asked his comrade for help. 'Heh! Alec give us a lift with this fella will you?' he pleaded. Armstrong refused. In the confusion of the retreat he had left the bolt of his light machine gun in place and was determined to go back to the hills and retrieve it. 'You've got no chance Alec,' Fanning warned him. The Mancunian paid him no heed. Leaping to his feet, he disappeared back through the groves. Fanning would never see him again. With the Moors a matter of yards away, he was then forced into a decision that would haunt him for the rest of his days. Abandoning the wounded man, he crept off alone. Heading eastwards through the olive groves hoping to find the Cookhouse he had left that morning, Fanning got hopelessly lost. With the enemy somewhere behind him and the sky overhead growing darker, he began to panic. 'I did a bit of squealing [and] screaming for my mother', he admitted, before being found by some Spanish troops who had finally come up to cover the open left flank. Together they went back to look for the wounded man, but he was nowhere to be seen. 'The Moors must have got him,' Fanning had no option but to conclude.[40]

CHAPTER 8
'THE MOORS WERE MOWED DOWN IN SCORES'

It was shortly before 6.00pm. The sun had sunk behind the hills on the far side of the River Jarama and the last of the light was seeping out of the day. Whilst the Moors on White House Hill readied themselves for an assault on the ridgeline, Harry Fry's machine-gun company were nervously awaiting their advance. As the Maxims had been silent all day, Pedro Pimentel, the Spanish officer in charge of Asensio's 8th Regiment, was convinced that victory was within his grasp. With the British companies cleared from the hills, all that stood between him and the plateau leading to the Valencia Road was a ridgeline held by a few dozen riflemen. Turning to Captain León, the commander of the 7th *Tabor* of Melilla, he ordered him to form his men into line, advance into the valley and sweep the ridge clear of what little resistance remained.[1]

What Pimentel did not know was that the British were waiting for him. Copeman and Aitken had been readying the Maxims for action all afternoon: the belts were loaded, the cooling systems filled with water and the gun teams, crouched behind their shields, were anxious to be given the order to fire. Joe Garber, a twenty-six year-old volunteer from the East End, had wanted to shoot as soon as the Moors had appeared on the hills opposite to cover the last of the rifle companies falling back across the valley floor. 'It was bleeding heartbreaking' to see one's comrades gunned down as they fled without being able to do a thing about it.[2] Nevertheless, Copeman refused to let the gunners fire. Threatening to box the ears of anyone who disobeyed him, he prowled up and down the line of Maxims glowering at his charges. Fry, nominally the leader of the 2nd Company, had already been cowed by the half-crazed Englishman. 'The least you have to bloody say mate, the better,' Copeman had warned him hours earlier when he had first learnt about the mix up with the ammunition, 'because when this is finished you're going to get your bloody head chopped off.'[3]

As he walked behind the guns, Copeman gave out instructions. 'Now look,' he began:

> This is what's got to happen. Not a bloody round has got to be fired [until my command]... And when I say 'Fire', you fire from the right to the left all together and keep going backwards and forwards until there isn't a bloody thing alive. They're here facing a good old bloody sailor [referring to himself] and you're going to get the show of your life. You'll never see how many men you can kill in a short time. These [pointing to the Maxims] are wonderful things you've got here. But don't fire until I say so because if you do there's anti-tank guns over there. They'll blow us right out of the bloody ground. They don't know we're here at the moment, so good luck, you haven't been noticed up to now.[4]

Despite Copeman's aura of confidence, doubts were niggling away at him inside. 'I was wondering if I had really trained these crews properly,' or if the guns would actually fire, he admitted.[5] Copeman was not the only one struggling to control his nerves. Beside him, manning the gun he had dragged across the ploughed field, Tony Hyndman was close to panic and Joe Garber's mouth was so dry that a lump had formed in his throat and he couldn't swallow.[6] To make matters worse, the shallow trench was half filled with wounded men who had been dragged back from the hills. John Henderson, the cabinet maker from Gateshead, noticed one casualty in particular. 'There was this ... big lad from London,' he recalled, 'lying there with his guts hanging out'. He was clearly in agony, but no one knew what to do to help him. As the volunteers waited for Copeman to give the order to fire, he died.[7]

At 6.00pm the Nationalists advanced. Although there could have been no more than 500 men, to the British troops waiting on the ridgeline, it seemed as though Franco's entire army was coming to get them. Copeman remembered they advanced in a long line, three or four men deep. Amongst the Moors and khaki-coated legionnaires were mounted officers. They had flowing red and blue cloaks and sabres drawn.[8] Garber remembered they were 'howling' as they advanced.[9] He thought that the troops, faces half hidden behind capes and cowls, 'looked like the devil himself'.[10] Another volunteer saw them firing machine rifles from the hip as they ran. Once they had reached the valley floor, the Nationalists saw the last of the British riflemen still retreating through the band of olive trees leading to the south. Turning towards them, some of the Nationalists opened fire. The rest continued advancing, moving ever closer to the ridgeline. By the time they were 200 yards away, it was all that Copeman could do to stop his men opening fire. John Tunnah remembered his comrades were literally begging for permission. One young gunner couldn't control himself. After cursing Copeman, he turned back to his Maxim, but before he could pull the twin triggers, the big man rushed over and laid him out with a single blow. With the Moors now climbing the ridge and only 50 yards away, a 'ruffle' went through the British line. Tunnah feared they might rout. Then Copeman gave the order to open fire.[11]

The hail of lead caught the enemy by surprise. 'As innocent as bloody babies they were,' Copeman remembered.[12] 'Within sixty seconds [the] ... five guns ... put over a thousand bullets among' them. Sweeping from right to left, the Nationalists fell in droves.[13] 'You might think to see men mown down as if a scythe was going through them wouldn't be possible, but this is literally what happened,' Tunnah recalled. 'It just stopped them like a stone wall.'[14] Copeman was equally impressed: 'the result was like mowing down wheat.'[15] In the Sunken Road, 100 yards back from the guns, Wintringham risked raising his head to see what was happening. 'As I stood up, I saw what every machine-gunner longs for, and seldom sees – enemy infantry in the open, with a skyline behind them and no good cover available.' From his vantage point he could make out Fry and a few others adding to the carnage with their rifles, whilst the Spaniards who had retreated from the Knoll were firing their Colt light machine guns. 'When they stopped [to reload] ... I could hear the two guns detached from Fry's company', firing away to the left.[16] One of these was crewed by Cyril Sexton, who remembered his gunner, Charlie Hart, a Yorkshire man who was a former reservist from the Royal Sussex Regiment, firing at and around the remains of the White House. 'Yorky' was a skilled shot and immediately began causing heavy casualties.[17] Wintringham, meanwhile, was transfixed by the carnage:

> The Moors could not reply; few could get their machine-rifles to the range before one of Fry's gunners got them [and as] the German heavy machine-gunners [who had been causing many of the British casualties all afternoon] had not [yet] reached the hill; their fire had died off because they were shifting their guns up. Only the Moors on the knoll to our right knew Fry's position with the accuracy that follows hours of watching; but their fire was ineffective, not an English gunner ducked.[18]

To the left front the last survivors from the rifle companies that had held the hills were now safely in the cover of the olive groves. 'They had passed the deepest point in the valley and were climbing towards the sunken road.'[19]

After recovering from the initial shock of the Maxim fire, a few of the Nationalists tried to retreat, 'individually or in small groups'.[20] Copeman ordered some of the gunners to fire behind them to prevent their escape. Seeing the route blocked, the veterans amongst them then threw themselves to the ground and played dead. Copeman was having none of it. 'Keep on bloody well firing,' he commanded, 'there's a lot of live bodies in that'.[21] By now the machine guns' cooling systems were bubbling over with the heat. 'For the final burst,' Tony Hyndman recalled, 'we all urinated into a steel helmet.'[22] The contents were then poured into the cooling jackets and over the barrels, which sizzled with the heat. Providing the liquid was not as easy as it may appear: 'you try peeing under fire,' another volunteer explained. 'All hell ... [was] breaking over your head and you'd be afraid to pull it out in case it got shot off.'[23]

After exhausting their second belts, the Maxims fell silent. Scores of Nationalist troops lay dead and wounded on the valley floor. Amidst the cries

Los Nacionales. This early propaganda poster depicts the unlikely alliance that was pitted against the Spanish Republic.

Moroccan *regulares* awaiting transportation to Seville, July 1936. In history's first airlift, the Army of Africa was carried across the Straits of Gibraltar by German Condor Legion planes.

'The Spanish See-Saw'. A Punch cartoon lampooning the foreign secretary's policy of Non-Intervention.

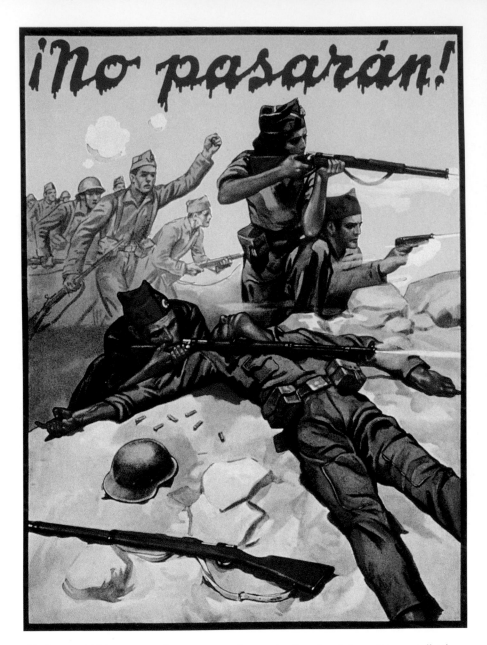

'*No Pasarán*'. This propaganda poster reused a popular French rallying call immortalized during the battle of Verdun. First used during the 1936 campaign in defence of Madrid, '*No Pasarán*' or 'They shall not pass' became one of the Republic's most powerful slogans.

The British Battalion banner. Richly embroidered and surmounted by a silver clenched fist, the flag was purchased with the proceeds of collections taken across Britain and presented to the battalion in November 1937.

Tom Wintringham, photographed in Madrigueras, July 1937. A committed communist and veteran of the Great War, the 'English Captain' led the battalion at Jarama until he was wounded heading a counter-attack on the second day.

Frank Ryan. An IRA activist and ardent Catholic, Ryan was a senior figure in the International Brigades.

The Jarama River. The photo above was taken on the west bank a few hundred yards south of the San Martín Bridge. In the background, looking east, are the hills climbed by the Nationalist troops before they met the British at White House Hill. The photo below was taken from the San Martín Bridge looking south.

The I-16 or Mosca was the Republicans' most advanced fighter plane. During the battle of Jarama the Soviets who piloted them enjoyed air superiority over the Nationalist pilots whose aircraft were both slower and less manoeuvrable.

Two members of Harry Fry's company manning a Maxim machine gun. Due to a mix-up with ammunition, the guns were out of action for the majority of the first day at Jarama, but were later put to deadly effect.

Sam Wild. 'A quick-witted, devil may care' Mancunian with Irish roots, Wild was wounded whilst retreating from the Conical Hill on the first day at Jarama.

The British Battalion on parade behind the front line at Jarama.

Moorish Infantry, Spain 1937. The British feared and demonized the Moors they faced at Jarama.

The Russian-built T26 tank was the most advanced tracked vehicle operating on either side during the Spanish Civil War. Nevertheless, it was of limited effectiveness due to the poor tactics the Republicans employed.

The Sunken Road. Formed over the centuries by farmers' carts repeatedly cutting into the thin Castillian soil, the Sunken Road became the battalion's key defensive line late in the second day of the battle.

A view from the Sunken Road looking west through the olive groves towards the ridgeline. The Jarama River lies out of sight nearly two miles beyond.

for help came the pathetic whinnying of the officers' wounded horses. Although in years to come, some of the British would be haunted by what they had done, that evening there was only elation. 'We cheered. We shouted abuse,' Hyndman remembered. The Nationalists, meanwhile, were 'strangely silent'.[24]

The fighting on the hills had cost the British dear. Of the 400 riflemen deployed, 100 had been killed and 145 wounded. Amongst the former were Clifford Lawther, the amateur north-east boxer with the 3rd Company and Fred Killick, the bank manager's son from Stockport whom Diamant had employed as one of his runners. In the confusion of the withdrawal, many of the survivors had become lost in the olive groves or retreated as far as the Cookhouse where they had started out that morning. A large group made up of the remnants of the 1st and 4th companies led by André Diamant returned to the Sunken Road by about 7.00pm. Another thirty or so, mostly from the 3rd Company, refused to go back and hid in and around the Cookhouse. Wide-eyed with fear, they spread stories of a complete collapse at the front. Some even fled the area entirely. Andrew Flanagan, the young Irish bricklayer who had fallen in love with a local girl during training, didn't stop until he reached Madrigueras over 100 miles to the east. Several other volunteers, like Sam Wild, David Crook and Walter Gregory, were still out in no-man's land.[25]

Knocked unconscious after being shot in his right hand, Walter Gregory awoke at dusk to find himself caught between the lines. Bullets were whipping overhead with alarming regularity as the occasional bursts coming from the hills the British had just abandoned were answered by Fry's Maxims on the ridge. After the slaughter on the valley floor, the surviving Moors had pulled back to the White House and Conical hills, where they were joined by some German heavy machine-gun teams who had moved up to give them covering fire. They were now busy digging in and establishing a new front line. Looking around him, Gregory saw scores of dead and wounded. Moors and British troops were mixed up together. Not daring to stand, Gregory crawled over to where Briskey had fallen an hour earlier. Seeing his company commander was dead, he then slowly made his way back to his own lines.

With his shattered rifle in his left hand, he dragged himself between the dead and wounded, who called out piteously for his help as he crawled by. The pain from his right hand was excruciating. Half the thumb knuckle had been ripped away. To make matters worse, the remnant of the bone was protruding through the open wound. As he crawled, it snagged on the ground, sending jolts of pain shooting up his right side. Eventually, Gregory reached some dead ground where he could safely stand and began making good progress. Having decided that he would be of no use as a rifleman in the near future, he determined to make his way back to the rear and find a dressing station. En route he came across a Spanish soldier, perhaps one of the men who had been ordered to fill the gap on the left of the British line. Gregory was delighted to see him. As well as having some bandages, which he used to strap the Briton's damaged hand, the Spaniard was also carrying a full water bottle. Having lost his hours earlier, Gregory took a long pull, only then realizing that it contained 'raw wood alcohol'. 'I have to admit,' the Nottinghamshire man confessed, '[it] probably pulled me round far faster than a mouthful of water could ever have done.'[26]

Meanwhile, David Crook and Sam Wild were still stranded in no-man's land. Huddled under cover in the strip of olive trees that led southwards down the valley, they were desperate for nightfall. Knowing that they would be picked off by the enemy troops now established on the hills above them if they tried to crawl out of cover, they waited patiently before making their move, despite the pain from their wounds. Crook had two bullets in his thigh and Wild had taken a burst of machine gun fire to his left side. A self-confessed 'cocky bastard', Wild was not afraid. 'Not because I'm a brave man, I just didn't feel [it],' he explained.[27] For Crook it was anger that made him determined to survive. Having seen so many of his comrades killed, he was adamant that he and Wild would make it back to their own lines. At last the sky darkened and 'a wisp of a sickle moon' appeared. It was a sight that Crook would never forget. 'Through the past 50 years,' he later recalled, 'I've never seen such a moon without thinking of Jarama.'[28] With the darkness now shrouding their movements, Sam Wild managed to stagger to his feet. Limping across the valley floor, he eventually reached the British lines. Before collapsing from blood loss and exhaustion, he sent some stretcher bearers out to fetch Crook. By the time they reached him, the ex-OTC man had managed to drag himself halfway across the valley floor. It had been an exercise in agony. 'My right thigh had turned to jelly and I had been inching my way along backwards sitting on my rump and pushing with my two hands and one good leg.'[29] After being carried back to the Sunken Road, he was reunited with Wild.

'We wounded were laid side by side,' Crook remembered, '[whilst] the doctors and nursing orderlies worked furiously dressing our wounds.' The casualties were then sorted by triage. The most serious were carried to lorries which had inched their way down the Morata road in the darkness. With their headlights off, so as not to attract enemy fire, they then turned into the Sunken Road. After being loaded into the makeshift ambulances, the wounded endured a painful journey over bumpy country tracks. Some, such as Henry Burke, 'a professional actor of ability' who had regularly trodden the boards for the Left Theatre Company in London before leaving for Spain, would not survive the journey.[30] Crook and Wild were more fortunate. Both ended up in first aid stations near Madrid. Others, such as Jim Prendergast, had already arrived at a hospital near Morata. Hours earlier, the Dubliner had been loaded onto an ambulance, alongside his company commander, Kit Conway, and fellow rifleman, Paddy Duff. 'Kit was in terrible pain,' Prendergast recalled. His intestines perforated in several places, the forty year-old was vomiting blood into the truck bed and could barely raise his voice above a whisper. Prendergast himself, having been riddled with shrapnel from a bursting shell, was feeling faint. 'After a while,' Prendergast remembered, Conway 'asked me if I was badly hit.' Shortly afterwards he lapsed into unconsciousness. Prendergast would never talk to Conway again.[31]

Others who had been wounded were taken further afield. Dan Gibbons, who had been hit in the right shoulder blade late in the afternoon, was driven all the way to the *Hospital Militar* in Castellon, a small town on the coast near Valencia. Gibbons was very pleased with his new home and would later send letters to the *Daily Worker* asking readers to send him books and cigarettes to aid his recovery.[32] Not all of the men wounded on the 12th were so fortunate. As his injury was not life threatening, Walter Gregory would be left lying at a clearing station half a mile behind the front line all night before a doctor was able to spare a few minutes to look at his thumb. Gregory's, however, was far from the most distressing case of neglect to emerge that night. At dusk, having been sent to the southern reaches of the Sunken Road to scout the battalion's open left flank, Jason Gurney stumbled across a sight that would stay with him for the rest of his days:

> I had only gone about seven hundred yards when I came on one of the most ghastly scenes I have ever seen. In a hollow by the side of the road I found a group of wounded men who had been carried back from ... the Casa Blanca Hill. They had arrived at a non-existent field dressing station from which they should have been taken back to the hospital, and now they had been forgotten. There were about fifty stretchers all of which were occupied, but many of the men had already died and most of the others would die before morning. They were chiefly artillery casualties with appalling wounds from which they could have little hope of recovery. They were all men whom I had known well, and some of them intimately... [Maurice Davidovitch was amongst them. He] lay on his back with a wound that appeared to have entirely cut away the muscle structure of his stomach so that his bowels were exposed from his navel to his genitals. His intestines lay in loops of a ghastly pinkish brown, twitching slightly as the flies searched around over them. He was perfectly conscious, unable to speak, but judging from his eyes he was not in pain or even particularly distressed. One man whom I was particularly fond of was clearly dying from about nine bullet wounds through his chest. He asked me to hold his hand and we talked for a few minutes until his hand went limp in mine and I knew he was dead. I went from one to the other but was absolutely powerless to do anything other than to hold a hand or to light a cigarette. Nobody cried out or screamed or made any other tragic gestures. I did what I could to comfort them and promised to try and get some ambulances. Of course I failed, which left me with a feeling of guilt which I never entirely shed... To this day I do not know what I could have done to help those poor wretches as they lay awaiting death in the twilight of that Spanish olive grove. They were all calling for water but I had none to give them. I was filled with such horror at their suffering and my inability to help them that I felt I had suffered some permanent injury to my spirit from which I would never entirely recover.[33]

CHAPTER 9
THE DARK
(6.00PM 12 FEBRUARY – 4.00AM 13 FEBRUARY 1937)

The fighting had been intense all along the line. To the north of the British position, the Franco-Belgians and the Dimitrov Battalion had suffered terribly. They had been involved in a running fire fight with Buruaga's 2nd Brigade. Outgunned and outnumbered, the Internationals had had the worst of the encounter. A quarter had been killed, including Grebenareff, the commander of the Dimitrovs. Five times the Nationalists had pushed them back, but on each occasion they had rallied and counter-attacked. Both sides had deployed tanks. German Panzer Is and Fiat tankettes had faced Russian T26s. Although the Republican armour had performed well, it had not been used in sufficient strength to punch a hole in the Nationalist line and several T26s had fallen prey to enemy artillery. Others had been taken out with petrol bombs or captured. By dusk, the remnants of the Franco-Belgians and Dimitrovs were holding a line several hundred yards back from the positions they had occupied that morning, but they were still in the fight.[1]

To the north of the XV Brigade, the fighting had been equally bloody. The Nationalists had captured Pajares Hill, a feature which dominated the centre of the battlefield and had been defended by the survivors of the XI and XIV brigades. Despite their resistance, they too had been forced to cede ground. Only on the far right of the Republican line had the Nationalists been held. On the outskirts of the village of Vaciamadrid, just a few hundred yards short of the Valencia Road, Spanish regiments had prevented the Nationalists from crossing the Jarama. Although under machine-gun and rifle fire, the Republicans' lifeline to the coast was still open. Whilst supplies, arms and ammunition trucks now had to make a brief detour to avoid being strafed, they could still get through to Madrid.[2]

––––––––––––––––

In the Sunken Road Wintringham did a headcount. Of the 400 men who had been holding the hills, only 125 had returned. One hundred had been killed and 100 wounded. Seventy-five were still unaccounted for. In the chaos of the retreat, they had scattered through the olive groves to the south and east of the British line. Some had even fled as far as the Cookhouse. Wintringham cursed his lack of foresight. If he had positioned a dozen of his best men on the far left flank at the start of the withdrawal, the stragglers could have been intercepted. Of the men that had returned, forty were survivors of the 1st Company, brought in by André Diamant, the plucky Egyptian who had emerged as a natural leader after first Conway, then Stalker had been shot. Diamant had led them back to the line singing the *Internationale*. Fifty-five others were from the 4th Company and thirty remained from the 3rd. Added to Fry's men, who had escaped the horrors of the day virtually unscathed, and the staff and runners who were directly under his command, Wintringham was left with 225 men.[3]

The remnants of the rifle companies were exhausted. Covered in mud, dust and gore, their clothes ripped by thorn bushes, ravenously hungry and with numerous small cuts and wounds, many were 'sleeping on their feet'. Others had already collapsed against the banks of the road and were snoring loudly. With the sun hidden behind the hills which lined the west bank of the Jarama 'it was ... bitterly cold'.[4] Whilst Frank Graham, the scholar from Sunderland, had kept his blankets and groundsheet, most of his comrades had not shown such prescience, having lost or discarded theirs through the course of the day. As the temperature plummeted, they huddled together for warmth. Amongst them was Jason Gurney, Wintringham's South African scout. On one of his many missions carrying messages through the olive groves that day, he had found a 'canvas and sheepskin jacket', which he now pulled tight around him.

Gurney was exhausted, but couldn't sleep: his brain insisted on replaying the day's nightmarish events:

> First ... the ... childlike excitement of moving up into the hills, seeing the enemy in the distance, the smoke of ... artillery fire ... staff officers and despatch riders rushing ... in all directions, the aerial dogfight and ... the pure theatre of war... Then the ... crescendo of violence, fear and excitement as our three infantry companies had been pounded to pieces.[5]

The last image, before he finally slipped off to sleep, was of the wounded he had discovered abandoned at the far end of the Sunken Road. Their faces would haunt his dreams that night and for many more to come.

Wintringham had more pressing concerns. The most urgent was the need to defend his reduced perimeter. Although it seemed unlikely that the enemy would attack after the battering they had received from the Maxims, their lines were only 700 yards away and a night assault could not be ruled out. As if to underline the point, bursts of tracer fire regularly lit up the sky. At a distance the bullets seemed to arc towards the British line agonisingly slowly, suddenly speeding up as they closed, then thumping into the soil around their positions. Knowing that five of Fry's guns were exposed 100 yards ahead of the line, Wintringham sent orders for the Scot to bring four back into the groves. The machine-gun commander was then ordered 'to establish a listening post in the valley, post sentries forward and begin to dig in'. By the time the messenger arrived, Fry had already begun to reinforce his position and sent back a note asking for picks and shovels. A quick search along the Sunken Road turned up half a dozen. Although each rifle company had been issued with thirty entrenching tools, they were heavy and awkward and 'were naturally the first things [the] men [had] "lost"'.[6]

Whilst searching for the shovels, Wintringham came across some dismounted International cavalry volunteers who had come up from the rear. The English Captain ordered them to take up positions 300 yards to the left. 'They moved off, grumbling ... an hour later... And we never saw them again.' Next, Wintringham went to find the commander of the Spanish infantry that had joined his line and asked him to move another company up to the Sunken Road. Wintringham did not think much of the Spaniard. 'His men were good lads but he was a nasty, softish paunch … [and] looked like a wood-louse.' Nevertheless, he promised to move some men up and eventually 'a few sleepy [ones]' appeared.[7] On his way back to the centre of the line, Wintringham met Sergeant Johnson of the 4th Company struggling with one of the Spaniards' Colts. A cartridge was stuck in the breech and the weapon was jammed solid. The Spanish infantry seemed entirely unconcerned by his dilemma. Groups of them 'were sitting around looking fatalistic'. Another was 'playing *flamenco* in a low wail'. Wintringham, however, was in his element and soon rectified the problem. 'I gave a tap on the cocking arm [and] the bent, jammed cartridge rattled loose.' With his gun ready for action, Johnson asked for a target. Pointing to the west, Wintringham told him to fire off occasional bursts around the skyline of White House Hill, 'just enough to keep the gun warm'.[8] As Wintringham continued his rounds, Johnson got to work. The Colt's muzzle flashes sent shadows dancing down the Sunken Road.[9]

Amongst the faces lit up was another of the battalion's 'celebrities'. Desmond Rowney was a cartoonist who had worked for the *Daily Worker* under the pen-name 'Maro' and was notorious for his less than flattering portrayals of George V.[10] As well as being a determined communist, Rowney was a Sandhurst-educated Great War veteran and 'an expert rifle shot' who had 'fought gallantly' throughout the afternoon.[11] By the light of Johnson's muzzle flashes, he sketched a 'Royal Rabbit Warren' strip for the amusement of his comrades. It was the last he would ever draw.[12]

At 8.00pm a red Studebaker truck driven by Josh Francis, the battalion's quartermaster, appeared. Edging his way up the road with the headlights off, Francis pulled to a halt and leapt out of the cab. He had brought up food, picks, shovels and ammunition. The men were ravenous. Many who had fallen asleep managed to rouse themselves to eat. There was soup, coffee and cold boiled rice. The men crowded round the back of the truck and Francis doled out their rations. Those who had them raised their dixies. Others, like Tony Hyndman, lifted their muddy hands and cold rice was pushed into them.[13] Due to the heavy casualties, there was plenty to go round. Hyndman helped himself again and again. After he had sated his appetite, the Welshman filled his water bottle, leant against the side of the Sunken Road and lit a cigarette. Wrapping the giant scarf that Giles Romilly's mother had given him tight around his middle, Hyndman felt a certain pride about his performance that day. 'What I dreaded most was not happening,' he explained. 'There were no tears yet.'[14]

After the men had eaten, Wintringham gathered them by the truck's tailgate to give out orders. All day the English Captain had felt himself somewhat removed from events and that night was no different. 'The stranger who was myself was no speech-maker,' he confessed. 'I said nothing of encouragement.'[15] Nevertheless, his orders provided some comfort for the men who were desperate for someone to take charge. The remnants of the rifle companies were then dismissed to catch a few hours sleep. They had borne the brunt of the day's fighting and would need to rest before morning. The 2nd Company and battalion staff were to provide men for sentry duty, digging parties and to form patrols. Stand-to was at three in the morning.

As the riflemen stumbled off, a messenger appeared from Brigade HQ. The dispatch he carried ordered Wintringham to fill the gap to his right with patrols, but first he decided to check on Fry. Picking his way through the olive groves, the English Captain suddenly suffered a crisis of confidence. He was not a soldier. He was a journalist and an academic, better suited 'to a quiet writing-desk or the clatter of a print shop' than the battlefield. A flurry of doubt passed across his mind. 'What on earth was I doing among these olive-trees, dusty earth ... [and] cold February hills, with hundreds of men to look after and lead in unequal battle?' Then, just as quickly as the feeling had assailed him, it passed. 'I snapped out of it,' he recalled, 'and got on with the job.'[16]

By the time Wintringham reached Fry's position, the orange flashes from Sergeant Johnson's Colt had been joined by two others, fired by groups of Spaniards alongside Sexton's Maxim crew 200 yards to the left. The tracers arced across no-man's land into the Nationalist held hills to their front. Not to be outdone, the Germans returned fire, their gunners intermittently seeking out the Republicans' lines. Adding to the show were pistol flares or Very Lights. Tracing high parabolas, the orange illuminations prompted flurries of fire and threw flickering shadows over the groves.[17]

In the 2nd Company's position, Wintringham was greeted by 'Yank' Levy. 'Here's the skipper,' the Canadian remarked jovially when he saw the Englishman approach. Wintringham could see that Fry's men had not been idle. As well as the low wall to their front, the gunners were now protected by a waist deep trench, running 100 yards along the ridgeline. Noticing their visitor, the men stopped work. 'It's the bleeding colonel,' one remarked playfully. The others sniggered whilst the joker leapt to attention and saluted with his spade. Spotting Fry, who was silent as usual, Wintringham suggested moving one Maxim to different points on the line and firing off occasional bursts at the hills, 'just to show the Fascists we were awake'.[18] As per Wintringham's order, a listening post had been established in the valley and sentries were patrolling the low ground to their front. After the mix up with the ammunition and the embarrassing confrontation with Copeman earlier that day, Fry was now firmly in command. To his relief, Fred Copeman had wandered off a few hours earlier. Dripping blood from the wounds to his hand and head and muttering something about bringing up stragglers, the former mutineer had disappeared to the rear.[19]

By the time Fry and Wintringham had finished talking, Fred Copeman had arrived at his destination. Knowing that many of the men who had withdrawn from the hills were still unaccounted for, he had taken it upon himself to find them and drag them back to the front. Once at the Cookhouse, Copeman met up with André Diamant who came up with an idea. The Egyptian proposed doing a sweep of the Cookhouse's wine cellars, cavernous structures dug into the sides of the hill that the battalion had climbed that morning, as it was one of the few places where the men could hole up out of the chill night air. Copeman agreed. The 'cellar' was lined with giant wine vats, 'each large enough to house a small family'. Copeman and Diamant were met by absolute silence. It was, the Englishman thought, 'the kind of silence which convinced me that many people were [there]'. Turning to his companion, he raised his voice to a stage whisper and announced his intentions. 'Give us those ruddy hand grenades, André,' he said. 'If there are any fascists in here we'll soon clear 'em out.' The men hiding in the cellar were not willing to call Copeman's bluff. Believing that the ex-Royal Navy man was just about crazy enough to carry out the threat, they announced themselves. 'Out they came looking rather sheepish,' Copeman recalled. There were fifty men all told. They were issued with rifles collected from the dead and marched back to the front.[20]

———————————

Back in the Sunken Road, Sergeant Major McDade had been put in charge of patrolling the battalion's open flanks. Wintringham was glad to have someone he could rely on as he later admitted:

> McDade's steadiness ... [and] his reassuring old soldier's bluff had been useful to me all throughout the day. He had been near me most of the time and as far as I could remember he had never volunteered a single suggestion; yet always one had the feeling that a wise old professional was letting the youngster find out for himself ... but keeping a sharp eye open for any real danger ... his lack of nerves, his quietness were good for me that night.[21]

Time and again, McDade trudged off down the Sunken Road, one or two men who couldn't sleep accompanying him, until he reached the Franco-Belgian lines on the far side of the Morata road. McDade would then turn around and retrace his steps to where the men were sleeping, before heading to the far south of the line, where the Spanish cavalry were supposed to be in support.

Meanwhile, the 2nd Company were still improving their position on the ridgeline by digging Maxim emplacements into the side of the trench. As they worked, the men could hear the Moors on the hills 700 yards away singing 'to keep their spirits up in the dark'.[22] Amidst the Arabic intonation, George Watters, one of the company's Glaswegians, noticed more familiar tones. 'One Welsh-speaking fellow was shouting at us about being Communist so-and-sos,' he recalled.[23] This could only have been Frank Thomas, the twenty-three year-old from Pontypridd who had been fighting with the 6th *Bandera* since the advance on Madrid. Later that night, when the Moors had stopped singing and even Thomas had tired of hurling abuse, another voice could be heard calling from no-man's land. A wounded Englishman, left for dead on the eastern slope of White House Hill, was begging for help.[24] 'Comrades, Comrades, I'm wounded,' he cried out over and over again. Although the sky was clear, the sickle moon threw little light across the valley and it was impossible to know exactly where the voice was coming from. With the enemy just 700 yards away, the men realized that a rescue mission would very likely end in disaster. Nevertheless, Watters recalled, 'one of our fellows was insisting that we should do something about it. It [was] ... horrible to hear a man's voice, calling hour on hour ... dying ... slowly, [and] getting fainter.'[25] At 1.00am, Captain Wintringham visited the trench for the second time that night and the Scots asked for permission to send a patrol into no-man's land to bring the man in. Wintringham refused. 'It would mean risking three fit men to rescue one wounded one ... [and] in this battle for Madrid's lifeline we had need of every rifle [we had].' The decision was not an easy one and caused the English Captain considerable turmoil. '[At that moment] I realized how utterly I loathed war,' he explained.[26] With that, the exhaustion hit him and Wintringham decided to snatch an hour's sleep. He knew he would need to be alert in the morning.

Despite the orders, with Wintringham gone, the Scots decided to act. As soon as their captain had disappeared into the night, George Watters and two others climbed over the low wall and snuck down into the valley. Watching them go into the 'inky black', Bill Meredith was awed by their bravery.

> Even if anyone could have reached him, even if he was not watched by the fascists ready to shoot down anyone who attempted to rescue him ... there was no certainty that any rescue party could find its way back to our lines. In spite of these obvious dangers [these] three comrades insisted that they be allowed to go.[27]

After inching his way down the steep slope to the valley floor, Watters stopped to explain his plan to one of his companions. 'You're so big in the mouth you can come out behind me with a grenade, and if there is any chance o' them getting us throw the grenade and get out o' it.' Watters then set out again, desperately trying not to make any noise. A few minutes later, he realized he was alone. The man with the grenade and the other who had left the trench with him were nowhere to be seen. Watters pushed on regardless, but the night began to play tricks on his senses. The further he edged out into no-man's land, the further away the voice seemed to be. Eventually he gave up and turned back, bumping into a British sentry on his way into the lines. As the man didn't recognize him, Watters was frogmarched back to Battalion HQ in the Sunken Road to have his identity checked before he was allowed to rejoin his comrades.[28]

At 2.00am Copeman and Diamant returned to the line with the fifty stragglers they had brought up from the Cookhouse. Diamant had been walking at the rear of the column with his rifle at the ready and was fairly certain none had managed to slip past him.[29] John Tunnah, a veteran of Lopera who had become the battalion's postman, recalled that some of those who had remained at their posts argued that the returnees should be punished for cowardice. A few even spoke of the firing squad, but one look at the men soon cooled their bloodlust. Some were still terrified. Others, edgy and upset, were at each other's throats as their fear turned to anger. They blamed each other for their retreat and Copeman for their humiliating return. 'If … [he] comes here I'll knock his … head off,' Tunnah overheard one man remark, but thought little of it. None of them had the courage to take on the ex-Royal Navy man. Far more of a concern was their morale. 'The whole thing was disintegrating,' Tunnah confessed. He slept little that night, worrying that at any moment the enemy would overrun them.[30]

Wintringham awoke forty-five minutes later. At first, Gurney remembered, he appeared totally confused. Although 'anxious to succeed in the role … in which he had cast himself, the realities had failed to live up to his imagination and he could no longer recognize himself,' the South African explained.[31] Wintringham had the curious feeling that the previous day he 'had been sleepwalking' and he knew that the situation was only going to get tougher. Stand-to came at 3.00am and fifteen minutes later the quartermaster, Josh Francis, arrived. His red Studebaker truck was packed with food and supplies. Gurney, who had slept for hours huddled up under his sheepskin jacket, was wrenched from his nightmares by the noise. Sensing 'a vast, looming monster bearing down' on him, the South African's first thought was that he was about to be crushed by an enemy tank. It took him a few moments to realize what was happening and compose himself.[32]

George Aitken, the battalion commissar, had hitched a lift with Francis. Climbing down from the cab, the Scot began doling out 'hot sweet coffee and a box of hugely thick bully-beef sandwiches'.[33] The men were revitalized by the food. Stamping their feet and nursing their coffee, they gathered round as Wintringham took control. Rifles clogged with dirt were cleaned, ammunition pouches and water bottles refilled and the stragglers reassigned to their companies. The troops manning the listening post were recalled and sentries were sent out to the left and right.[34] More through stubborness than judgement, the battalion had survived their first day and night in combat and Wintringham now seemed to have recovered some of his determination. Nevertheless, no-one knew what fresh hell the new day would bring.

CHAPTER 10

DAWN

(4.00AM–12.00 MIDDAY, 13 FEBRUARY 1937)

The first false light of dawn found Fry's men 'searching the valley with aching eyes'. At 4.00am they sensed movement: the enemy was gathering for a fresh attack.[1] Wintringham was unconcerned. The Maxims had already proved their worth; the gun pit, which they had only just finished digging, was now waist deep and each weapon had plenty of extra belts filled with the correct ammunition. If the Nationalists were to attempt another advance across the open ground, the 2nd Company would be ready for them.[2]

With the centre secure, Wintringham turned his attention to the flanks. Overton, who had 'pulled himself together during the night', and the fifty-five men who remained from the 4th Company, were ordered to take up position 100 yards to the right of the Maxims.[3] From there they could watch the dead ground that snaked up from the valley floor to the rear of Fry's position. They would also be close enough to the machine gunners to counter-attack should the Nationalists try to rush them. For the first two hours of the previous day's battle, Wintringham and his staff had occupied the same position. The English Captain knew the area well. Although there were only olive trees for cover, to the front the ground sloped steeply away to the valley floor providing an excellent field of fire.[4]

The remains of the other two rifle companies were positioned out on the flanks and slightly to the rear. André Diamant, in command of the 1st Company which now numbered fifty-eight men, was ordered to move to the far left of the line, whilst the remnants of Briskey's company were sent down the Sunken Road to the right. The British line now formed an arc, stretching across over half a mile of groves.[5] Wintringham and his staff had taken up position 200 yards behind Fry, three olive trees back from the Sunken Road. Remembering Macartney's warnings that a straight, shallow trench could become a death trap if caught by enfilading fire, Wintringham was glad to get the bulk of his men out of the Sunken Road.

Just before dawn, Wintringham received some bad news. Alex McDade, the battalion sergeant major, had been wounded. Calm, efficient and reliable, the stocky Irishman had been a major comfort throughout the trials of the first day. Whilst patrolling the battalion's right flank, he had been hit in the arm by a stray bullet fired from a considerable distance. 'Maybe they used a microscope to get me,' McDade had joked as he was helped to the rear. Wintringham would miss 'his quiet assurance' badly.[6]

Elsewhere on the front, Fred Copeman was looking out towards the horizon. Across the groves, away from the enemy lines, dawn was breaking and already there was 'a dull red line in the east'.[7] Wintringham also noticed the change. 'The stars seemed fainter [and] the sky was paling'. The new day was approaching with alarming rapidity; 'almost as quickly as a theatre curtain opens,' he recalled. 'In a few minutes it was daylight and the battle … continued' once more.[8]

The opening act of the second day saw Fry's Maxims at the forefront of the action. In the forward trench, his men had been hearing movement in the valley beneath them for the better part of an hour. Now, in the growing light, they could see what had been causing the commotion. Bill Meredith noticed 'a company of fascists coming forward on our left'. The troops were the 1st *Tabor* of Tetúan. Following the battering their countrymen had taken the previous evening, Colonel Asensio had reassigned the unit to the 8th Regiment during the night. It seems that no-one had bothered to inform their commander, Captain Perales, of the presence of the enemy machine guns on the ridge, however. Overnight the only fire had been coming from Sergeant Johnson's Colt, a couple of Spanish guns and the solitary Maxim that Wintringham had ordered to open up from different positions up and down the line.

Clearly Perales thought that his men could take the ridge with a single decisive thrust at dawn. Oblivious to the danger, his men were now advancing straight into Fry's field of fire.[9] Three guns were deemed sufficient to counter the threat. 'We trained [the Maxims] ... on them [and] allowed them to advance within eight hundred metres [875 yards], then let them have it.' As the guns chattered to life, the Moors scattered. Most of those not killed or wounded in the opening burst tried to flee back to the hills.[10] Others stood their ground and returned fire. The guns swept across them again and broke their resistance, leaving only a handful to run or crawl to safety. 'Never have I seen men retreat so quickly,' Meredith recalled. 'It was a complete rout.'[11] Having learnt from Copeman's able demonstration of the previous night, Fry ordered his gunners to fire behind the fleeing troops to cut off their retreat. Several more were killed, before the remnants regrouped beyond the hills.

Positioned 200 yards to the rear, Wintringham had heard 'the clatter' of the guns. Loath to abandon his command post, he 'bit down ... [on his] impatience' and sent a runner forward to gather news. As the guns fell silent, the man reappeared and breathlessly blurted out the news: The valley was 'full of Moors and fellows in khaki'. 'How many?' Wintringham demanded. 'Best part of a Brigade, Comrade Fry thinks.' 'How near?' 'Well down, and running like hell.' 'Towards us?' Wintringham inquired. 'Gawd no!' the runner replied.[12] Wintringham soon had further cause for good cheer. Although the Spaniards who had joined them the previous day had disappeared during the night, another unit had replaced them and was digging in on the battalion's left flank. The new arrivals were from the famed Lister Division, a key element of the elite 5th Regiment. Trained by communist advisors sent from Russia, the 5th had introduced discipline to the Republican Army and had helped forge the brave yet disorganized militias that had defended Madrid the previous summer into a solid fighting force. Their commander, Enrique Lister, was one of the Republicans' most prized officers. 'Young, aggressive, ruthless and ... brave', Lister was a stocky man, whose cheeks dimpled when he smiled, giving him an almost childlike appearance.[13] A dedicated communist, he had been forced into exile in 1931 and his subsequent adventures had seen him travel across the globe. He had taken part in the uprising against the Cuban dictator Machado.

Later, he had travelled to Moscow to study in the famed Frunze Military Academy before returning to his homeland to fight in the war. By February 1937, Lister had risen to command a brigade, which boasted new rifles and machine guns and three light field pieces. Wintringham's left flank was secure.

At about the same time that Lister's men appeared, thirty British reinforcements arrived on the right wing, bringing the battalion's strength up to 250 men. These were some of the veterans of the fighting at Lopera. Previously assigned to the Brigade Guard based in Morata, they had been called forward during the night.

———————————

Following their failed attack, the Nationalists facing Wintringham's battalion made no further attempts to better their position that morning. Whilst their comrades to the north of the Morata road advanced against the Franco-Belgian and Dimitrov battalions, the men of Asensio's 8th Regiment were content to bide their time. Occasionally bursts of machine-gun fire or rifle shots were exchanged, but otherwise a relative calm descended over the valley. The rising sun burnt off a blanket of morning mist, revealing another perfectly blue sky. As the day heated up, the visibility steadily improved. Far off to the north-west Madrid appeared out of the haze, its cluster of towers glinting in the sun. Enjoying the warmth, Jason Gurney sat amongst the olives to the east of the Sunken Road, listening to the fighting to the north increasing in intensity. As the British would later discover, the Franco-Belgians and Dimitrovs were taking 'a terrible hammering'.[14] Even further to the north, the Thaelmann Battalion was also in serious trouble. In the previous day's fighting they had lost all their heavy machine guns and on the 13th all their Colts jammed. In one attack alone both the battalion commander and political commissar had been killed. Although relieved to be out of the worst of it, the British knew their respite would be brief. 'One half of us cherished the hope that the battle had drifted away [from] ... us,' Gurney recalled, 'but behind this lay the horrid certainty that our time was coming.'[15]

By 10.00am the British had crawled out from behind their defences and were stretching their limbs in the sun. The last of their cigarettes, Woodbines from home or Spanish anti-tanks, were sparked up and savoured. Others, unable to relax, pestered Wintringham for his field glasses. Having noticed occasional puffs of smoke from the Nationalist lines as snipers tried to draw a bead on them, they wanted to try their hand at 'some fancy shooting at a thousand yards range or more'. Glad to be 'in the quiet trough of the wave', Wintringham was happy to oblige.[16] Raising the sights on their Russian rifles, some men took pot shots whilst a spotter, watching the bullets fall, called out adjustments for range. Meanwhile, Cyril Sexton's Maxim crew, positioned out on the left flank, were also thinking about how to get their own back on the enemy. After making a dawn trip to the arms cache set up in the Sunken Road for extra ammunition, Sexton had spent the morning observing the Nationalists on White House Hill. They had been busy preparing their positions overnight and were now well established. Several foxholes had been dug amongst the trees and bushes and the enemy seemed particularly concentrated around the farmhouse that had taken so much punishment the day before. Having made his observations, Sexton set out for the Sunken Road to report his findings to Wintringham.[17]

In Fry's forward trench, James Maley was also enjoying the respite. It was a beautiful day, the Glaswegian remembered; there was 'hardly a sound' and 'no-one to shoot at. I sat there thinking about home and wondering what I'd be doing.' As it was a Saturday, Maley realized that he would 'probably be going to Parkhead to watch Celtic'. The thought was unsettling. 'It was a bit strange to be there in Spain, fighting the fascists, while everything was going on normal back in Glasgow,' he explained.[18] Although Maley would not find out for several months, it would be business as usual at Parkhead that afternoon. One goal down at half time, the Bhoys would come back to thump Albion Rangers 5–2.[19]

Other volunteers thought of their loved ones. George Aitken, the Scottish commissar, had a wife and son in London. Both had cried when he had told them of his decision to go to Spain. Harry Fry's wife was in Edinburgh, Danny Gibbons's had been writing regularly ever since his train had departed for Dover and Jason Gurney had a girlfriend who had modelled for him back in the King's Road. 'She was a bad model,' the South African remembered. 'She couldn't keep still and frequently started to get sexy when I wanted to draw, but I loved her dearly and never tired of looking at her.' She had 'the most glorious body' Gurney had ever seen: 'blonde hair, tight curled ... A high, rather narrow forehead... A long neck ... [and] broad shoulders [which] ... set off a pair of small but perfect pear shaped breasts which pointed outwards from one another, giving them a magnificently arrogant appearance.'[20]

Tom Wintringham's love life was considerably more complex. The English Captain was forever falling in and out of love. Although he had been married since 1923, he had indulged in numerous affairs. Nevertheless, his wife, Elizabeth, had stuck by him and whilst the couple had not lived together for several years, she still wrote regularly and cared for Wintringham deeply. In the first two years of their marriage, Elizabeth had given birth to two children. The first, Robin, had died in his cot at the age of six months. A year later their second child, Oliver, was born. Wintringham had then moved in with another woman, Millie, a colleague from the British Communist Party, who bore his third child in September 1931. Five years later, whilst reporting for the *Daily Worker* in Barcelona, Wintringham had met Kitty Bowler, an American journalist who was also covering the war. Revolutionary Barcelona was a powerful aphrodisiac and they had embarked upon a breathless affair. Two months later Wintringham had left Catalonia to join the International Brigades. Having learnt of her lover's frustrations with the machine guns the battalion had been issued with through his subsequent letters, Kitty had consulted two experts based in Valencia and then set out for Madrigueras in early January. After spending a few days with Tom, Kitty had returned to Barcelona, leaving the thirty-nine year-old pining like a lovesick teenager. On 27 January he had put down his feelings in a heartfelt letter. 'You made me strong again,' he confessed. 'I am happy and will remain so, just so long as you, my love, my darling, my everything exist.'[21]

Unknown to the English Captain, since he had left for the front, Kitty had come to the attention of André Marty, the brigade's chief commissar. Through the communists' network of informers, Marty had learnt of Kitty's interest in the machine guns and leapt to the conclusion that she was a Nationalist spy. Her arrest ordered, Kitty was bundled into a staff car and driven back to Albacete. Although arriving late at night, she was immediately ordered into his office as she later recalled:

Behind a rolltop desk sat an old man with a first class walrus moustache. He was sleepy and irritable and had pulled a coat on over his pyjamas... To my surprise my mass of Spanish papers did not interest him in the least. Even my UGT [General Workers' Union] card and pass were thrown back in my face, contemptuously. My past was all that interested him... At the end of the hour he read out the charges ... 1) Travelled from Albacete to Madrigueras without a pass. 2) Penetrated into a military establishment. 3) Interested yourself into the functioning of machine guns. 4) Visited Italy and Germany in 1933. THEREFORE YOU ARE A SPY.[22]

Three days and nights of interrogation followed before she was finally released. Although Bowler later pleaded ignorance, according to Marty her release had one strict condition: that she leave the country immediately. As Kitty returned to Madrigueras hoping to catch up with Tom, she believed the issue was at a close. Marty's madness would eventually catch up with her, however, and when it did, it would be Wintringham who paid the price.

Whilst the British at Jarama continued to enjoy a few hours of relative tranquillity, overhead the skies were anything but quiet. Earlier that morning a flight of twelve Nationalist bombers had passed by to bomb Morata de Tajuña. At 10.30am, after the distant sound of explosions in the east had signalled the mission's success, the bombers swung back towards the British lines. As they passed overhead two Republican fighters intercepted them. With the remnants of the 1st Company, André Diamant was transfixed by the battle that ensued. After several minutes of rattling machine-gun fire, the Egyptian saw two Nationalist machines fall from the skies in flames. The rest then gunned their engines and fled for home. Later, Wintringham heard a flight of Russian bombers passing high overhead. Five minutes later, a few of their escort, snub-nosed Russian Moscas, swooped down to attack the Nationalist positions on the ground. With their machine guns chattering, the little fighters took it in turns to strafe the enemy lines.[23]

At 11.00am Cyril Sexton's reports on the Nationalist positions on White House Hill finally bore fruit as the French 75s placed on the road to Morata opened fire. With the shells bursting around their positions, several Nationalists abandoned their foxholes and fled to the rear. It was the moment Sexton and his gun crew had been waiting for. As the enemy broke cover, their Maxim chattered into life, killing or wounding several before they could reach safety. Several belts later, the shelling ceased.[24] By now the sun had reached its zenith and the day was hot and still. To the south of the British positions, the Spaniards of the Lister Brigade, having travelled all day to reach the front line, were exhausted. Several lay sleeping in the dappled shade of the olive trees and Wintringham noticed that one man had strung up his towel as an awning to provide more protection from the sun.[25]

At midday Dave Springhall, the XV Brigade's assistant commissar, found Wintringham behind the Sunken Road. The son of an insurance agent, 'Springie' had been born in Kensal Green in 1901. At the age of fifteen he had joined the Royal Navy, but was dismissed after just four years for distributing 'seditious' material amongst the ratings, including an article he had written for Sylvia Pankhurst's publication *Worker's Dreadnought*, entitled 'Discontent on the Lower Deck'. Following his dismissal, Springhall joined the CPGB and was watched closely by the security services from that point on. In 1924, after rising through the ranks of the YCL, he visited Russia as a delegate at the Fourth Congress of the Young Communist International and two years later was jailed for his activities during the General Strike. Springhall was a serious man, completely dedicated to the cause, who had once told a comrade that he would 'sooner be shot than expelled from the party'.[26]

Although things had been quiet that morning on the British section of the front, Wintringham knew it was only a temporary reprieve and was determined to have everything ready for the next Nationalist assault. As soon as Springhall reached his position, he reeled off a list of complaints: the Maxim belts had been filled with the wrong ammunition; the Franco-Belgians were too far to the right; the Spaniards had taken an age to move up on his left flank; and the entrenching tools he had been promised were yet to arrive. Springhall made a note of each, before discussing the reason behind his visit: Colonel Gal was preparing a counter-offensive to relieve the pressure on the battalions to the north. The remnants of the British Battalion were to take centre stage in the attack.

Another of the International Brigades would support them alongside the Lister Brigade and fifty Russian tanks which would advance in two sections, one on either of the battalion's flanks. Seeing Wintringham's growing disbelief, Springhall added that the Nationalist positions on White House Hill would be heavily bombed before his men were given the order to move out. Nevertheless, the English Captain was anything but reassured. Alongside him, Jason Gurney overheard the conversation. The South African was equally incredulous. 'There was at least a brigade of Moorish infantry in front of us with all their machine guns and artillery intact, nevertheless, we were supposed to charge down the hill and drive the Fascists back across the river. It was nonsense,' he concluded.[27]

After Springhall had left, Wintringham began to prepare for the advance. There was no set time, but he understood that when the tanks appeared he should follow. As the 1st and 3rd companies had had the worst of the previous day's fighting, he decided they should not be involved. Instead, the thirty newly arrived reinforcements from the Brigade Guard, forty of Overton's company and thirty of Wintringham's staff would be sent. That made 100 men all told. It was a pitifully small amount for an advance against the Moors on the hills opposite, even if they were seriously compromised by the airstrike that Springhall had promised. Realizing he would need everyone he could muster, Wintringham set off for Fry's forward trench, hoping the Scot could spare him some men.[28]

Although the morning had been quiet, over the last hour the volume of machine gun fire whipping overhead had been steadily increasing. By the time Wintringham left for the ridgeline, it was approaching the levels of the previous afternoon. Some 300 yards of olive groves separated him from his destination. Moving out, he noticed the trees twitching and rustling as the bullets scythed through the leaves. Reaching the Sunken Road, Wintringham paused for a breather. Whilst he gulped in lungfuls of the crisp spring air, he noticed a gap in the bank targeted by the enemy gunners who were hoping to catch one of his men unawares. Gathering himself, the English Captain then leapt over the side for the final dash to the ridgeline. The 100 yards seemed to stretch out for an eternity. '[It] was like wading into breakers,' he thought. 'The *crack-phht* of bullets … came in a regular rhythm as the guns traversed, interweaving … a swinging net of lead.' Although the gunners were not aiming specifically at him, the psychological effect of being under continuous fire was appalling. Running through the groves, he experienced a gut sinking feeling. It reminded him of days spent in church 'as a small boy when told that God was everywhere and could see everything'.[29]

When Wintringham reached the ridgeline, Fry insisted no-one could be spared. Although the forward trench had been as quiet as any other sector of the British line that morning, things were now beginning to heat up. Over by the Knoll, 800 yards to Fry's front right, the Nationalists had been manhandling a light artillery piece into position and other enemy troops had been seen sighting machine guns and mortars all along the front. It seemed as if a barrage was imminent and Fry expected it would be followed by an all-out assault on his position. Since the action at dawn, Fry's guns had had few clear targets to aim at. The enemy mortars and machine guns were well sighted and under cover and the artillery piece was hidden behind a large tree. Nevertheless, the British had had two notable successes. Throughout the course of the day, the Nationalists had been trying to establish a machine-gun post in a trench which they had dug during the night 500 yards from Fry's line. The British, whose position overlooked the enemy trench, had allowed them to set up their guns five times, then concentrated the fire of two of their Maxims on the trench until they had killed all those inside. The Nationalists did not seem to learn and continued to repeat their mistake. The Canadian, 'Yank' Levy, had also managed to pick off a few of the enemy artillerymen over the course of the morning. Every now and then, one would be foolish enough to stick his head out from behind the tree, prompting Levy to rattle off a quick burst from his Maxim. The Canadian's fire was deadly accurate and his tally was steadily mounting.[30]

'Yank' Levy was an experienced gunner and widely held to be one of Fry's best men. Born in Hamilton, Ontario in 1897, Levy had been brought up in the nearby town of Windsor and in Cleveland in the USA. After a spell in the Merchant Navy, he had joined the British Army's 39th Battalion. Better known as the Jewish Legion, the battalion and its sister unit, the 38th, fought the Turkish Army in the Jordan Valley in April 1918. Levy served as a machine gunner and achieved recognition as the battalion's boxing champion, before being invalided home after a gas attack and a bout of malaria. Back in the States, Levy had married Mary Prezenter and in 1919 the couple had a daughter. The following year, he travelled to Mexico to fight under General Goméz in the final stages of the revolution. Levy's later adventures also saw him working as a gun-runner supplying Nicaraguan guerrillas and he even served for a short while with the Sandinistas with whom he planned an armed robbery in Philadelphia in 1927. Tipped off, the police intercepted the gang before they could carry out the hit. Levy and his companions were arrested and sentenced to twenty years' imprisonment. In February 1933, however, his appeals for leniency were answered and he was deported to Canada where he worked as a stevedore and labour organizer before travelling to Europe to join the International Brigades.[31]

Disappointed by Fry's refusal to lend some men for Springhall's forthcoming attack, Wintringham set off for the 300-yard dash back to his position behind the Sunken Road. This time the Nationalists were waiting for him. As soon as he left the cover of the trench, two machine guns opened up. For every step he took he could hear three or four bullets whizzing across the valley and kicking up the white soil around his feet. As he closed on the Sunken Road, the gunners' fire became increasingly accurate. 'One ... bullet ... twitched the front of my tunic,' he remembered, 'cutting a half-round hole ... just in front of my trouser buttons. "Too near", I thought, and dropped behind an olive-tree root.' Wintringham was pinned down for several anxious moments by the cross-fire, before a break enabled him to scramble to safety. Bent double he made it back to his position beyond the Sunken Road. As he got his breath back, Wintringham thought about their chances in the upcoming attack. If the enemy machine gunners could shred the coat of a single man from 800 yards, what would their fire do to 100 men advancing across the open space of valley floor? The answer did not bear thinking about.[32]

CHAPTER 11
THE FEINT
(12.00 MIDDAY—4.30PM, 13 FEBRUARY 1937)

An hour after Springhall had informed them of the forthcoming attack on the Nationalist lines, Wintringham and his men were still waiting. There was no sign of the T26s and the intensity of the firing to the north was increasing. Then Springhall reappeared. Growing ever more impatient for the off, the two officers watched as a flight of three Republican bombers came out of the east. The 'heavy' bombing of White House Hill that Springhall had promised was anything but impressive. The biplanes unloaded just three or four bombs each. Each burst wide of the mark, showering the Nationalists with mud and stones but doing little real damage. The bombers then turned in a wide arc. Forming line nose to tail, they went in one after the other on a series of strafing runs that proved equally ineffective. The machine-gun bullets whizzed and cracked around the enemy positions, but the Nationalists in their foxholes were too well dug in. After ten minutes it was all over. Concluding their final pass, the bombers swung back to the east, climbed and disappeared into the haze. Wintringham was singularly unimpressed. The Nationalist machine-gun fire peppering his positions continued unabated and the English Captain estimated that forty Hotchkiss guns were now trained on his men. 'The valley, I hoped and believed, could be held from our side by seven Maxims twenty years old,' he recalled, so 'how could I hope to cross it against the fire of six to seven times that number of modern guns?'[1] There was nothing else to do but continue waiting. Unless the tank support proved considerably more effective, any infantry attack on the hills would be suicidal.

**The Morning Feint and the Afternoon Attack on the Machine-Gun Company:
13 February 1937**

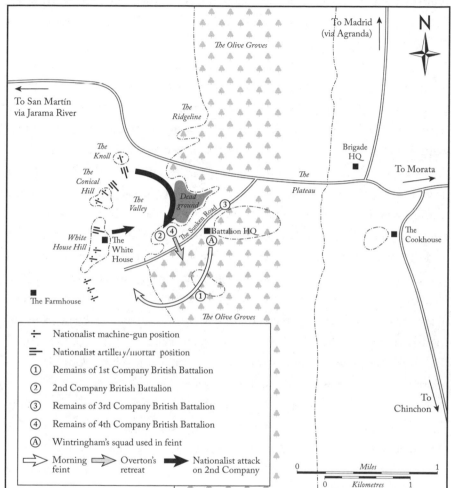

Despite the logic of his reasoning, Wintringham knew he had to do
something to relieve the pressure on the battalions to his north. At any
moment the Thaelmanns, Dimitrovs or Franco-Belgians could buckle under
the mounting pressure. One breakthrough could be enough to compromise
the entire line. 'If we could not make a real attack,' he thought 'we must
[at least] put up a bluff, [or] make a distraction.' Anything that would refocus
Asensio's attention and relieve some of the pressure to the north could prove

invaluable. Scanning the Nationalist lines from his position in the groves, Wintringham remembered an old maxim he had learnt in the Great War: when 'facing a much stronger opponent, be cheeky – so long as you do not weaken your defence thereby'.[2]

Leaving the rest of his men in the defensive positions he had assigned them at first light, Wintringham gathered a thirty-strong party to make a feint against the enemy's right flank. The newly arrived reinforcements from the Brigade Guard provided most of the troops, whilst others were taken from battalion staff. Amongst those selected were several 'picked shots'. Wintringham chose the dour yet reliable Scots commissar, George Aitken, to lead them, but first he would take them into position himself. The party set off to the east. Looping round away from the Nationalist lines, they travelled in a large arc that eventually took them round to the south side of White House Hill. Wintringham told the men not to make any particular effort to hide themselves. He wanted to draw the Nationalists' attention and make them worry about what was afoot. If he could convince the enemy that a major attack was about to be launched against his southern flank, then perhaps he could draw some of the pressure off the battalions to the north. After half an hour scrambling through the groves, the men emerged due south of the enemy gunners on White House Hill and about a quarter of a mile to the left of Fry's position.

Wintringham ordered his men into pairs and then sent them crawling forward to find cover. Big Manuel, the Cuban, and 'Phil the boxer' were the first to advance. 'Go ... as far as you can,' Wintringham called after them as they slithered forward on their bellies, 'but don't get into trouble.' Soon all the sniping teams had moved up. Whilst one of each pair, equipped with field glasses, acted as a spotter, the other kept up a steady harassing fire, aiming to provoke the enemy gunners into a response. Wintringham looked on in approval. 'We probed nooks and tore to pieces a Moorish *burnous* hanging over a bush.' His plan soon started working and the enemy began to return fire. Nevertheless, the range was extreme and the danger minimal: so much so that an exhausted Wintringham even managed to snatch a few minutes' sleep. Later he was woken by the crack of a Russian rifle fired inches from his head and crawled over to Aitken's position. 'I'll come back,' he assured the

Scot. 'Keep up the fire. Don't go forward unless the tanks come up, or the Spaniards move forward. I'll go and see Fry.' With that Wintringham slithered back into the groves, got to his feet once under cover, and set off on a looping run for the ridgeline.[3]

Back at Fry's forward trench, things had taken a turn for the worse. As Wintringham and Aitken had been moving into position, the Nationalists had opened up an artillery barrage centred on the 2nd Company's position. Both field guns and mortars were used. The former were positioned on the far side of the Knoll and beyond the Morata road, whilst the latter were far closer in. Between the Knoll and the ridgeline was a wrinkle of dead ground which the Nationalists had now occupied. From there it was only 600 yards to Fry's trench, well within range of the Moors' 50mm Valero mortars, which were now raining a steady stream of high explosive on the British position. Fry's men were glad of the work they had put in the previous night. Despite the storm of shrapnel shrieking overhead, the men were safe in their trench behind the low wall. 'Yank' Levy was even managing to return fire at some of the Nationalist gun positions on the far side of the Morata road. Alongside the Canadian, Fry was manning the central Maxim. Bill Meredith later remembered the Edinburgh man's impressive calm. Occasionally drawing on his pipe, Fry would squeeze off a few rounds at any Nationalist who appeared, whilst all the while the artillery was showering them with stones, olive branches, roots and dirt. As Bill Meredith watched, a shell burst yards away from their position. Shards of hot shrapnel sliced into the wall, shattering the stones. Fry was unmoved. Taking a long pull on his pipe, he turned to Meredith and asked him insouciantly – 'Did I hear something?' Meredith was impressed: 'For a novice like me under a first bombardment, this serenity represented the height of quiet courage,' he explained.[4]

At 2.00pm, 'Yank' Levy's attention was drawn by blurred movement to his right. Looking round, he noticed 'a group of 25 Spaniards on the plateau 300 yards [away] ... running like hell toward the enemy battery just beyond the road'. Around 50 yards behind them was a second group, double their number, apparently in pursuit. Deciding that the lead group were the enemy and that he was witnessing the start of the long promised attack, Levy ordered

Arthur Doran, a volunteer from Weston-super-Mare, to open fire. Before Doran could pull the Maxim's twin triggers, however, Levy saw a Russian T26 pursuing both groups and realized that they must both be the enemy. Doran managed a few bursts. A handful buckled and fell before they reached cover and disappeared from sight.[5] The tank rolled up the road, drew level with the ridgeline then ground to a halt. If this was Springhall's big attack, Levy was distinctly unimpressed.

The T26 was a formidable sight. At 15ft long, 8ft wide and weighing nearly 10 tons, it was heavier and better armed than the Nationalist machines and its 45mm cannon could destroy anything the enemy could deploy on the battlefield. With a top speed of 20mph, it was highly manoeuvrable and if used correctly could have swung the battle in the Republicans' favour. Rather than deploying them on a narrow front in overwhelming numbers as the Wehrmacht would do to such devastating effect in 1939, however, at Jarama the Republicans were overly cautious with their prize machines, thereby largely nullifying their effectiveness. Wary of the enemy anti-tank guns, the T26's three-man Russian crew were under strict orders not to expose themselves. Instead, they performed swift raids, popping up from the dead ground to fire off a salvo of shells before reversing into cover. After idling for a few moments level with Fry's forward trench, the tank spotted by Levy duly obeyed orders and reversed out of sight.

Shortly afterwards, Overton arrived in the 2nd Company's position. Once again, the former Welsh Guardsman had lost all self-control and was half mad with fear. Having taken off his boots and puttees, he had run through the groves in his socks. 'What are you doing here?' Fry demanded. Wide-eyed, Overton was unable to answer. Fry continued to fire off questions, but all were ignored. Only when asked why he had taken off his boots, did Overton reply: 'I can run better,' he explained, and with that he leapt out of Fry's trench and ran back to his company's position a few hundred yards to the north-west. Watching him zigzag through the groves, Fry and Levy were not exactly inspired with confidence. They were right to worry. Overton's cowardice would soon cost them all dear.[6]

Meanwhile, a quarter of a mile to the south, Aitken's thirty men were also coming under artillery fire. The feint had proved remarkably successful.

Worried that the Republicans were attempting to outflank him, Asensio had ordered a heavy barrage on their position and by the time Wintringham managed to return, Aitken had been forced to withdraw 60 yards to get his men out of the worst of the fire. The move had proved too late for some. Several had been hit by shrapnel and Phil the boxer was amongst the dead. Nevertheless, Aitken's band had actually grown in strength. Hearing the shooting, a few men from Briskey's 3rd Company who had been hiding in the groves since the previous afternoon, had mustered the courage to join them. Satisfied that Aitken was doing all he could, Wintringham returned to the Sunken Road.[7]

At 3.00pm the English Captain got a telephone message from Colonel Gal, brought to him by a runner as he was inspecting the far right of the British lines. To his disbelief, Wintringham was ordered to advance at once, regardless of tank support. If he failed to do so, the message threatened, Gal would have no choice but to have him arrested. Realizing that Gal had little idea of the situation on the ground, Wintringham ignored the order. His battered battalion were in no position to advance. If anything, the artillery fire coming down on Fry's trench was increasing. Despite the excellent cover, two of his men had been hit and it seemed ever more likely that the Nationalists were about to attack. Running forward to the ridgeline, Wintringham got a panoramic view of the entire front. The effects of Aitken's feint were wearing off and the Nationalists had once more taken the initiative. On the right, the Dimitrovs had been pushed further back and the gap between their line and the British position was increasing. As Wintringham scanned the valley through his binoculars, flashes of movement caught his eye. Using the natural cover, the Moors were advancing into the dead ground to Fry's front right. Slowly but surely they were working their way closer to his position. Only the presence of the remnants of Overton's 4th Company, who were sniping at the brown figures as they shuffled forward, was holding them in check.[8]

At 4.00pm Wintringham went back to Aitken's position to order the Scot to withdraw. Starting in an hour he was to pull his men back to the Sunken Road directly behind the forward ridgeline. If the Nationalists tried to launch an assault on the machine gunners, Aitken's men would be able to counter-attack. Wintringham did not want the Nationalists to know what he was up to, so told

Aitken to stagger his withdrawal. The men were to move back in pairs with a five-minute gap between each whilst the rest of the section kept up harassing fire. André Diamant's company, who had also been on the left flank throughout the day, were given similar instructions, only they were to start moving half an hour after Aitken's men had begun. Far to the left rear of the front line, the Egyptian had had a quiet day. Following their exertions on the 12th, his men were no doubt glad of the respite, but their isolation had its price. Whilst the rest of the battalion had eaten, Diamant's men had had no food all day.[9]

'By these methods,' Wintringham later confided in his memoirs, 'I believed I could gather enough support to beat off what was obviously coming: a big attack on Fry in the last hours of the evening.' What the English Captain did not realize, however, was that the 2nd Company's position had already been compromised. During the afternoon, the Nationalist artillery barrage had shattered Overton's nerves and shortly after Wintringham had left Fry's trench for the last time, his cowardice overcame him. 'Yank' Levy witnessed the moment Wintringham's plans fell apart. At 4.00pm he was distracted from his vigil watching the Nationalist gunners by the Knoll by some particularly accurate artillery fire. Two shells in quick succession fell on Overton's position. With nothing other than olive trees as protection, the men of the 4th Company were dangerously exposed. Red hot shrapnel shrieked through the branches, threw up clods of earth and showered the men with leaves. Albert Charlesworth, the twenty-two year-old metal polisher from Oldham was amongst those hit. 'An artillery shell ... exploded near me and I went [flying] through the air.' Charlesworth landed heavily. 'My left arm refused to move,' he recalled.[10] The twenty-two year-old's battle was over. He was carried back to the Sunken Road, loaded onto a lorry and sent to a dressing station behind the lines. With Charlesworth gone and another of his men wounded and crying out for help, Overton snapped. Leaping to his feet, he turned his back on the Moors picking their way through no-man's land and ran. The fifty riflemen under his command only hesitated a few seconds. As Levy looked on, the whole company started to retreat and were soon flying through the groves. The Canadian was amazed by the sight. '4 company [were] running hell ... for leather to the rear with O[verton] leading by about 25 yards.'[11]

Fry also witnessed the retreat and immediately realized its consequences: without Overton's men, his right was exposed. The Nationalists could work their way round using the dead ground and out-flank him. Calm as ever, Fry reacted by re-positioning one of his guns. The crew were ordered to move 50 yards to the right to cover the dead ground that Overton's flight had left unguarded. The gun would only stay in position for a matter of minutes, however. The Nationalist fire was too heavy and the crew were dangerously exposed. Moments later, a runner leapt into Fry's trench with a message from Overton urging the machine gunners to withdraw. 'Yank' Levy remembered Fry's reaction. 'Knowing how yellow he [Overton] showed the day before,' the Canadian recalled, 'Fry [went] to the rear [to check if there were any substance to the order] and returning tells us we are to hold our position at all costs and pay no attention to anything O[verton] may say.'[12]

At 4.30pm, one of Fry's men spotted the Nationalist commander's headquarters on the hills to their front. Knowing that Brigade HQ would be interested, the Scotsman looked around for a runner to take the information to Wintringham. None were in sight so Fry asked Bill Meredith if he would take the message instead. 'Sure,' he replied. 'I took [it], ducked my head as low as I could and ran like hell for our front line.' After searching for some time, Meredith found Wintringham. As Fry had predicted, the English Captain was delighted with the information 'and scribbled out [a] reply'. Meredith then 'began to cover the two hundred metres [219 yards] [back] to the Company.' Suddenly the guns that had been pounding their positions all afternoon fell silent and for a few moments an eerie calm descended over the battlefield. Then the Nationalists launched their attack. Before Meredith could rejoin his comrades it would all be over.[13]

CHAPTER 12
CAPTURE!
(4.30–6.00PM, 13 FEBRUARY 1937)

'Yank' Levy was the first to see them coming. Groups of twenty-five to fifty Foreign Legion troops were picking their way across the valley floor. Advancing in short bursts, they used the cover well. George Leeson, the former Royal Navy gunner, also noticed their advance. 'Men [were] ... running down the skyline from the top of the hill position they'd held.'[1] They crossed the valley then disappeared into the dead ground to the British right. After alerting Fry to the danger, Levy leapt out of the trench to have a better look. Jogging for 50 yards, he came to an area of the ridgeline that overlooked the dead ground. Sure enough, there they were. A large body of Nationalists had formed and were waiting for the order to advance. Running back to his position, Levy ordered Private White, one of the company's messengers, to return to the area and report back on the Nationalists' movements. A few moments later he was back, saying he had seen nothing. Exasperated, Levy drew a quick sketch of what he had seen and, entrusting it to White, sent him to find Wintringham and ask for instructions. As he left the trench the Nationalist artillery, which had been an ever-present menace since noon, fell ominously silent.[2]

Not realizing the significance of the lull, Levy turned his attention back to the Nationalist gunners by the Knoll 800 yards to his front right. Throughout the day he had been picking off those brave or stupid enough to reveal themselves and by the afternoon he had notched up a tally of kills. 'I ... [was] aiming at this tree [beside their position],' he recalled, 'when to my amazement' a fascist soldier popped up '20 yards in front of me ... directly in line with my sights'. At first Levy was too shocked to react. Maurice Goldberg, a London Jew manning the gun to his left, also saw the unexpected arrival. 'Blimey, who's that?' he asked no-one in particular. Someone else shouted 'Who are you?' and for a few moments indecision ruled. 'We had ... received rumours that we [were] ... going to be relieved,' Levy explained, '[so] some of the boys thought that this was one of our Spaniards who somehow had gotten ahead of us.'[3]

The gunners' confusion was understandable. They had been in combat for over thirty hours. Although some had snatched a few hours sleep during the night, others had been awake ever since they had jumped off the trucks at the Cookhouse early the previous morning. They were physically and mentally exhausted. To make matters worse, the battlefield at Jarama was horribly disorientating. 'You didn't know what was happening,' Frank Graham recalled. 'It was very rough country.'[4] Friends and enemy alike seemed to appear from the unlikeliest of places. Donald Renton, the 2nd Company's political commissar, remembered that the Foreign Legion's uniforms also added to his men's confusion. They 'were not unlike those of our Spanish loyalist units'.[5] A final factor was that the Nationalists, knowing that the machine gunners would experience a moment of doubt, took advantage by pretending to be their allies. Some shouted 'camarada!' as they approached. Others gave the Republicans' clenched fist salute and sang the Internationale as they advanced. Bill Meredith, at that moment returning to the forward trench from Battalion HQ, was also unsure as to how to react, but for a different reason. 'I had no doubt that here was a mass desertion from the fascist lines,' he explained.[6] George Leeson was also taken in. As he watched the enemy advance, a man beside him stood up and called out, 'cease fire, don't shoot'. Others raised their rifles in welcome, little realizing the fate that awaited them.[7]

'Yank' Levy, on the other hand, smelled a rat. Depressing his Maxim's twin triggers, the Canadian let out a rolling burst of fire. The soldier who had popped up 20 yards ahead of him was the first to be cut down. Then all hell broke loose. Dropping their pretence, the Nationalists opened fire with their rifles and hurled hand grenades into the 2nd Company's trench. Levy saw the gunner to his right, Arthur Doran from Weston-super-Mare, firing wildly for a few seconds before the grenades silenced him forever. Levy shouted at Doran's number two to take over, but he too had been killed in the explosion, 'on his knees in the same position he was while feeding the gun'. Levy then saw a group of five Nationalists running towards him, demanding that he cease fire. They were just 20 yards away. As he swung his Maxim towards them, another group appeared, coming out of the olive groves behind him. One of them opened fire with 'a small … sub-machine gun'. The bullets whipped round Levy, but left the Canadian unscathed. Another then threw a bomb. Levy dropped to the floor, his face against Doran's still warm body, and counted to four. To his great relief, the grenade failed to explode.[8]

By now the Nationalists were pouring into the trench. Some were firing their guns from the hip, others had reversed their rifles and were using the butts to batter the British into submission. Donald Renton was hit in the legs by a burst of machine-gun fire. Harry Fry was shot through the arm, the bullet shattering the bone to smithereens. Jimmy Rutherford, a nineteen year-old from Leith, was knocked to the ground and George Watters was hit round the head by a rifle butt and rendered unconscious. In other areas of the trench some of the volunteers were fighting back. Panayiotis Katsaranos, the leader of the battalion's London Cypriots, was 'cracking skulls with his rifle butt' until he was surrounded and 'the fascists riddled him with bullets'.[9] Meanwhile, Bill Meredith had taken cover in the groves 20 yards away. A growing look of horror spread across his face as he realized what was happening. 'More and more fascists were swarming over the top' and within minutes the fighting was over. Amongst the twenty-seven survivors taken prisoner was Ted Dickenson, Fry's second-in-command. Standing with his 'legs wide apart and [his] back straight as a poker [he] still appeared every inch a soldier', Meredith recalled. 'He was looking at the fascists with contempt written all over his face and it was obvious that his capture would never shake his calm courage.'[10]

'Yank' Levy, meanwhile, had also recovered his composure. As the Nationalists had swarmed into the trench he had played dead, waiting for an opportunity to escape. 'As soon as the fascists had passed [over] me, I got up and made a dash for the rear.' Johnny Stevens, a young Londoner, broke cover with him, but they were both out of luck as Levy remembered:

As [we] ran ... a fascist ... [came] out of the grove and ... [started] motioning me to the trench. Stevens, who was ahead of me, [was] also told to get back. I shout[ed] at him to keep running [and said I'd] ... keep between him and the gun but he turned about and followed me back.[11]

Bill Meredith was also about to make a run for it when a Nationalist spotted him, brought his rifle up to the shoulder and fired. The Northumbrian was lucky. 'I saw the puff of smoke but have no knowledge where the bullet landed.' As he turned to run, he caught a final sight of Levy. Two Nationalists had lunged at the Canadian, caught him and dragged him back to the trench. Meredith had seen enough and set off full tilt towards the Sunken Road:

With fascists firing at my back and our battalion returning fire, the air seemed thick with lead. I never expected to reach the line. My back was shrinking from the bullets I expected to plough into it at any moment, and at the same time I was afraid of one of our men firing a little too near and hitting me instead.[12]

The Northumbrian's luck held. 'Somehow I covered the two hundred and seventy five metres [300 yards] ... unharmed' and dived into the Sunken Road. Looking up, Meredith saw that he had dropped at the feet of Tom Wintringham.[13]

The Foreign Legion troops, meanwhile, had turned the captured Maxims around and opened fire on Wintringham's position. In addition to the machine guns, Jason Gurney recalled, 'there must have been a couple of hundred riflemen firing high expansion bullets'. These were dumdums which exploded on impact. As well as causing horrific wounds, the noise they made was utterly bewildering. The secondary explosions made it seem as if riflemen were all around them. 'I think at this particular moment we were all a little mad,' Gurney remembered:

The sheer weight of noise was tremendous... People were running around shouting and behaving in all manner of peculiar ways. Wintringham bawled at us to fix bayonets ... [and] we all clustered round against the bank ready to go over the top. It was rather like some totally improbable incident out of the *Boy's Own Paper*, and quite futile: a handful of men proposing to charge about two hundred yards into the face of eight Maxim guns and an unknown number of ... infantry.[14]

Caught up in the excitement, Wintringham stood up in the Sunken Road. Waving the stick he used for removing machine-gun blockages above his head, he called on his men to counter-attack. As well as Gurney, John 'Bosco' Jones and a handful of others fumbled their bayonets into place and prepared to follow him. Also there was Bert Overton. The former guardsman was having another of his more rational moments and had briefly regained control. 'I'll never forget [what happened next],' Jones recalled. Wintringham climbed up onto the bank and 'wallop he got one in the leg'.[15] The bullet had hit the English Captain just above the knee. His leg buckled and he crashed to the ground, blood pumping from the jagged tear in his flesh. As Wintringham dragged himself back to cover, up stepped Bert Overton to replace him. Perhaps inspired by his captain's example or half mad with the thrill of battle, he briefly overcame his cowardice to lead the charge.[16]

Forty men followed Overton. Only six would come back. 'The fascists in front were waiting for us,' Jones recalled.[17] Within seconds half of the British had been mown down by Maxim and rifle fire. Bobby Quail, the weight lifting champion from South Hylton, was hit in the hand, Jimmy Wheeler was killed instantly and the man next to Jones got a bullet 'straight in the mouth' and was thrown back into the road.[18] Alec Leppard, a nineteen year-old from Finsbury Park, and Cyril Pencot were also wounded seconds after leaving the trench. The rest ignored the casualties and ran on. Jason Gurney felt as if he were in a trance. 'I was running with my head down, imagining that my helmet would protect my face ... with absolutely no idea what I would do ... if ... I got to the other side.' Sixty yards through the groves, he looked up and, to his horror, found that he was alone. Thirty-five men had already been hit. A trail of dead and wounded led all the way back to the Sunken Road. The five survivors had gone to ground. Noticing an olive tree stump nearby, Gurney decided to join them. 'The heap of earth' built up around the trunk 'was only eighteen inches wide and one foot high, but ... provided cover for my head.'

With 'an enormous mass of metal tearing at the air above' him, the South African flattened his body into the contours of the ground. 'I lay ... close to despair,' he later confessed.

> I had no thought of prayer ... nor did I think back over my past life, nor any of the other things that people are supposed to do in the face of imminent death. But I did feel very unhappy in no ... specific way. I wasn't frightened of being killed but of being mangled ... a living man, smashed out of shape, caused in me a reaction of the purest horror... The thought of being torn and broken terrified me.[19]

Realizing he would be hit if he stayed where he was, Gurney got to his feet and ran for the Sunken Road. Bullets flashed past as he zigzagged through the trees until at last the trench appeared in front of him. Without breaking stride, he flung himself into it and 'rolled to a stop on the far side'.[20]

Meanwhile, in Fry's forward trench, George Watters had regained consciousness. '[The British] were all standin' ... wi' their hands up in a line,' the Glaswegian recalled.[21] Moving between the prisoners, the Nationalists began seeking out their leaders. Ted Dickenson, the company's Australian second-in-command, immediately realized what was going on. Whilst giving Fry some first aid for his shattered arm, he ripped the insignia off the Scot's uniform so the Nationalists would be unable to identify him.[22] The act undoubtedly saved his commander's life. Dickenson, on the other hand, would be less fortunate. James Maley, the twenty-nine year-old Celtic fan who had been dreaming of Parkhead just a few hours before, remembered that the Foreign Legionnaires 'were making threatening gestures ... that they were gunna cut our privates off'. One approached the Glaswegian and started asking questions in rapid fire Spanish. Seeing that he couldn't understand, the Spaniard punched him in the face instead. Tommy Bloomfield, a fellow Scot, saw a priest amongst the enemy. Seeing a mortally wounded volunteer, he 'took out his crucifix' and was about to administer the last rites when one of the Nationalist officers pointed out that he was a 'Rojo'. The priest ceased his ministrations and moved on. Bloomfield was disgusted. He would never look at a clergyman in the same way again.[23]

With the threat of a second British counter-attack looming, the Nationalists decided to move the prisoners away from the front line. The Foreign Legion stayed with the Maxims and a Moroccan unit took over escort duty. The British were tied together with wire wrapped round their wrists and thumbs. Harry Fry was in agony. The bonds had forced him to adopt an unnatural position, tearing open the wounds in his arm. Meanwhile, the British in the Sunken Road were still firing wildly as the prisoners were led away and several were hit and killed by their own side. 'There was a lot of dead ground ... and the Fascists ... [were] able to keep ... [in] cover,' Renton recalled, but they 'compelled us' to march across the high ground, fully exposed to the fire.[24] On the far side of the valley, the prisoners were ordered to make a sharp turn which finally brought them under cover. The Moors then ordered them to halt. Phil Elias, a volunteer from Leeds, asked permission to smoke. It seemed to have been granted, but as he reached into his inside pocket, a nervous Moor fired a burst of sub-machine-gun fire at him from close range. Stitching across his stomach, the bullets cut Elias in two and also killed John Stevens, a young YCL member from Saint Pancras who was standing behind him. The Moors, however, had only just begun and singled out Ted Dickenson for special treatment. Although his quick thinking had saved Fry, the Australian had forgotten to remove his own Sam Browne, a wide leather belt that was only worn by officers. Seeing it, the Moors pulled him out of the line and gave him an ultimatum: either fight for the Nationalists or die. Dickenson chose the latter. 'He marched up to a tree like a soldier on parade,' Bloomfield remembered, 'did a military about-turn, and said "Salute comrades!"' The Moors advanced until their rifles were nearly touching his head before opening fire. Dickenson's skull was blown to pieces.[25]

By now the men in the Sunken Road were in a state of panic. Rifle bullets and rounds from the captured Maxims were still thumping into the olive trees around them. Leaning against one side of the trench with the blood still pumping out of his shattered thigh, Wintringham observed the chaos. Having returned from his failed counter-attack, Overton was demanding that the entire battalion be given permission to withdraw. The English Captain was having none of it. Knowing that the remnants of his battalion were all that stood between the Nationalists and the Valencia Road, he dismissed Overton's request out of hand. It would be Wintringham's final contribution to the battle. Although the bullet that had struck his leg had missed the bone, the muscle had been badly torn and he had lost a lot of blood.[26]

Nearby, Jason Gurney watched as 'one of [his] ... closest friends in the battalion', buckled under the pressure. '[He] was rushing round enmeshed in a cocoon of protective insulated wire ... [and] had obviously gone completely mad,' the South African remembered. Crying, 'I have captured the Fascist communications!', the man leapt up onto the bank and was immediately 'shot dead by a burst of machine-gun fire. It was horrifying, but it seemed to be the best thing [for him],' Gurney recalled. 'My only feeling was one of infinite pity mixed with relief.'[27]

At that moment George Aitken, the Scottish commissar who had been leading the diversionary attack on the far left flank earlier that afternoon, dived into the road after a mad rush through the groves. 'The fire was tremendous. It was a sheer miracle that I managed to get through.'[28] After seeing that Wintringham was out of action, the Scot took over command. First he ordered two stretcher bearers to carry his captain to the rear, then attempted to bring order to the battalion, now just 150 strong. Overton, meanwhile, was still insisting they withdraw. '[He] told me that as a regular soldier ... he felt the position was hopeless,' Aitken recalled, but the Scot, like Wintringham before him, was adamant that they hold.[29] Frustrated, Overton disappeared to the north. Running down the Sunken Road, he spread his defeatism amongst the men, muttering to himself and anyone who would listen that they were doomed and had to withdraw.

Aitken was left to make the best out of the situation. Realizing that guarding his flanks was his first priority, he called for volunteers to move out to the right. Twelve men stepped forward. By 5.45pm they were in position. Bill Meredith, the Northumbrian from the 2nd Company who had managed to escape capture, was amongst them. '[Our] nerves were ... frayed,' he recalled, 'as the position was very precarious.'[30] Later, Meredith's group was joined by the 2nd Company's sole remaining Maxim. Having been positioned on the far left flank since the opening day, Cyril Sexton's gun crew had not been captured with the rest of their comrades. When ordered to relocate, Sexton had been most put out. His position had been well fortified and afforded a sweeping field of fire across the entire left flank. The new position 'at the start of the olive groves about ten yards behind the sunken road' by contrast, was 'terrible'. Sexton's line of sight to both the front and the left was almost entirely blocked by the trees and they were out of sight of the bulk of the battalion. Isolated and alone as night began to fall, the small cluster of men awaited the next onslaught.[31]

CHAPTER 13

THE SECOND NIGHT

(6.00PM 13 FEBRUARY – 6.00AM 14 FEBRUARY 1937)

That evening a lone reinforcement arrived at the Cookhouse. Jock Cunningham, a cantankerous Scot, who was 'idolised by his comrades', was the original commander of the 1st Company.[1] The thirty-four year-old from Coatbridge had been suffering from flu ever since the battalion had arrived in Chinchon on 9 February and had been unable to join the men at the front line. That was about to change. 'Still sick with fever', Cunningham heard his men were in dire straits. Dragging himself from his sickbed, he hitched a lift to the Cookhouse with a passing ambulance, arriving 'some time between dusk and midnight' on the 13th. After listening to a garbled account of the action from Tiny Silverman, the battalion's chief cook, Cunningham packed his pockets with ammunition and cigarettes, gathered a handful of stragglers and headed towards the sound of machine-gun fire at the front.[2]

Jock Cunningham was one of the longest serving British volunteers in the International Brigades. His baptism of fire had been at Madrid in November 1936. Fighting alongside eighteen other British volunteers in the 4th Section of the Commune de Paris Battalion of the XI International Brigade, Cunningham had performed heroically. Armed with an assortment of ancient rifles that had to be loaded one bullet at a time, the 4th Section was thrust straight into the action. After marching down the Gran Via, they were tasked with defending a ridgeline in the Casa de Campo, a sprawling area of parkland on the western outskirts of Madrid. On the morning of 9 November 1936 the Nationalists pounded their positions with artillery fire. As soon as the barrage lifted, the Moors were sent in. By the time the Internationals were ordered to pull back, only five of the British section remained. Despite the setback, the XI Brigade and their sister unit, the XII, later returned to the fight and were instrumental in holding the rebels on the outskirts of the city.[3]

In December 1936 Cunningham fought at Lopera as a section commander with the British and Irish Company of the XIV Brigade. After the battle he replaced Nathan as company commander and led the unit at Las Rozas. The survivors joined the British Battalion at Madrigueras at the end of January 1937. Fred Copeman, who rarely had a good word to say about anyone, met Cunningham at the training base. 'Jock was an ex-army sergeant,' the Englishman wrote, 'handsome and really lovable, [and] tough as they come.'[4] Walter Greenhalgh, a Mancunian from the 1st Company, thought Cunningham an 'inspiration' and John 'Bosco' Jones remembered him as 'a very brave lad'.[5] George Aitken was another of the Scot's admirers. The commissar recalled that his incredible bravery and disregard for enemy fire stemmed from a belief that he was invulnerable. 'Cunningham thought that nothing could happen to him,' he explained. 'He [went] ... about as if he led a charmed life.'[6]

Cunningham's family had a proud military tradition. His father, John, had fought in the Boer War and six of his brothers had been in the British Army. Jock himself had served with the Argyll and Sutherland Highlanders, but his military career had been anything but plain sailing. In 1929 he had led a mutiny over pay and conditions in Jamaica. George Aitken later heard the story. 'He was tried, found guilty and sent to the glasshouse [at Aldershot], but they didn't break [him]. He went on hunger strike 3 or 4 times ... [and] when the Home Office person came in [to interview him] he threw his chamber pot in his face ... in fact he was such a bloody nuisance that they were glad to get rid of him.' Impressed by his determination, the British Communist Party campaigned for Cunningham's release.[7] As a party organizer Aitken grew to admire Cunningham's charisma and bloody minded determination. '[He was] very forceful and very effective at close quarters,' he recalled. If anyone could organize the battalion following Wintringham's departure, it was Jock Cunningham.[8]

As the Scot was advancing to the front line, Wintringham was still waiting for treatment on his wounded thigh at the dressing station. Beside the English Captain lay Walter Gregory, the runner from the 3rd Company who had been shot in the right hand the day before. Gregory had been waiting for attention for twenty-four hours, but could not complain. 'Compared to most [of the wounded] ... I would have qualified as A1 for immediate military service,' he explained. The scenes at the dressing station were appalling. 'There were wounded troops lying all over the place with more arriving all the time. There was a shortage of doctors, nurses and medical supplies and even the most gravely wounded simply had to be left lying in the open air.' That night Wintringham and Gregory were taken to separate hospitals. It took the latter 24 hours to reach Murcia on a slow-moving train.[9] Wintringham was more fortunate. He reached the hospital at Elda-Petra near Valencia on the same night that he was hit. After arriving he penned a quick note to his American girlfriend, the journalist Kitty Bowler. 'Dear Kitty,' it began, 'hit in the thigh while trying to organize a bayonet charge. Damn these out of date sports. Nice wound. 2 days hard fighting. Done well, [but] lost all too many. Love, Tom.'[10]

Meanwhile, the situation in the Sunken Road had improved. 'With ... darkness, the firing ... died down,' Gurney remembered. 'The enemy were obviously satisfied with their ... work and had no intention of pressing on until the following day.' After thirty hours of intense combat, the South African was close to collapse. 'I was ... physically and emotionally exhausted so I lay down against the bank of the road and fell into a deep sleep.'[11] George Aitken, on the other hand, could afford no such luxuries. The Scottish commissar was busy organizing the men. Patrols were sent out to the left and the right to ensure the enemy were not attempting to outflank them. To make matters worse, morale was low. Willie Lloyd, the Welsh veteran of Lopera and Las Rozas, was worried about what had happened to his friend from Aberaman, Bob Condon. They had been split up on the first day and Lloyd had not seen him since. 'News came through that the whole of [Condon's section] ... had been wiped out,' Lloyd recalled, and he began imagining what he would have to tell his friend's mother.[12] Many of the survivors were half-crazed with fear. The adrenaline of the first two days had worn off and the men began to realize their mortality. John 'Bosco' Jones recalled that they were 'very depressed so many lads had been lost' and the battalion was on the verge of collapse. 'Half [of us] wanted to stay and half to run.'[13] Alone on the right flank, Cyril Sexton's gun crew also passed a sleepless night, jumping at shadows. 'It was a night of dismay and alarms... Everyone seemed to be on edge.'[14] The survivors were asleep on their feet and their imaginations began to play tricks on them. With the moonlight playing over the olive trees, the gnarled branches turned into Moors coming after them in the dark.[15]

Not long after nightfall, the Nationalists fired a Very flare over the British lines. Arcing high into the sky, it came down swinging on a parachute, casting flickering shadows over the faces below. By chance, the flare landed in the centre of the Sunken Road, right on top of the battalion's ammunition store. 'There was a tremendous explosion', then all 'hell was let loose'.[16] Startled into action, the Nationalists opened up with their Maxims, light machine guns and rifles and several of the British returned fire. In the confusion, some of the volunteers believed they had been attacked by some sort of secret weapon. Thick black smoke filled the road, 'making some think of poisonous gas'.[17] Several fumbled with their Czechoslovakian gas masks, whilst others ran. Bert Overton was amongst the latter. Shouting 'liquid fire!' and yelling at his men to fall back, he vaulted over the eastern bank of the road and disappeared into the olive groves.[18] Fifty men followed him. Bill Meredith saw them fly by. Wide-eyed with panic they resembled frightened game. 'What's happening?' Meredith called out. 'We've been ordered to retreat,' came the reply. Meredith joined the stampede, only coming to his senses several minutes later. 'About six of us turned back,' he recalled.[19] Aitken, meanwhile, was trying to rally the rest. Running up and down the road he 'managed to prevent the majority from disappearing ... though [by the time order was restored] we had already lost damn near half the battalion.'[20]

At about 10.30pm Aitken ordered André Diamant, the Anglo-Egyptian who had taken over command of the remnants of the 1st Company on the 12th, to lead a patrol out to the left flank. Half an hour later, Diamant made contact with the Lister Brigade which was holding the line to the south.

The Spaniards told him that 'their position was good' and Diamant made his way back to the Sunken Road.[21] Later, Jason Gurney awoke to find himself alone. It was bitterly cold, and no-one was to be seen 'apart from a few dead bodies. This had been the worst day of my life,' the South African remembered. 'There was no point in staying where I was and I simply wandered off to look for Brigade HQ.' By the time he found the staff bunker, situated in a number of dugouts half way down the road to Morata, it was starting to get light. George Nathan, the battalion assistant chief of staff, took pity on the South African and offered him some bread and coffee. It was obvious Gurney was on the verge of collapse.

> The bloodshed and chaos of the previous day had not bothered me at the time but now a reaction began to set in. My mind kept going back over the events of the last few days since the wounding of Francis; the waste and desecration of the olive groves, the finding of that ghastly collection of wounded derelicts and my inability to do anything for them, finally the killing and the total collapse of any semblance of order in the Sunken Road. I had often read about the sense of moral collapse which pervades a defeated army, but it was quite a different thing to experience it.[22]

Gurney had suffered a mental breakdown and would have no clear memory of the next few days' events. In the weeks that followed he remained with Brigade HQ as a runner and later joined the American Abraham Lincoln Brigade.

Jock Cunningham was half a mile away from the line when he heard the ammunition exploding. Half an hour later some of those that had fled with Overton came rushing by. 'Where's the battalion?' Cunningham demanded. 'This is the battalion,' they replied. 'Where's the enemy?' the Scot continued. 'Not far ahead: two hundred yards.' Cunningham's presence calmed the men and they joined the growing crowd he was leading back to the line. He now had fifty or sixty soldiers under his command.[23] On reaching the Sunken Road, Cunningham was shocked by what he saw. The remnants of the battalion were in stark contrast to the 'boy scout parade' that had left the Cookhouse two days before. Most of the hundred or so who remained were asleep, aside from a few sentries who stood shivering here and there, leaning on their rifles. Cunningham shook them awake. The men were filthy. Dust and gore covered their uniforms. Their sweat streaked faces were blackened with mud. During the night all had seemed lost, but with the coming of dawn the men took heart. Jock Cunningham was there.

CHAPTER 14
TANK ATTACK!
(6.00AM–2.00PM, 14 FEBRUARY 1937)

Cunningham's arrival brought fresh hope. Although small in stature, the Scot's presence and calm reassurance worked like a lucky charm. Having survived for two days and nights against the best the Nationalists could throw at them, the men were not about to give up now. Amongst those Cunningham had brought up from the Cookhouse was Bob Condon, Willie Lloyd's friend from the valleys of Aberdare. The two men had not seen each other since the morning of the 12th and Lloyd had feared the worst. 'When I saw ... [him] returning unhurt, it was like a sight from heaven,' Condon later explained. 'I had been worrying about him and about the loss to his family [for the past forty-eight hours].'[1] Jock Cunningham was a whirlwind of energy. Two strong outposts were ordered to investigate the ground to the left and the right. Neither found any sign of the enemy. A third was then sent forwards to Fry's old trench. Creeping up in the half light of dawn, they discovered the position was occupied by a company of Moors. Cunningham led the charge. Taken by surprise, the Africans retreated. The British recaptured some of the Maxims lost the previous night before pulling back once more.[2]

Later that morning, Cunningham decided to abandon the Sunken Road. Although offering some cover from the front, without the buffer of Fry's trench the position was a death trap. As the ground rose ahead of it, any attackers could advance to within 100 yards before being discovered. To make matters worse, the road ran straight north–south with few deviations so could easily be enfiladed by flanking fire. A single machine gun set up to fire along its length could wipe out the whole battalion. Cunningham thought the rising ground behind the road a more suitable defensive position. It afforded a better field of fire and the olive trees provided some cover.[3]

Now just over 200 strong, the battalion moved back in two stages. Whilst the machine gunners were setting up their Maxims in the groves behind the road, the riflemen remained behind to cover them. As the Nationalists were expected at any moment, it was a nervous time. 'The riflemen, poor cunts, were scared to death,' Bill Meredith recalled. The Maxim crews seemed to take an age before they were ready, but finally the infantry were given the signal to fall back. Once in their new positions, the men were ordered to dig in.[4] The work was exhausting and soon their thoughts turned to food. Some had not eaten for three days. At about 8.00am Diamant sent four men to the rear to bring up supplies. They never returned. Cunningham then ordered Bill Meredith and two others back to the Sunken Road to see if any food had been left behind. The young Northumbrian was sure the enemy would be waiting for them. 'We thought ... [that] the fascists ... would realize that the road ... had been vacated ... and would occupy it themselves.'[5] Weighed down by the canteens of their comrades, the three men crept forward to the road and then proceeded along it until they stumbled across a large urn of coffee, abandoned the night before.[6]

Over on the right flank, Cyril Sexton's gun crew were amazed to see a solitary figure out in the open approaching them from the Morata road. '[He] was a telephone lineman recovering wire since [Brigade HQ] were short of it,' Sexton recalled. 'We asked if he had seen anything of the enemy, the reply of "No" surprised us.'[7] Isolated away from the main line, Sexton's crew had a relatively quiet morning. Leonard Bibby, the twenty-five year-old who had served in the Territorial Army, even had time to write a letter home to his brother Harold. It would be the last he ever wrote.[8]

At 9.00am Cunningham received orders from Brigade HQ. Unaware of its tactical disadvantages and determined not to concede any more ground, Gal insisted that the British reoccupy the Sunken Road. Reluctantly, Cunningham obeyed. Meredith was given the unenviable task of informing the gun crews who had spent the last few hours digging in. 'As I went round, I was called every

Tank Attack! 14 February 1937

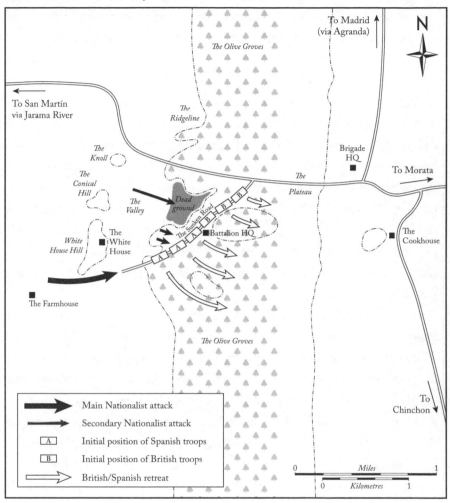

fucking name they could lay their tongues to,' he recalled.[9] Although the coffee had raised the men's spirits, food was still a pressing concern. Cunningham suggested that Aitken go back to the Cookhouse to bring up some supplies and see if he could rally any more stragglers. The Scot agreed and set out shortly after 9.00am.[10]

Cunningham spent the rest of the morning organizing the defences. Diamant's men and 300 Spaniards from the Lister Brigade brought the battalion up to strength and soon it held a line along the Sunken Road of about a mile in length. Light machine guns and Maxims had been set up at regular intervals and the men were positioned every three or four yards. Though tired and hungry, they seemed determined to resist. A further boost came with the arrival of a second detachment of men from the Brigade Guard. These were the veterans of Lopera and Las Rozas who had been based in Morata for the first two days of the battle. Amongst them, in a good position behind a small pile of sandstone, was Michael Economides, one of the battalion's British Cypriots. The former waiter recalled that although there was still no food, some letters from home reached the line that morning and were distributed amongst the men. It must have seemed surreal to read about domestic concerns back in London, Glasgow and Dublin to men who for two days and nights had been fighting for their lives.[11] Later, Jock Cunningham walked past the position Economides was defending. 'I remember one man ... [beside me said that he had] no helmet,' the Cypriot recalled. '"All right," Jock said to him, "take mine" [and] threw it [down] to him.'[12]

Later, Cunningham asked for volunteers to recover a light machine gun tripod that had been left in no-man's land. Cyril Sexton and William Ball, the former receptionist for Great Western Motors in Reading, agreed to go. Whilst the rest of their gun team provided covering fire, they sprinted across no-man's land. The Nationalists opened up from their positions just 15 yards away from where the tripod had fallen. Nevertheless, the mission was a success and they were soon back in their own lines. Cunningham rewarded each man with cigarettes he had brought up from the Cookhouse. He then split up Sexton's gun crew. Yorky and Sexton were left to man the gun, whilst the rest, including Bibby and Ball, were given rifles and told to join the line. Cunningham needed every man he could get. Sexton would never see Bibby or Ball again.[13]

André Diamant was delighted that Cunningham was in charge. The two men had served together at Lopera and Las Rozas and shared a mutual respect. 'We discussed the position of the battalion,' Diamant recalled, 'and he agreed with me to draw back my company to the olive trees at the other side of the road.'[14] After ordering his men to relocate, Diamant walked up and down the line four times to do a headcount. In total, 215 of the British Battalion remained. Seconds later a runner arrived from Brigade HQ. He was carrying a sketch map of the front and a note written by George Nathan. Diamant looked at the map then handed the note to Cunningham. The Egyptian recalled:

> The front was in the form of a half moon. At the extreme left [was] the Spanish battalion, covering three quarters of the ground to the [south of the Morata road] ... we had to cover the other quarter... On the right ... [were] the Franco Belge, Dimitrov and Thaelmann [battalions].[15]

The map also revealed a large gap between the British and the troops to their north. Cunningham ordered Diamant to extend the line to cover it, but at first there were simply not enough men. Then, at 10.00am, the Scot sent twenty-eight reinforcements to the right wing. The gap was plugged and the line was complete. Nathan's accompanying note was full of optimism. 'Sit tight,' it read, 'at one o'clock our tanks will advance through those gaps on your right and left. Meanwhile dig in and await further instructions.'[16]

By midday the heat was terrible. Now that the coffee was finished the men were suffering from thirst. The situation became so desperate that the machine gunners were asking for volunteers to urinate in their water bottles so that they could use the liquid to cool the guns. In the early afternoon, the Nationalist artillery opened fire. Under the constant pounding, the men grew ever more nervous and some lost control. Tom Spiller, the volunteer from Hawke's Bay, was crawling down the Sunken Road with the shrapnel fizzing overhead, when he noticed a thirty-four year-old Londoner whom he had first met in Madrigueras. The man was weeping uncontrollably. 'What's the trouble comrade?' Spiller shouted above the gunfire. In between sobs the man explained that he was terrified that he would panic and take the whole battalion with him. 'Well,' Spiller replied, 'when nightfall comes I'll see that you're taken out of the line, you're no good if you can't stick it.' As he finished speaking, a shell exploded 15ft away. 'It blew one ... [man] to pieces and bits ... off another one... Flesh and ... bone hit me on the face and hit this chap I was with too,' Spiller remembered. 'Of course, he really screamed blue murder then.'[17]

Elsewhere, Bill Meredith was passing on Cunningham's latest instructions to the machine gunners. As well as giving each crew a specific range and direction to shoot at, the Scot had insisted that they hold their fire until his command. As Meredith reached the last Maxim, a low grumbling came rolling through the groves. For a few moments many of the volunteers were jubilant. Their first thought was that their tank support had arrived, but it soon became clear that the advancing T26s had been captured earlier in the battle and were now manned by the enemy. Rattling up the Sunken Road, the tanks hit the Spanish Republican troops in the flank. With no anti-tank guns and precious few grenades, the Republicans were hopelessly outmatched. Within ten minutes they had fled. Seeing their comrades flying, the British left also crumbled. Exhausted after three days in the line, Joe Garber, the twenty-six year-old from the East End, was convinced he was doomed. 'We're finished here,' he thought as he saw the tanks closing in on them. His only wish was for a swift, clean death. 'I hope they just catch me through the back of the head and have done with it', was the last thing he remembered thinking before he fled into the groves.[18]

Tom Spiller was on the battalion's extreme left flank when the Nationalists attacked. 'I saw tanks dropping over into the Sunken Road away to our left and then chasing the Spaniards back,' the New Zealander recalled. Fearing that the enemy armour would loop round their positions and cut off their retreat, he too decided to flee while he still had the chance. Crouching as low as he could, he sprinted north along the road away from the Nationalist armour. The tanks came rolling up after him, flaying the road and olive groves with machine-gun and cannon fire.[19]

Following up the armour were Moorish infantry. Willie Lloyd heard them 'howling and screaming to frighten us' and Bill Meredith remembered them coming 'over the top in their thousands. They had aeroplanes with them and an intensive machine gun fire covered their advance.' The enemy aeroplanes dived from the rear of the British positions, strafing the Sunken Road as the Moors closed in.[20] As Meredith looked on, a wave of panic spread along the Republican line. With the Spaniards on the far left broken, the British in the centre and on the right also began to crumble. 'The slaughter was terrible,' Meredith remembered.[21] At one point the Scot saw five men running in a huddle. A burst of machine-gun fire caught them before they reached the trees and four were cut down. Not everyone fled, however. A Welsh volunteer nicknamed Taffy, 'the only man [on the left of the line] ... not [to] retreat ... saw the fascists advance ... [and] went out to meet them'. Before he had gone more than a few dozen paces, he was killed, his body 'more full of lead than a drain pipe'.[22]

Ball and Bibby, Sexton's gun crew members who had been reassigned to the rifle line, also held their ground. Spotting an abandoned Maxim, they began firing at the advancing troops. Within minutes the Nationalists were upon them. Remembering the carnage the captured guns had caused in the Sunken Road on the 13th, Bibby and Ball refused to retreat until they had removed the Maxim's bolt, thereby rendering it useless. The job done, they leapt from the road and ran. Ball survived to join up with Cunningham, but Bibby was shot through the head. A tank then rolled over their position, crushing the Maxim beneath its tracks. Elsewhere, Willie Lloyd and Bob Condon noticed a wounded man with three bullet wounds in his legs and stopped to help him. Fashioning a cradle from their crossed rifles for him to sit on, they hurried to the rear.[23]

In the centre of the British line, Jock Cunningham was one of the last to withdraw. Grabbing his binoculars as Ball rushed up to join him, he watched the T26s working their way up the line. 'Suddenly a shell burst right beside them.' The explosion tore Ball's leg off, showering Cunningham with gore. For a few minutes Ball lay on the ground, 'blood passing from his ... wound and reddening the soil' before he was carried to the rear. Tommy James, a Great War veteran from Rotherham, noticed Jock Cunningham scowling with rage. 'I will never forget the look [on his] ... face as he kicked loose soil over the blood.'[24] With the tanks now a matter of yards away, Cunningham quickly regained his composure. James saw him 'quietly giving instructions [to a handful of men]' explaining that the best place to be was right up close to the tanks as that way they couldn't bring their guns to bear.[25] To demonstrate, he 'actually [started] walking round the tank' to the amazement of the men still left in the position. When he finally decided to clear out, Bill Meredith and two others ran with him. By now the entire road was in chaos. 'Men were going down like ninepins.' A burst of fire caught the man to Meredith's right in the arm. Cunningham bandaged him as they ran, not daring to slow down until the sound of firing was behind them.[26]

Tom Spiller, meanwhile, had run into the volunteer who had been weeping uncontrollably a few hours before. Too terrified to move, he lay in the bottom of the road as the enemy drew ever closer. Looking behind him, the New Zealander saw twenty Moors bearing down on them, an image that would remain burned into his memory for years. 'They were coming in echelon formation ... [and] had these flowing Moorish cloaks on, with a red hat like a little flower pot... And ... were screaming blue murder above the din of ... battle.' Spotting an abandoned light machine gun, Spiller decided to return fire. 'Can you use this bloody thing?' he yelled to the man beside him. 'Yes,' he replied, seeming to gain some resolve from Spiller's determination. 'Well, let these bastards have it.' However, the Moors were already too close. As soon as the volunteers opened fire, two or three hand grenades burst around them. The force of the explosion threw Spiller's companion on top of him. Struggling out from underneath him, 'Kiwi' decided that discretion was the better part of valour. After stuffing his pockets with as much rifle ammunition as he could carry, he leapt over the bank of the road and ran.[27]

On the right of the line the British fared somewhat better. Faced only with foot soldiers, for a while they held their own. After listening to the gunfire and tanks rolling in on their left, Cyril Sexton remembered the moment he first caught sight of the enemy. 'On our front we could see shadowy forms advancing... Yorky opened fire whilst I was feeding the belt.' Surprised by the Maxim fire from their front, the Moors took cover, while Yorky swung his gun round to the left and fired off another belt through the trees. 'To our left,' Sexton recalled, 'the sound of battle increased ... and then I could see our troops retreating from the sunken road to the olive trees behind. The ... road was [soon] ... empty ... except here and there were bodies.' Alternating between sending bursts to their left and their front, Sexton and Hart held the Nationalists at bay for several minutes until disaster struck. 'We had a stoppage,' Sexton recalled. 'I carried on firing with my rifle whilst Yorky tried to clear [it]', but it was no good. They didn't have the right tools for the job. After Sexton had fired a final clip from his rifle to keep the Moors' heads down, Hall removed the gun's bolt and the pair retreated, zigzagging through the trees to throw off the enemy fire.[28]

Another group of holdouts were led by the Boxing Parson from Killarney, the Reverend Robert Hilliard. Without anti-tank guns or hand grenades, their resistance was doomed from the start. Nevertheless, the four men stood their ground as the Nationalist tanks rumbled closer. Hilliard's companions were soon killed and the reverend himself badly wounded.[29] Michael Economides, the British Cypriot who had been posted with the Brigade Guard, was another who resisted until the last. From his position in the Sunken Road, he saw the Moors advancing in groups of three and four towards him. Perversely, Economides was delighted. Although he had fought at Lopera and Las Rozas, he had never had such a clear sight of the enemy before. Sliding his rifle forward between the sandstone blocks he had used to build a parapet, he went to work. The Cypriot became completely absorbed in his own personal fire fight. Shooting clip after clip he hit several of the enemy, whom he thought were Spanish troops. 'I must have ... hit more than one,' he remembered, 'because they were big enough and near enough [so as I couldn't] miss.' Minutes later, as he looked up from his endeavours, Economides realized he was alone. His companions had long since fled, but he had been so engrossed that he had not noticed a thing. With the Nationalists advancing ever closer, he realized that his position would soon be overrun. Getting to his feet, he ran north along the Sunken Road, before leaping over the bank and zigzagging through the trees to the east. 'As I was running, I felt a bullet [drill through my calf].' At first there was little more than a burning sensation and he continued for several paces before he threw himself to the ground. Luckily, the bullet had passed directly between the fibula and tibia without breaking either. With blood running down his leg and the bullets whistling all around, Economides crawled on, making for a shallow ridgeline 30 yards away which would protect him from enemy fire. Once under cover the adrenaline wore off and the pain became excruciating. The cartilage between the bones had been burnt by the bullet and each movement was agony. After what seemed like an age, the Cypriot reached the ridgeline and pulled himself to his feet. Hobbling on, he made his way back to the dressing station where his wound was cleaned and bandaged. Despite the pain, Economides' tattered calf was the least of his worries. 'They cut off the shoes I had on,' he remembered. 'They were a damn good pair ... I [had] brought from Millet's in Oxford Street before I went [to Spain].'[30]

As Economides was receiving treatment, Tom Spiller was still fighting his own rearguard action. After sprinting 100 yards into the groves to the east of the Sunken Road, he had taken cover behind a tree trunk and was firing off clips at the Moors who had thrown the grenades and overrun his previous position. Every time he had to reload he would move to a different spot so as not to draw too much attention to himself. He need not have worried. The Moors were fully occupied competing 'with each other to see how many of our wounded they could bayonet'. Often it took more than one of them to finish off the British casualties. 'The first [would] ... let fly with his bayonet ... and the chap would grab [it] ... as it came down, but then another would ... get him in the side.' The Moors were merciless. 'Some of those chaps must have got about twenty or thirty bayonet holes through them,' Spiller recalled.[31] At one of his positions, the New Zealander came across the Jewish volunteer he had seen in the Sunken Road a few minutes before. The man had been wounded in the thigh by the grenades and was now terrified that the Moors would find him and finish him off. 'I didn't speak to him at all,' Spiller remembered, 'I was too busy trying to knock those Moors over.' Nevertheless, the volunteer grew ever more desperate and began begging Spiller for help. 'He grabbed ... [Spiller's] right leg', but the New Zealander was having none of it. 'I had to kick him off in the [end],' he admitted. The man was appalled. 'He screamed and roared ... [as] of course he could see what was happening only twenty or thirty yards away.' Eventually the fear overcame him and he lost control of his bowels.[32]

Having moved to yet another firing position, Spiller found himself beside Bert Overton. The Welsh Guard had returned to the front following his flight on the night of the 13th, but was still struggling to keep himself under control. 'He was very nervous, he knelt down and tried to fill a [rifle] magazine: he wasn't using clips, just fiddling with single rounds and he just couldn't get them in.' Moments later Overton was hit. 'He suddenly screamed. A bullet [had] ripped the side of his rifle to pieces and he fell back out of my vision.' Moments later Spiller also fell back. 'Two wounded jokers were ...

screaming and roaring at me [to help them], but I had to retreat and leave them there.' Later, they were killed as well.[33]

Another holdout was André Diamant, the Anglo-Egyptian in charge of the remnants of the 1st Company. Diamant had thirty men with whom he withdrew in controlled stages. After firing from one position for several minutes, they would pull back to the next ridgeline, where they once again took cover and opened fire. In this way he was 'able to hold up the [enemy] advance ... five or six times'. By about 4.30pm, Diamant had reached the final position, a ridgeline on the edge of the groves. To the east the Cookhouse was visible. Beyond it lay the Valencia Road. To buy some time for the last of the wounded to be carried down the hill to the rear, Diamant formed a defensive line with heavy stones, from behind which the men sniped at any targets that became visible. Despite being under 'a very heavy fire', the Egyptian 'had the crest of the hill in front ... more or less under control'.[34] With Diamant were Sexton and Hart, the machine gunners who had been holding the right flank of the Sunken Road until their Maxim had jammed. Having made their way through the groves, they had also reached the final ridgeline. 'Here we met up with a few of the Battalion ... laying behind the last trees,' Sexton recalled. 'Behind us I could see the Madrid Valencia road in the distance.'[35] After holding the position 'for a considerable period of time', Diamant eventually gave the order to withdraw. Picking themselves up, the men made their way down the slope to the Cookhouse. Nothing now stood between the Nationalists and the Valencia Road.[36]

CHAPTER 15

THE GREAT RALLY
(2.00PM—12.00 MIDNIGHT, 14 FEBRUARY 1937)

The Cookhouse had been in turmoil all day. When George Aitken arrived mid-morning there was a rumour that a retreat had been ordered all along the front line. The men were desperate to get away and the exodus was building. Groups of mixed nationalities were falling back to Morata with little or no organization. Some were on trucks, others on motorcycles and the majority on foot. Unsure whether the withdrawal had actually been ordered, Aitken decided to check for himself. Boarding the battalion's sole remaining lorry, he ordered the driver, Alexander Foot, an ex-Royal Air Force (RAF) man, to take him to Divisional HQ in Morata. Half an hour later, Aitken was in conversation with several staff officers. They had no idea where the rumour had originated and told the Scot to return to the front line and hold his position. On the journey back, Aitken passed 'a score or more' of British volunteers heading in the opposite direction. Ordering Foot to pull over, he leapt from the lorry and demanded that they follow him back to the front. 'I said "there's no retreat, go back, turn round",' he remembered. Initially, the men were less than enthusiastic and Aitken was forced to employ desperate measures. 'I think it was the only time I had my revolver out all the time I was in Spain,' he recalled.[1]

By the time they arrived at the Cookhouse, the situation had deteriorated. The buildings and olive groves were filled with dead, wounded and dying men. 'Moaning and screaming' for help, they were largely ignored.[2] Bemused survivors from the front were milling in the courtyard. Most were British, but

The Great Rally: 14 February 1937

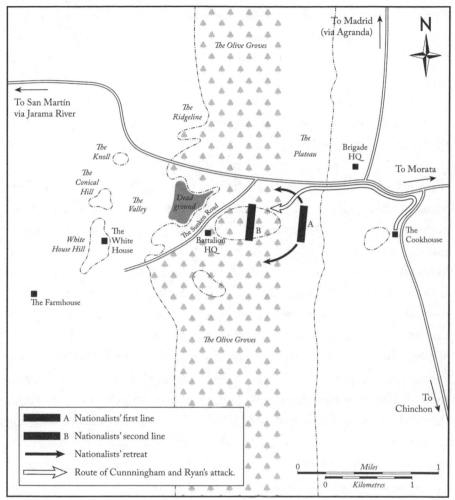

some Spanish troops from the Lister Brigade were also there. Others were French, Belgians, Germans or Slavs from the International Brigades. 'All ... had similar stories to tell of comrades dead, of conditions that were more than flesh and blood could stand, of weariness they found hard to resist,' recalled Frank Graham, the young scholar from Sunderland.[3] Trucks were leaving for Morata overfilled with desperate men, whilst others clung to the sides. It was a case of survival of the fittest. All was chaos and no one was in charge. The overriding emotion was one of panic. 'Dispirited by heavy casualties, by defeat, by lack of food [and] worn out by three days of gruelling fighting', the men were desperate to get clear before the Nationalists arrived. Nervously, they glanced towards the western ridgeline where occasional rifle reports indicated that Cunningham, Diamant and a handful of holdouts were still keeping the enemy at bay.[4] Others were straggling down the slopes. Some were helping wounded comrades and a few hobbled along using their rifles for support.

Tom Spiller, the New Zealander who had been in the thick of the fighting on the third day, reached the Cookhouse in the late afternoon. 'I thought the war was over,' he confessed. Convinced that they were just moments away from capture, he decided not to allow himself to be taken alive. 'I thought ... I'm holding onto this ammo, and I'll get some more, and I'm going to be a guerrilla fighter in the mountains.'[5] Bill Meredith, the Northumbrian who had narrowly escaped capture with the rest of the machine-gun company, recalled 'a scene of indescribable confusion... Truck after truck [was] streaming by' loaded with 'unharmed men' whilst by the roadside 'dozens of wounded' were left to fend for themselves. Disgusted with the situation, one man grabbed a rifle and threatened to open fire if the drivers did not stop.[6] Elsewhere, a British doctor, who had done sterling work for the first two days, lost all self-control. Yelling 'The Fascists are coming', he decided to abandon his charges and 'go while the going was good'. After hauling himself onto a passing lorry whose driver 'was torturing his gears', the doctor leant from the window to give one final garbled order before being whisked to safety. 'Cooks! Cooks!' he called, '[the] Fascists are coming! Poison the soup! Poison the soup!' With a call of 'Drive on, driver, drive on', he then disappeared into the east.[7] Luckily for the Republicans, Tiny Silverman and his cooks were solid men and rather than fleeing for their lives, they kept cooking. The smell sent Joe Garber wild with hunger as he hadn't eaten for two days. 'We rushed in[to] the building,' the cabinet maker from Whitechapel remembered. 'There were tins of garlic sausage being heated up and we grabbed a whole lot.'[8] Some recalled vast urns of hot soup, thick ham sandwiches and cups of hot coffee, whilst others witnessed men 'lying about on the roadside, hungrily eating oranges that had been thrown to them by a passing [truck]'.[9]

Frank Ryan, the Irish commissar attached to the XV Brigade, was attempting to bring some order to proceedings when he noticed a young Spanish officer struggling to control his unit. 'His hand bloody where a bullet had grazed the palm, he was ... fumbling with his automatic, in turn threatening and pleading with his men.' Sensing bloodshed was only moments away, Ryan decided to take charge. After ordering his translator Manuel Lizarraga, a Spanish-speaking Filipino attached to Brigade staff, to calm the officer, he commanded the men to form up. 'They stumbled to their feet,' the IRA man recalled, in 'one line of four'. Others then began to join them. 'Adjusting helmets and rifles' they too fell into line and soon Ryan had a crowd of men, both British and Spanish, under his command. Nearby, Jock Cunningham was also busy organizing the troops. Seeing his efforts, Ryan marched his group towards them and the two officers joined forces. Cunningham ordered a headcount and found he had 140 men. 'Unshaven, unkempt ... [,] grimy' and covered in the blood of their wounded comrades, they were a motley bunch.[10] Nevertheless, they were determined to resist.

With Ryan and Cunningham at its head, the column advanced to the north, leaving the wounded at the Cookhouse, then turned west down the Morata–San Martín road as the sun sank into the groves ahead of them. At first they marched in silence. 'Whatever popular writers may say,' Ryan would later explain, 'neither your Briton or your Irishman is an exuberant type. Demonstrativeness is not his dominating trait.' Nevertheless, Ryan thought a song would raise their spirits. 'I remembered a trick of the old days when we were holding banned demonstrations.' Urging the men to 'Sing up!', he led them in a rendition of the *Internationale*. The transformation was remarkable. 'Quaveringly at first, then more lustily, then in one resounding chant the song rose from the ranks. Bent backs straightened; tired legs thumped sturdily; what had been a routed rabble marched to battle again as proudly as they had done three days before.'[11]

As the column advanced, its numbers swelled. 'Spaniards and everybody came out to see us and cheer us, and sing like mad. Men who were streaming back [from the front] stopped and joined us.' French survivors of the Franco-Belge battalion and Slavs from the Dimitrovs were amongst them and soon the *Internationale* was being sung in several different languages. Others were yelling the Republican war cry of '*No Pasarán!*' (they shall not pass). Ryan noticed that Jock Cunningham was the only one not joining in. 'Hands thrust into his great-coat pockets', the Scot 'trudged along [silently] at the head of his men', trying to work out what he was going to do when they encountered the enemy.[12]

Halfway back, with the battlefield now shrouded in shadow, the column passed a solitary figure by the side of the road. It was Colonel Gal, the brigade commander. Ordering them to halt, he gave 'a very quiet, very sensible speech' which Aitken translated for the men.[13] Bill Meredith recalled his words:

> He said that the decisive moment of the battle had come ... and I believe for once ... [he] was right. [He] told them that the [Valencia] road ... must be saved; that the battalion had shown a quality of endurance that he had rarely seen in many years of warfare [and] that our retreat had left a gap in his line he could not fill with any other unit.[14]

When Gal had finished, Cunningham stepped smartly forward to salute him. 'We'll go up and fill that gap,' he declared.[15] Turning to the men, Cunningham told them 'that [although] it would be certain death to go back [, the colonel] ... wanted to know whether ... [they] would do it.' To the Scot's immense pride, 'not one said no'.[16] Marching on, they passed a Spanish unit, who 'caught the infection'. They took up the song, Ryan recalled, and 'deployed to [our] ... right'.[17]

Cunningham knew that sooner or later he would have to swing the column to the left to fill the gap in Gal's line. The Scot had never been up the Morata road before, however, and misjudged the distance. At dusk, when they finally broke to the left, they emerged a few hundred yards behind the Nationalist line. The next few hours were chaotic and confusing. With bullets whipping overhead in the dark, the men advanced individually or in small groups. Rushing forward a dozen paces, then throwing themselves to the ground, they fired blindly into the night. 'We advanced inch by inch,' Bill Meredith remembered. 'We crawled on our bellies for three hundred yards, shoulder to shoulder, packed tight. We would lie and give five rounds then advance.'[18] Hearing the troops behind them, the most advanced Moorish picket panicked and 'ran without firing a shot'. Looping round the British, they joined their second line. The Nationalists' position was still a strong one: the Moors were supported by German heavy machine gunners and Foreign Legion troops. Nevertheless, they were starting to panic. A few hours ago they had believed the British were broken and the battle was won. Now they were being attacked by an unknown number. Maybe this was the general counter that they had been dreading?

Frank Ryan recalled the chaos that night. The men were mixed up and disorientated and orders were being shouted in a variety of languages. Trying to regain some control, the Irishman told Manuel, his Filipino translator, to help out. Yelling over the gunfire, he asked him, 'What's the Spanish for "Forward"?' '"Adelante!" yell[ed] Manuel, and wave[d] the Spanish lads on.' The next minute, as a wave of gunfire swept overhead, the order changed. '"Abajo!" [Manuel cried.] And down they flop[ped] to give covering fire.' Looking to one side, Ryan noticed a 'burly French officer ... waving a ridiculously tiny automatic' who was also caught up in the fire-fight. At one stage he sought out Ryan to ask for grenades. There were none, but the Frenchman led his men forward regardless. With a cry of 'En Avant!' he disappeared into the night. Ahead appeared cones of blue-red flame pinpointing the positions of the German machine gunners. The Internationals crawled up to within striking distance, then fell upon them with fixed bayonets.[19]

Tom Spiller was on another part of the line. 'What a shambles it was that night!' the New Zealander recalled. 'After a short while I didn't know whether I was coming or going; there were flashes all around me left right and centre.' In the darkness Spiller found himself stumbling over the dead and wounded, only discovering whether they were friend or foe when he put his hand down to touch their faces.[20] Unknown to Spiller, his 'cobber' Fred Robertson, a fellow countryman from Hawke's Bay with whom he had travelled to England from New Zealand, was amongst them. During one of several chaotic bayonet charges, which saw the men screaming through the night, Robertson had been shot and killed.[21] When he found out, Spiller was devastated. 'I felt ... like crying,' he later wrote.[22]

Elsewhere, Frank Ryan had a similar experience. After tripping over a corpse at his feet, he identified it as one of their own. Realizing they had regained their old lines, Ryan gave the order to halt and dig in. Cunningham and a few others had advanced even further, but a messenger later brought them back. Working through the night, the troops constructed a series of rifle pits strung out in a rough line through the groves. When dawn broke it became clear that Ryan and Cunningham's counter-attack had been successful. On the left, contact was made with the Listers and on the right the Dimitrovs had also forced the Nationalists back. All along the line, the enemy had been held. For now at least, the Valencia road was secure.[23]

PART THREE
CONCLUSIONS

There's a valley in Spain called Jarama,
That's a place that we all know so well,
For 'tis there that we gave up our manhood,
And most of our old age as well.

From this valley they tell us we're leaving,
But don't hasten to bid us adieu,
For e'en though we make our departure,
We'll be back in an hour or two.

Oh we're proud of the British Battalion,
And the marathon record it's made,
Please do us this little favour,
And take this last word to Brigade.

You will never be happy with strangers,
They would not understand you as we,
So remember the Jarama Valley,
And the old men who wait patiently.

ALEX McDADE, APRIL 1937

CHAPTER 16
FROM JARAMA TO BRUNETE
(15 FEBRUARY–JULY 1937)

The fighting of 14 February marked the peak of the Nationalist offensive at Jarama. Although fierce fighting continued until the 27th, the day of a doomed Republican counter-attack spearheaded by the newly arrived American volunteers of the Abraham Lincoln Battalion, the positions captured by the British on their third night in action were held until the end of the war. Both sides dug in and the battle slowed to a defensive stalemate reminiscent of the Great War. Nevertheless, Jarama was celebrated by the Republicans and the CPGB lauded the efforts of the British Battalion in the pages of *The Daily Worker*. Conway, Ryan, Fry and Wintringham were all singled out for special praise and, in a particularly purple piece of prose, Harry Pollitt hailed Cunningham as 'the British Chapayev'.[1] In reality, the battle had been horrendously costly for both sides. Up to 20,000 Nationalists and 25,000 Republicans had been killed. Of the 500 British volunteers who had advanced into battle on 12 February, roughly 150 were dead and a similar number wounded. As a result, the battalion was no longer able to function as an entirely British unit and from that point on Spaniards were drafted in to fill one of its four companies.[2]

Aside from two short breaks, the majority of the battalion remained on the Jarama front until June 1937. During this period the line was relatively quiet. One report, for example, recorded that in a whole week there had been 'practically no casualties, save Dr Brodsworth who was hit ... by a spent bullet'

Spain: February 1937–August 1938

THE ARAGON CAMPAIGN
and
THE BATTLE OF EBRO

Zaragoza
Quinto
Ebro River
Belchite
Caspe
Móra
Gandesa
Alcañiz
Batea
Seguro
de Baños
Calaceite
Mediterranean Sea

➡ Republican attacks
⇨ Nationalist counter-attacks

B a y
o f
B i s c a y

Atlantic Ocean

Irun
FRANCE
Ebro River
Figueras
SPAIN
Zaragoza
Barcelona
PORTUGAL
Brunete
Madrid
Teruel
Vinaròs
MINORCA
Navalcarnero
Mondéjar
Benicas
MAJORCA
Talavera de la Reina
Tagus River
Valencia
IBIZA
Albacete
Mediterranean Sea
Pontones

SPANISH MOROCCO

0   *Miles*   200
0   *Kilometres*   200

Territory captured by 8 March 1938

Gains made between March 1938 and 29 July 1938

in a particularly private area. 'They saved his John Thomas,' the report continued, 'but the boys now call him "The Yid".'[3] Sporadic attacks, sniper fire and artillery also took a toll. On 14 March Jock Cunningham was badly wounded by machine-gun fire whilst blocking a Nationalist flanking manoeuvre. Two bullets hit his left arm and a third lodged deep in his chest. In his absence, Fred Copeman took over command. Cunningham made a slow recovery and on his return in late May was promoted to major and given a staff role in Brigade command. He would never lead the battalion again and his belief in his own immortality was also badly shaken. As Aitken recalled, from that day on Cunningham was far more careful and took extravagant measures to avoid enemy fire.[4]

On 23 March George Aitken's exemplary conduct was rewarded with promotion to Brigade commissar. The Scot was replaced by a new arrival, Bert Williams, whose first major job was to chair a battalion meeting convened on the night of 27 April to look into Bert Overton's actions at Jarama. The former Guardsman's culpability for the machine-gun company's capture was established beyond doubt, his case unaided by the revelation that whilst in hospital he had falsely claimed the rank of captain and had been drawing the equivalent pay. Found guilty of desertion in the face of the enemy and impersonating a senior officer, Overton was sentenced to work in a labour battalion. Often this was tantamount to a death sentence, as those convicted were given the most dangerous jobs and exposed to heavy fire. One veteran openly admitted that this was the case, stating that the labour battalions served as 'an expedient means of getting rid of a soldier who had become a dangerous embarrassment'.[5]

Overton was not the only member of the battalion in trouble with the communists in April 1937. Andrew Flanagan, the young bricklayer who had deserted on the first day at Jarama, had since returned to duty, but then went absent without leave for a second time. After asking for permission to return to Madrigueras to marry the Spanish girl he had fallen in love with, he was granted five days, but made no attempt to return and was arrested a week later. Flanagan spent one month in prison for the crime. Following his release a doctor declared him unfit for further service and he was dismissed from the battalion. A report written in late 1937 provides the last clue as to what became of the couple. 'Since [his release] ... he has been living with his woman ... on the charity of [her] ... family,' the archivist recorded. Whether Flanagan remained in Spain after the war is unknown.[6]

Throughout March and April many others also went absent without leave. Following the hell of the first few days of the battle and the monotony of weeks in the trenches, the temptation to slip away from the front line to the relative comforts of Madrid often proved irresistible. Albert Charlesworth, the metal polisher from Oldham, was one of several who succumbed. In April 1937 he disappeared from the lines only to return several days later and was put on punishment fatigues for ten days as a result. John Mudie, a twenty-four year-old Labour Party member and former chauffeur, also deserted. As he was already considered a 'rotten [,] ... lumpen element' by the battalion commissar, he was imprisoned in Valencia and only released three months later after he and thirteen other British inmates had gone on hunger strike in protest at being jailed without trial. After his release Mudie got into trouble for drunkenness and his record also notes that he was later hospitalized in Pontones with venereal disease.[7]

Another who deserted was Tony Hyndman. After his experiences on the second day at Jarama, the Welshman suffered a mental breakdown and begged George Nathan to keep him out of the front line. Nathan was sympathetic and, due to Hyndman's fluent German, made the Welshman a Brigade runner, responsible for maintaining contact with the Thaelmann Battalion on the British right. After the front had stabilized, Hyndman, who was by now suffering from a stomach ulcer, and his companion from Madrigueras, Jon Lepper, who was also sick from an eye infection, were sent to Albacete, where the camp commissar put them to work in the XV Brigade's news department. Both were later ordered back to the front. Terrified of returning and increasingly 'paranoid concerning the Communist Party', Hyndman and Lepper deserted.[8] By May 1937, they had made it undetected to the coast, but then disaster struck. In Valencia, having been spotted leaving a meeting with the British Consul, they found themselves arrested. The imprisonment that followed 'was a steady progress through jails, camps, then more jails', with lice, fleas, interrogations and beatings playing regular roles in their captivity.

'Our ailments became worse,' Hyndman recalled, especially Lepper's, who often cried with pain. 'Then one day our cell door was opened, and our names were called. We were for release. It was a trick, surely,' the Welshman thought, 'they would shoot us and then tell our friends we had been killed fighting at the front, like heroes.'[9]

In fact, a far more benevolent fate awaited Hyndman. Whilst Lepper was sentenced to a period in a labour camp, the young Welshman's contacts guaranteed him special privileges. Such was the British Communist Party. Whilst professing equality, it was as corrupt and riddled with favouritism as the systems it derided. Hyndman was returned to Albacete, where Harry Pollitt, on one of three visits to Spain throughout the course of the war, had good news for him:

> 'Don't be afraid, comrade ... what with your family and your friends, you have been more trouble to me than the whole British Battalion put together.' He put his arm across my shoulders, and handed me a letter. 'Here, read this and tell me what you think.' It was from Stephen [Spender, the famous poet and Hyndman's ex-boyfriend]. It told me that I only had to tell the bearer of the letter what I wanted, and he would arrange it. I replied that I wanted to go home. I was ill. Harry ... said I would be on my way within a week.[10]

Pollitt was true to his word.[11]

By the end of May, those wounded during the opening days at Jarama began returning to the front. Walter Gregory, the 3rd Company's runner who had had his right thumb shot off was amongst the first to arrive. Having enjoyed his time recuperating in the countryside of Murcia, he returned refreshed and ready for action. A few weeks later, David Crook, who had been shot in the thigh near the Conical Hill, also returned to the line. Many others who had been wounded were not so fortunate. William Ball, the crack shot from Reading who had had his leg torn off by a tank shell, had died shortly after being stretchered from the field. The Reverend Robert Hilliard, also hit on the 14th, survived a little longer. Five days after the tank attack, whilst recovering in Benicasim, Hilliard's hospital was hit during a Nationalist air raid. One of the bombs damaged the structure of the building and a wall fell in and crushed him. After his burial, his personal effects, a passport, a CPGB membership card and a pocketbook containing private letters were sent home to his wife.[12]

In May 1937 street fighting broke out in Barcelona. Although resulting in few casualties, these skirmishes were a manifestation of a serious split in the Republic. On one side was the increasingly influential Communist Party, on the other the anarchists and the POUM, old-school Marxists who favoured Trotsky over Stalin. Essentially, the former believed that winning the war was everything, whilst the latter stressed the importance of the social revolution above all else. Unwilling to negotiate, the communists determined to eliminate their opponents by any means available. Over the next few weeks several members of the opposition disappeared. The leader of the POUM, Andreas Nin, was arrested, imprisoned and after a brutal interrogation, executed by the Spanish Communist Party's secret police, the SIM (Military Intelligence Service). His body was never recovered.[13]

A few British veterans of Jarama were present in Barcelona that May. One was David Crook, the Cheltenham graduate who had carried a volume of Shakespeare's *Tragedies* around the battlefield. Following his recovery from the wound he had sustained on the 12th, Crook had been recruited by the KGB as a spy to report on the activities of foreigners fighting with the POUM and the anarchists. As a direct result of his actions several were imprisoned by the communist secret police operating in Barcelona, at least one of whom, Landau, an Austrian anarchist, was deported to Russia where, presumably, he was later shot. 'I was in those days in a state of blissful ignorance of Stalinism,' Crook explained:

> How else could I have done the things I did in my twenties? As for Landau, he was
> evidently an enemy of the Soviet Union, so he was an enemy of mine. I had gone
> to Spain to fight in a life and death struggle. I was willing to risk my life and had
> no compunction about being responsible for that of an enemy. My conscience,
> then, was clear.[14]

Following the communist crackdown in Barcelona, the International Brigades were also purged of the politically undesirable. In the British Battalion, at least two veterans of Jarama suffered the repercussions. Frederick Freedman, a thirty-two year-old Englishman who had long been noted for his 'Trotskyite views ... [and] trouble making', was imprisoned in Madrid, where he was later joined by Walter Rowlands, a former mechanic who had been in the YCL until 1934, before turning to 'Trotskyism'.[15]

At the end of May the remnants of the British Battalion still at the front line received some excellent news: the machine gunners of the 2nd Company captured on 12 February had been released. In the weeks that followed, the story of their adventures began to circulate through the lines. After Elias, Stevens and Dickenson had been shot by the Moors, the rest of the prisoners had been handed over to the Guardia Civil who protected them from the crueller instincts of their front line comrades. They were then taken to a holding area in San Martín de la Vega, a nearby village, where they were kept for two days before being moved to Navalcarnero, a town 20 miles to the south of Madrid. There they had their heads shaved, were fingerprinted and then interrogated by Merry del Val, the son of a former Spanish ambassador who had spent several years in London. The volunteers were determined to give nothing away. 'Yank' Levy, who had previously been imprisoned by the American authorities following an attempted armed robbery in Philadelphia, 'coached' the others as Tommy Bloomfield recalled: 'Everything he told us to say was the truth, even though it was a pack of lies. Questions and answers were, "Why did you come to Spain?" "To do a job of work." But we didn't add [that] the work was to defeat fascism.'[16] Donald Renton, the company's political commissar, was even more calculating in his responses. 'Our business was to try and mislead the enemy about the actual strength of the Battalion and so build up a conception ... of an enormous mass of men and matériel ... ready to resist [the] fascist onslaught,' he explained.[17]

Afterwards, the prisoners were subjected to some brutal treatment. Basil Abrahams, a former baker from Hackney who had his twenty-second birthday whilst in captivity, recalled that they were crammed nine at a time into small cells, 'and for 5 nights ... were constantly beaten by the Moors'.[18] Later, they had a stroke of good fortune, which played a major role in their eventual release. A *Daily Mail* reporter who happened to be in town at the time took several photos of the prisoners standing on a flat bed truck which later appeared in a gloating article typical of the paper's pro-Franco stance. The photographs were irrefutable proof that the men were still alive and prompted a demand for their release from the British government as well as a visit from the local consul. The story was widely publicized and the photos were shown at local cinemas across the UK. In Paisley James Maley's mother was delighted when she recognized her son as she had had no news from him for months. She eventually persuaded the projectionist to cut the frames from the newsreel for her to take home.[19]

After Navalcarnero, the prisoners were sent to a concentration camp in the grounds of an old pottery factory in Talavera de la Reina. During the day they were forced to build roads and at night witnessed regular departures of the 'agony wagon': a truck which took the condemned off to a local graveyard to be shot. Tommy Bloomfield thought that it was only a matter of time before the British prisoners joined them:

> In the morning when the death wagon had gone they would say to us, 'esta tarde todos muertos' – this afternoon you all die. When it had gone in the afternoon, we were told 'esta noche todos muertos' – tonight you all die, then when that one had gone we were all told 'mañana todos muertos' – tomorrow morning you all die.[20]

Despite such threats, they remained at Talavera for three months. A final move saw the men transferred to Salamanca where they were tried for 'aiding a military rebellion. Five, including Harry Fry, George Leeson and Jimmy Rutherford, were sentenced to death, the remainder to twenty years' imprisonment.[21] Neither sentence was carried out. In May the prisoners were informed that Franco had pardoned them and an exchange for Italian officers captured by the Republicans was arranged.

Tommy Bloomfield was relieved to hear the news. Conditions in captivity had been appalling:

> During my three and a half months in prison, I cannot remember having a bath or a wash. Neither did we have a change of clothes. We could pick the body lice off the outside of our trousers they were so plentiful. [And] they were so fat that when

you cracked half a dozen between your thumb nails, you had to scrape your nails

on the floor to kill more.[22]

Beatings and interrogations were a common occurrence and medical care was non-existent; 'most of us fell ill,' Jimmy Rutherford recalled.[23] On 30 May, having signed an agreement that they would not rejoin the Republican forces, the prisoners were taken to the French border crossing at the ancient city of Irún. There they were forced to walk through a jeering crowd of Franco supporters, before being handed over to the French police to begin their journey home. At Dover British CID interviewed and fingerprinted them, but no charges were pressed despite their being in breach of the Foreign Enlistment Act. For the majority it was the end of their Spanish adventure. James Maley choose to remain in Glasgow, George Watters was too sick to return and Donald Renton was considered too valuable to the CPGB to be allowed to go back. Harry Fry, Tommy Bloomfield and Jimmy Rutherford, on the other hand, decided to return in defiance of the agreement they had signed with the Nationalists. They would rejoin their old unit within six weeks of their release.[24]

Back at the trenches of Jarama, Jason Gurney, who had transferred to the Lincoln Battalion in protest at Fred Copeman's appointment as battalion commander, had been shot by a sniper.

I was moving along the trench peering through the fire holes, when suddenly

I felt as if there had been an enormous explosion in the centre of my brain. I was

not conscious of any pain and as I fell to the ground, I remember thinking, quite

calmly, 'I wonder if it's killed me?'[25]

Gurney had been wounded by an explosive bullet in the right hand 'which had laid it open for about two and a half inches ... and left a hole large enough to take a hen's egg'. As the hand had been pressed against his forehead, many of the splinters had passed through into his face, and his eyes had also been damaged. Although his eyesight soon returned, the bullet ended Gurney's military career and within weeks he was back in England.[26]

In July the British Battalion finally left the trenches for good. Before they departed, the corpses of comrades killed in the groves were disinterred and gathered together for reburial in a communal grave just behind the front line. A hastily constructed memorial was erected to mark the site. Helmets and rifles stood atop a large slab of stone inscribed with the names of the fallen. A funeral service was then read by Aitken and Copeman and the battalion withdrew from the line as Tommy James recalled:

> It seemed like leaving some treasured and hallowed spot. I felt sadness and pride. The identified and unidentified slept, known and unknown, beneath the ... Spanish soil. I felt a tightening of the throat [as we marched away and gave them my own salutation:] Salud Comrades! Farewell Jarama![27]

Back in Britain, stories of the appalling losses the battalion had suffered were beginning to get through. At first, reports were confusing. Some casualty lists were made available to family members, but they were often incomplete or inaccurate and those seeking further confirmation had to resort to tracking down their relatives' comrades in Spain. As late as April 1937, Edgar Wilkinson's family were still unsure of his fate. On the 12th his aunt wrote to the Sunderland student, Frank Graham, requesting information. 'He is down on the list as wounded and I have written to his mother to say that he is alive, and well,' she explained, 'as she must not have shocks according to doctors [as] she is in a very critical state of nervous[ness].'[28] Graham had the unhappy task of informing her that he had witnessed Eddie's death two months before.

Mrs S. McCleary, another veteran's mother, would have to wait until 1938 before her worst fears were confirmed. Her twenty-four year-old son, John Black, had sent her his last letter on 11 February just before the battalion had gone into action. Mrs McCleary had received it a month later and had not heard from him since. Her subsequent appeals for information are held in the Comintern archives in Moscow. 'I have had no word from him since that big fight on the beginning of February,' she wrote in July 1937. 'I was wondering if you have ever met him or could ... get to know where he is or if he is dead or alive. The suspense is awful.' The recipient was either unwilling or unable to help, however, and four months later another letter arrived at the British Battalion's headquarters, in which Mrs McCLeary explained:

> It is almost eight months since I had my last letter from him ... that was the beginning of February, if you knew him would you be so kind enough to write and let me know if he was taken prisoner or has been killed in action as his belongings were sent to his girl friend in Brighton [at the end of February] ... which he said should [happen if] anything [were to] happen to him.[29]

Still there was no reply. At the end of the year, Black's girlfriend wrote the last letter that appears in his Moscow file. 'He wrote to his parents and myself three or four letters, and the last time we heard from him was February 11th of this year.'[30]

How and when Black's mother took the news of her son's death when it finally reached her is not known, although surviving documents show that other grieving parents were remarkably stoical. Having received confirmation of his son's death in early March, William Ball's father wrote to the CPGB in reply. Far from blaming Pollitt and his party, the letter merely informed them that the contents of any parcels that arrived in Albacete addressed to his son should now be distributed amongst his comrades.[31]

As other families learnt of their losses, funerals and memorial services were arranged across the country. At many, Communist Party representatives or wounded comrades back from the front made speeches extolling the virtues of the fallen and insisting that their sacrifice had not been made in vain.

Meanwhile, the war in Spain went on. After leaving the Jarama front, the survivors of the British Battalion spent 'a few glorious days' sunbathing and swimming in the river at San Lorenzo de Escorial. All too soon, however, they were ordered back into action. This time, Fred Copeman, with Sam Wild as his newly promoted second-in-command, led them to the north-west of Madrid to take part in the battle of Brunete. Designed to encircle the Nationalist forces besieging the capital, Brunete was the government's first major offensive of the war. Around 50,000 troops, 136 pieces of artillery, 128 tanks and 150 aircraft were used. Initially, the sheer scale and ambition of the project caught Franco off guard. Most of the forward units made considerable gains on the first day, 6 July, but, in the sector where the British were held in reserve, an advance supported by T26 tanks was repulsed at the village of Villanueva de la Cañada. That night the battalion were ordered to attack. As they were about to go in, a crowd of civilians was seen approaching from the village. When they got close to the British lines, it became clear that there were Nationalist troops amongst them, herding them forward and using the civilians as a human shield. Suddenly, someone opened fire. Within seconds the road was covered in corpses. Old men, women and children lay amongst the Nationalist dead.[32]

Incensed by the trick, the British rushed forward, pushing the Nationalists before them. 'We lighted the streets ... with bursting grenades as we drove the Fascists to the centre of town,' one of volunteers recalled. Although the move was successful and the village fell, several British casualties were caused. Amongst them was Bill Meredith, one of the few men to have escaped the 2nd Company's capture at Jarama. Meredith, who had been promoted to section commander, 'had gone to help a wounded man lying in the road'. The casualty turned out to be a Nationalist officer, waiting to dispatch one last Republican with a loaded pistol. 'Bending over in the semi-darkness, [Meredith] ... received a bullet in the heart.'[33] Walter Gregory, the runner who had been shot in the hand at Jarama, was also hit. On the first day of the battle, whilst crawling along a drainage ditch in an attempt to outflank a Nationalist position, he was wounded in the arm. Fortunately for Gregory, the bullet had lost much of its velocity by passing through the forehead of a comrade advancing ahead of him. Nevertheless, it was enough to see the Nottinghamshire man sent to Madrid for a second stint in hospital.[34]

That night few Nationalist prisoners were taken. Disgusted by the enemy's trick and burning for revenge over the death of Meredith, the British were in no mood to show any mercy. Sources are reticent as to what exactly happened that night, but a couple of quotes are revealing. Copeman admitted:

> [I] didn't have much hope that many [prisoners] would be taken... I gave instructions that No.2 and No.3 Companies were to clear the houses. Charlie Goodfellow could be relied upon not to allow any licence, but I was not so sure

> about Alec [Cummings], who had waves of cynical contempt for what he termed
> 'misplaced sentiment'.[35]

A second report, although of admittedly dubious origins, added the following details.

> When we had finished not a Fascist got away alive. They had slaughtered old men,
> women and children. We went in there, lined them up, made them dig a trench
> and shot every one... Some managed to escape over the fields, or thought they
> could, but we sent the cavalry after them, and they were cut to pieces.[36]

There is some evidence that Frank Ryan may have ordered the execution. That at least is what the Nationalists believed, as later events revealed.[37]

The next day, the battalion were ordered to swing their advance to the south-east. A high ridgeline, which the volunteers named Mosquito Crest, had to be taken. It dominated the approaches to the capital and its capture would force the Nationalists to lift the siege of Madrid. Frank Graham, the Sunderland student who had fought in Bill Briskey's company at Jarama, was amongst those attempting to capture the heights. 'We tried [for] five days to take the hill ... [but] it was impregnable... Once we'd lost the surprise ... we should have just dug in and waited.' With hindsight Graham believed the battalion's inability to capture the ridge was decisive, not only in the battle, but in the entire Civil War. 'Of course there were many big battles [that] took place,' he admitted, 'but ... I think ... that a lot of us realised that the war had been lost at that point... After that it was only a question of prolonging it as far as possible until [political] changes could be taking place in Europe.'[38]

By 13 July the Republican advance had ground to a halt and the Nationalists began a series of counter-attacks which would eventually drive the government forces back to their original lines. This final phase of the battle was extremely arduous for the British. With little food and virtually no water, they fought a series of rearguard actions against ever-increasing numbers in the burning heat of high summer. Franco threw all his reserves into the battle and his troops enjoyed air-superiority for the first time since February. The skies above

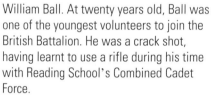

William Ball. At twenty years old, Ball was one of the youngest volunteers to join the British Battalion. He was a crack shot, having learnt to use a rifle during his time with Reading School's Combined Cadet Force.

Walter Gregory recovering from the wound he suffered at Jarama.

George Nathan. A veteran of the Great War, Nathan dressed like a typical British Army officer during his service with the International Brigades. Complete with driver, swagger stick and pipe, he breezed around the battlefield in a motorcycle sidecar.

John 'Bosco' Jones. Before travelling to Spain, Jones had fought Oswald Mosley's Black Shirts at the battle of Cable Street, the British Union of Fascists' biggest defeat.

Donald Renton. The political commissar of the 2nd Company, Renton was wounded then captured on the second day.

A well-earned break. Members of the British Battalion resting behind the lines at Jarama, 1937. Frank Graham, the student from Sunderland, is sitting fourth from the right. Immediately to his left, hiding his face from the photographer, is Giles Romilly, Winston Churchill's nephew.

Wounded from Jarama. Walter Gregory, the 3rd Company's runner, is second from the right in the bottom row.

Members of the 2nd Company captured at Jarama on 13 February 1937. The Glasgow Celtic fanatic, James Maley, is second on the right. Partially obscured next to him is Jimmy Rutherford. Another of the 2nd Company's Scots, Rutherford returned to Spain following his release, and was promptly recaptured and executed. George Leeson, a former Royal Navy machine gunner from Ireland, is fifth from the right. Harry Fry, the company commander, stands two places to Leeson's right. Bert 'Yank' Levy, the moustachioed former bank robber and gun runner, is standing alone on the left wearing a cap. Two places to Levy's right is Tommy Bloomfield and beside him is Donald Renton, the company's political commissar.

Burial of a British soldier amongst the olive groves at Jarama.

The International Brigade's Farewell Parade, Barcelona, 29 October 1938.

Members of the British Battalion leaving Victoria Station, London, on their return from Spain, December 1938.

Officers and staff of the British Battalion pictured alongside some Spanish comrades. Sam Wild can be seen kneeling on the right, wearing a dark shirt. This photo is believed to have been taken around the time of the push across the Ebro in 1938.

The ruins of Belchite. The most fought-over town of the war, Belchite played host to the British Battalion in September 1937. After the Republic was defeated Franco decided to preserve the ruins as a monument to the war.

The International Brigade Memorial at Jarama. Before the author's visit, the plaque was vandalized by members of the Falange, a Spanish fascist movement.

The Conical Hill. Of the 143 men of the 1st Company who held the feature on the afternoon of 12 February nearly half were killed or wounded.

The peaks of the Pyrenees seen from the battlements of the Castell de Sant Ferran in Figueras. The majority of the British Battalion were quartered in the castle for a few days en route to Madrigueras.

This humble memorial to the British Battalion overlooks the valley where the first two days' fighting took place. The rise on the right in the foreground is where Fry's company belatedly set up their machine guns. To the left are the hills that the British rifle companies held on the afternoon of the 12th. The skyscrapers of Madrid are just visible on the horizon.

A close-up of the memorial. The plaque reads 'To Kit Conway and the other 200 internationals of the British Battalion who died for liberty'.

Brunete and Villanueva thrummed incessantly with the aero engines of German bombers which pounded the Republican positions daily and any Russian fighters who took to the air soon fell prey to the Condor Legion's latest technological advancement, the Messerschmitt 109.[39]

The battalion suffered horrendous casualties at Brunete. Of the 331 British volunteers that Copeman had led into battle, just forty-two effectives remained by 25 July when they were withdrawn from the front line. Hundreds had been killed or wounded, including several veterans of Jarama. Alex McDade, Wintringham's sergeant major, was killed on the first day. Bert Overton was another early British casualty. Working with the labour battalion, Overton had been killed 'by a shell while carrying munitions to a forward position'.[40] On the final day of the battle, George Nathan, the XV Brigade's former assistant chief of staff, died in an air raid whilst leading some reinforcements to the front line. 'We were among big grey rocks in the foothills of the Guadarrama mountains,' one eye witness recalled, '[when] a piece of a heavy bomb from a German Junker plane hit him low in the back and penetrated deeply. He was rushed to hospital in Madrid but died early ... the [next] morning.'[41] Nathan's body was returned to the front for burial. Cunningham and Gal cried as his coffin was lowered into the grave.[42]

Others veterans of Jarama were wounded at Brunete. André Diamant was struck by shrapnel in a bombing raid and would eventually lose his right leg and Albert Charlesworth, the metal polisher from Oldham who had fought in Overton's 4th Company, was also hit.

> I don't know if it was a bullet or a stone chipped by a bullet that caught me across the nose and little bits went into my eye. It didn't seem bad, there was no blood. Anyway, two days later I could not open it, it had gone solid with pus and the like so I had to go to hospital.[43]

Tom Spiller's wounds were much more serious. Two bullets hit the New Zealander in the leg and one caught him in the shoulder. After recovering in a Spanish hospital he returned to Australasia to recruit more of his countrymen for the Republican cause. During the battle for Mosquito Crest, Sam Wild was hit whilst arguing with his comrades about football.[44] 'We were standing talking with three or four others,' Fred Copeman remembered, 'when suddenly three of them fell in a line. One [anti-tank] bullet had passed through all of them.' The first man was shot through the head, the second, 'a young Spanish lad … got it through the stomach' and 'Sam caught it low down in the thigh'.[45] Copeman himself was injured by bomb fragments. Although the wound was thought to be minor at the time, it would cause complications which would come back to haunt him.

Desertion reached an endemic level at Brunete. Especially in the latter stages of the battle, many took the opportunity to flee after dragging wounded comrades back from the front line. Sidney Silvert, a tailor who had been wounded on the second day at Jarama, deserted on 12 July. When he was caught, at first he was shown pity and was found a job repairing clothes at Camp Luckacs. The leniency did not work and he deserted once more, this time heading for Madrid. After he deserted for a third time, the authorities finally lost patience and he was imprisoned in the provincial jail at Albacete. Although it seems that most deserters were picked up after spending a few days in the bars and brothels of Madrid, Barcelona or Valencia, others managed to avoid capture and made it all the way back to Britain. A report in the Comintern archives in Moscow notes that the Scottish Ambulance Unit, a charitable organization which provided care for the wounded on both sides during the conflict, abetted several attempts. One of its members, a Communist Party stalwart named Maurice Linden, left the unit in protest after getting wind of the scheme. Linden attested that one deserter, named Doran, had been found refuge in Madrid where he was 'housed … for some time [by an anarchist group] before he … was evacuated to Valencia'. The same report went on to state that 'there is some general talk among the British comrades that in Madrid there is a house in which there is to be found a woman who assists comrades to desert. From this it would appear that even in the Battalion itself there is some liaison with the evacuating group.'[46]

With morale at an all time low, political disagreements amongst the battalion's senior staff also came to a head. The military officers, represented by Cunningham and Copeman, resented the influence of the political commissars. The former 'had never had much enthusiasm' for the latter, Fred Copeman recalled.[47] The soldiers saw them as interfering in matters they did not understand. Aitken, Cunningham and Copeman were all called back to London as a result. The subsequent meeting of the Central Committee took place at the CPGB's headquarters at King Street. Accusations of incompetence and excessive ambition were made by both sides. The issue of Copeman's 'irrational behaviour' was raised and Aitken was criticised for failing to resist orders 'which [had] sent the British into impossible positions where they had been decimated.'[48]

Cunningham was singled out for a particularly vicious attack. As he had been in charge of co-ordinating the movements of the entire brigade, Harry Pollitt, the leader of the CPGB, blamed him for the fiasco at Brunete. Whilst Cunningham excelled at inspiring the men and leading small-scale actions, it seems he was not cut out for the more tactically demanding role of Brigade command. The man who had shortly before been hailed as the 'British Chapayev' was now pilloried for being 'politically [and] ... theoretically ... crude'. He was also accused of being delusional and labouring under 'great pretences' and considering 'himself more intelligent than ... Marx, Lenin [and] ... Stalin'.[49] The grilling seemed to go on forever as Copeman recalled:

> For over an hour I watched Jock's simple, sincere attempt to face up to the criticisms of people who had seldom had to risk their own hides ... he was having to face insinuations which amounted to nothing less than hints at fascist tendencies, and in one case to temporary insanity.[50]

As Copeman revealed many years later, behind the accusations of military incompetence lay a political motive for Cunningham's removal from the front line. Jock was not considered a loyal Party man. Pollitt disliked him and feared that he was too independent and single minded to be easily controlled. Eventually, as the attacks grew ever more vehement, the Scot cracked under the pressure. 'Jock finally broke down,' Copeman remembered. 'The cynical disregard for all he had done, coupled with the self-satisfied claims of the intellectuals and the unconcerned counting of casualties, was too much.' Seeing that their differences were too great to be reconciled, Pollitt decided that Cunningham and Aitken should remain in England for the rest for the war. Copeman, on the other hand, was deemed to have shown 'an impartial attitude' and was therefore considered fit to return.[51] Aitken was appalled by the decision. In a letter to Pollitt he complained that sending Copeman back after he had had a nervous breakdown was 'a grave mistake'.[52] Nevertheless, Pollitt stood by his decision. For Cunningham and Aitken it was the beginning of the end of their attachment to the Party. Copeman, on the other hand, still enjoyed its full support. After getting engaged to Kitty, his flame-haired Scottish sweetheart, he made his way back to Spain.[53]

CHAPTER 17
THE NATIONALIST BREAKTHROUGH
(AUGUST 1937–APRIL 1938)

In mid-August the British moved to the Aragon front. The battalion had been reinforced since the defeat of Brunete and was now 400 strong, although half were Spanish troops.[1] Military command had decided on a new offensive aimed at capturing Zaragoza and diverting Franco's attention away from the Republic's rapidly crumbling enclave in northern Spain. The British were held in reserve during the XV Brigade's first major action of the offensive, an attack against the town of Quinto. Nevertheless, Tom Wintringham, who had taken up a role on Brigade staff after recovering from the wound he had sustained at Jarama, took part in the vicious street fighting that ensued. In a letter to his eight year-old son O.J., Wintringham described the climax of the battle – an infantry assault backed by armour on a Nationalist strongpoint in a ruined church.

> Our tank straddled a street corner and started firing at the church, whoof BANG clatter, clatter, clatter – the clattering was bits of roof and wall falling down. I walked down the side of the street, scouting. I wanted to find a house we could set on fire so that it would set fire to the church. I was just having a good look round, nipping round corners and doors very quickly so they couldn't shoot me, when WHACK – a bullet hit me on top of the shoulder. It didn't hurt much but my arm went all wibbly-wobbly.[2]

The wound proved more serious than Wintringham first thought. The bullet had shattered his shoulder blade driving bone splinters through the flesh, one of which settled in his elbow and later became infected. As a result, Quinto would be Wintringham's last action in Spain. After several months in hospital he was allowed to return home and reached Britain in November 1937.

After Quinto had fallen, the British Battalion took centre stage. They were ordered to take Purburrel Hill, a fortified position on the outskirts of town that was holding up the offensive. On the first day, the hill proved a tough nut to crack. According to a subsequent report, 'its defence-system included barbed-wire, tank-traps, artillery and machine-gun emplacements, bomb-proof magazines and dug-outs'.[3] Several volunteers died before nightfall put an end to the assault. The next day, after a fierce artillery bombardment, anti-tank guns were hauled into position to pound the pillboxes to dust. When the infantry went in for a second time resistance was light and the position was captured without the loss of a single man.[4]

The battalion's next target was the town of Belchite, another Nationalist stronghold which had been surrounded and cut off by the Republican advance. The British helped repulse an enemy column attempting to break the siege and then settled down to starve the defenders out. With Belchite's surrender on 5 September, the battalion once more moved to the rear with the rest of the brigade. During a ten-day lull, Harry Fry and Jimmy Rutherford rejoined the battalion and the former took over command. On 11 October 1937, the British took part in an assault on another Aragonese town, Fuentes de Ebro. The attack was led by the 24th Spanish Battalion, who rode into action on the backs of forty-seven tanks. The rest of the XV Brigade also took part.[5]

The operation was a disaster. Artillery and air support were almost entirely ineffective. The Spanish troops fell off the fast-moving tanks, some were crushed under their tracks and the rest could not keep up with their advance. Cut off from their infantry support, the Republican armour fell prey to Nationalists armed with petrol bombs and grenades. The Republican infantry also suffered from the lack of support. Without the tanks to protect them, the British had to advance across over 600 yards of open ground. On 13 October Harry Fry led the assault 'through a barrage of artillery fire'.[6] He was cut down and killed in the first dozen yards and the attack ground to a halt. Ten days later, the battalion, now reduced to just 150 British troops, was pulled out of the line. To everyone's relief, they were sent to Mondéjar, a village where they had previously rested following the trials of Jarama.[7]

At the end of October, after several weeks attached to Brigade staff, Fred Copeman rejoined the battalion. The Englishman was suffering from undiagnosed stomach pains and his leg had swollen below the knee. To make matters worse, morale in the battalion was at a low ebb. 'Things were not going too well,' Copeman remembered; 'most of the older volunteers were fed up ... and unless a tighter grasp could be kept the new [ones] ... would be likewise affected.'[8] Copeman cited twin factors for this malaise: continuing infighting between anarchists and communists and a series of desertions from the battalion that had gone unpunished. Adding to the men's dissatisfaction was a government decree incorporating the International Brigades into the Spanish armed forces. Effectively, this meant that there would be no going home until the war was won. Before he could address these issues, however, Copeman's appendix burst and he was rushed to hospital.

> Within two hours I was on the operating table [at Alcañiz]. At first I thought that a serious appendix was the only problem ... [but] I later found out that ... a small piece of metal [from the wound he had suffered at Brunete] had passed up the left leg from the knee, between the bone and the muscle and entered the lining of the stomach.[9]

It was the end of Copeman's military career in Spain. After spending months in a succession of hospitals, he was repatriated in April 1938.[10]

The battalion, now led by Copeman's second-in-command, Bill Alexander, remained at Mondéjar until December. During this time they received several illustrious visitors, including Paul Robeson, the internationally renowned American singer and actor, and the Labour Party leader, Clement Attlee. On Christmas Day Harry Pollitt made the second of his three visits to the battalion. The Communist Party leader brought individual food parcels from Britain and a feast of pork, nuts and wine was laid on. A series of sporting events completed the festive calendar. An Englishman won the boxing, but, despite the swirling snows of winter, both British teams were soundly defeated by the Spanish at football.

On 17 January the battalion went back to the front line. The men were needed to resist a Nationalist counter-attack following the Republicans' capture of the town of Teruel eleven days earlier. The fighting took place in the mountains during the worst winter on record. Conditions were appalling. As well as the enemy, the troops had to battle freezing temperatures, biting winds and 30ft-deep snowdrifts. Along with the Mackenzie-Papineaus, a Canadian battalion which had been incorporated into the XV Brigade, and the German Thaelmann anti-fascists who had fought at Jarama, the British rifle companies dug into defensive positions in the frozen ground in a valley to the north-west of the town, whilst the machine gunners held a ridgeline above them. On the 19th there was a terrific artillery bombardment on the British positions. The riflemen suffered terribly. Twenty-one British volunteers were killed.[11]

Whilst the battalion was at Teruel, one of the darkest episodes in its history took place. The commander at the time, Bill Alexander, later recalled the event:

> In the mountains north of Teruel ... two men [Patrick Glacken and Peter Kemp] were caught on their way to enemy lines. One was carrying a map giving the Battalion positions with precise machine-gun locations – information which in Nationalist hands could have led to heavy casualties and defeat. There were very bitter feelings in the ranks against them. They were taken to the rear, court-martialled and sentenced to death.[12]

Although Alexander is rather coy about their fate, Richard Baxell, author of *British Volunteers in the Spanish Civil War*, has since pieced together the story. Whilst Kemp, who it seems was the instigator of the plot, was executed by his fellow volunteers, Glacken's punishment was similar to that handed out to Bert Overton after Jarama. Ordered to join a labour battalion, he was digging fortifications when the position came under heavy artillery fire. Glacken was killed in the barrage. Few of his comrades mourned his loss.[13]

At the end of January, the remains of the battalion were withdrawn from Teruel, only to be thrown into the front line once more on 16 February. This time their mission was to attack Nationalist positions at Segura de Baños, a town 40 miles to the north. The assault was aimed at relieving some of the pressure on the Republican troops still holding Teruel in the face of an aggressive Nationalist counter-attack. On 12 February, just before going into the line, the battalion celebrated the first anniversary of Jarama. The men were given 'double rations of bacon and eggs with real English tea'.[14] Four days later, a night attack was made on the Nationalist lines. Although the British made some progress at first, they were eventually thrown back in disorder after suffering several casualties. Bill Alexander was wounded in the shoulder and Sam Wild, the penultimate rifleman to leave White House Hill at Jarama, took over command.[15]

On 9 March 1938, as the frigid plains of Aragon were warmed by the bright spring sunshine, Franco launched a devastating attack against the Republican lines. Around 150,000 men, 700 guns, 150 tanks and 600 aircraft, including the newly arrived German Stuka dive-bomber, were used. The Republicans had never seen anything like it. Exhausted after their efforts at Teruel, they were soon routed. On the first day of the offensive, Colonel Juan Yagüe y Blanco's Moroccan Corps advanced 22 miles. It was the largest territorial gain since the opening months of the war. The International Brigades were rushed to the front to plug the growing gaps in the line, with the British Battalion returning to Fuentes del Ebro. On their way they met a tide of Republicans fleeing before the Nationalist advance. When the enemy arrived, the British soon found themselves surrounded. At first they were forced back to Belchite, but within hours they were driven back from that position too. The retreat soon lost all sense of order and for the next week scattered bands of Republicans fanned out across the Aragonese plains, desperately trying to stay ahead of the Nationalist advance. With the enemy columns occupying the roads and Condor Legion aircraft strafing and bombing any Republican build ups, the men were forced to travel cross-country.[16] Frank Graham, the Sunderland student who had seen Beckett and Sprigg die at Jarama, briefly documented the chaotic retreat. 'Over the mountains, to Caspe, the only way there, no roads at all, just over the mountains. We had to work by more or less guessing the direction to get there. We arrived in Caspe [on 15 March], terrible journey, never stopped walking ... no food, no water.'[17]

At Caspe the remnants of the battalion reformed and were ordered to fight a rearguard action to buy time for other units to withdraw. During the ensuing battle, which lasted twenty-four hours and saw much hand to hand fighting, Sam Wild and three others were momentarily captured. Whilst the Nationalists were distracted looting their packs, the four men flew into them using their feet, fists and even a tin of bully beef as improvised weapons. Within seconds the Nationalists were out cold at their feet. 'We thought it best not to hang around,' Wild recalled. 'By the time the fascists ... realised what had happened we were a good few yards away.'[18] On 16 March the battalion withdrew once more. Frequently under air attack they made their way to Batea, which they reached the next day. In the town some semblance of order awaited them.

Thanks to their rearguard action at Caspe, the Republicans had managed to organize enough men to hold the line. Food, water, supplies and a handful of reinforcements reinvigorated the survivors. Walter Gregory recalled:

> Day after day ... men wandered into the town either alone or in small groups to be given a 'right royal' reception by their comrades who had presumed them dead or captured. That so many men did manage to reach Batea after losing contact with their units says much for their determination. With no provisions, frequently without ammunition, moving by night and hiding by day and with nothing but the most rudimentary of maps to guide them, they had made their way through territory thick with enemy patrols to the safety of the brigade, and were still prepared to take up where they had left off.[19]

To such men, the comparative comforts of Batea were well received and over the next week the battalion's ebbing morale got a much needed boost. The respite was to prove brief indeed.[20]

On 30 March, whilst the Republicans were still reeling, the Nationalists launched the second phase of their spring offensive. Fast-moving columns led by Italian tanks spearheaded the advance. The move caught the Republicans off guard. Having left Batea, the British Battalion were withdrawing down a road on the outskirts of Calaceite when they met the enemy as Walter Gregory recalled:

> As we turned a bend in the road, we ran foul of a column of enemy light tanks...
> Another group of tanks [then] broke cover from a wood on our flank and Italian
> infantry in large numbers [also] entered the fray... All hell broke loose as [the]
> enemy ... poured fire into the leading companies of the Battalion and as soon as
> the order was given to scatter and make for the hills we broke into ones and twos
> and sought cover wherever we could find it.[21]

Fortunately, the machine-gun company, which had been in the rear of the British column, reacted quickly to the situation. Setting up two of their guns on the high ground to the side of the track, they managed to set one of the tanks on fire. In the confusion, many of the men escaped. But a large number of the 1st Company, who were at the head of the column, were captured and fifty others were hit by gunfire. Of the veterans of Jarama, Frank Ryan and Jimmy Rutherford were amongst those taken prisoner. Six weeks later, Rutherford was recognized by his interrogators as one of those captured at Jarama over a year before. Having signed a pledge promising he would not fight again, Rutherford must have known what was coming. On 24 May 1938 he was executed by firing squad. He was just twenty years old.[22]

The survivors of Calaceite once more found themselves split into small groups and behind enemy lines. Moving ever eastwards towards the Ebro River as spring gave way to soaring summer temperatures, they tried to avoid the Nationalist patrols sent into the hills to track them. Albert Charlesworth, the twenty-three year-old from Oldham who had fought under Briskey at Jarama, found himself in the company of a red-haired Welshman, whose name he later forgot. Terrified of capture, they kept running until they reached the town of Mora del Ebro, then jumped on a train to Barcelona.[23] Walter Gregory was in charge of another group. Leading a dozen men, he skirted the main roads, moving by night. Then, on 2 April, four days after the Italian tanks had broken the battalion, Gregory's men met sixty more British survivors at the junction of the Batea–Calaceite road. Together, they decided to make a stand.

Moving south-east of the nearby town of Gandesa, they found 'an ideal defensive position' where the road passed through a narrow cutting, bounded on both sides by steep, rock-strewn slopes. By the time the first Nationalists appeared, several stragglers of various nationalities had joined them and their band was 200 strong. 'We successfully repulsed the Nationalists' leading cavalry patrols with little difficulty,' Gregory recalled, 'and an infantry attack which took place early in the afternoon was a rather half-hearted affair and posed no real threat.' Later an Italian armoured car tried to force the position, but it was set alight by a well-sited Republican machine gun. Although his men had resisted well, Malcolm Dunbar, the highest ranking British volunteer present, realized that they could not hold out for ever. As the blazing sun slipped behind the Nationalist-occupied hills, he led the bulk of the Republicans to the south-east towards the Ebro, leaving Gregory and a handful of men behind as a rearguard. The Nottinghamshire man's position was probed throughout the night. The first to try were a Nationalist cavalry patrol. They rode at the British full tilt with carbines blazing. 'I ordered my volunteers to take up positions among the boulders on the upper crests of the hill,' Gregory remembered. 'We struggled into place and returned their fire.' Realizing they were no match for infantry in such broken terrain, the riders wheeled away 'in search of an easier target'. Gregory was struck by the romance of the scene. 'The dying rays of the sun flashed red on their sword blades as they made off, and I was left to think how incongruous mounted men appeared in the twentieth century war we were fighting.' The Nationalist artillery were the next to try to dislodge the dozen British volunteers, but their efforts also proved in vain. Only a few minor wounds were caused 'by shell and boulder fragments which whistled through the air in the wake of each incoming volley'.[24] At midnight Gregory decided his job was done and pulled back towards the Ebro.

First light found the group approaching the Móra bridge, one of the few crossing points over the Ebro that the Republicans hadn't already blown. The scene was chaotic. Trucks, tanks, heavy guns and columns of walking wounded were pouring down the road. The bridge acted as a bottleneck and a huge queue had formed. Amongst the military personnel and equipment were hordes of civilians also fleeing the Nationalist advance. Bill Rust, a *Daily Worker* journalist, vividly captured the scene:

> The refugees were mostly women, and every other one was carrying a small child; others held parcels or balanced them on their head in the Spanish manner. A tinny din of bells heralded the approach of a herd of goats, which was quickly followed by a flock of sheep hustled along by yelping dogs. Donkeys and mules passed by, laden with household effects – a bundle of bedding, a canary cage and a gramophone-horn. Down the road came the refugees, wending their way through the guns and military lorries, their canvas shoes dragging along the hot and dusty road.[25]

To many, the retreat over the Ebro seemed like the death knell of the Republic. Since the Nationalist offensive had begun four weeks earlier, Franco's troops had advanced 100 miles. On 15 April Italian units reached the sea at Vinaròs, driving a wedge between Catalonia and the rest of the government held territory, effectively splitting the Republic in two. Tens of thousands of troops had been killed, wounded or captured and tons of war matériel had fallen into Nationalist hands. In a conflict where the front line had remained largely static ever since the defence of Madrid in 1936, such territorial losses were catastrophic. Nevertheless, the Republican generals had one last ace up their sleeve.

CHAPTER 18

THE EBRO OFFENSIVE AND THE FAREWELL PARADE

(APRIL–OCTOBER 1938)

In the first few weeks of April, the British Battalion regrouped on the west bank of the Ebro. Dozens of stragglers who had become separated in the retreat after Calaceite managed to rejoin them, many having to swim across the river to reach the Republican lines. To the surprise of many, Franco changed the direction of his offensive after reaching the Ebro. Instead of crossing the river and crushing the remains of the Republican Army in Catalonia, his troops turned south towards Castellon and Valencia, but were held by a strong defensive line in the Levante. This bought time for the Republicans in Catalonia to reorganize and a temporary re-opening of the French border between March and May allowed 18,000 tons of badly needed equipment and ammunition to be brought in. Although well received, the supplies would prove too little too late.[1]

The British Battalion spent the spring months in a variety of locations to the west of the river. Under Sam Wild's leadership their morale, badly deflated after the catastrophic reverses in Aragon, slowly recovered. New recruits coming across the Pyrenees provided a boost and along with the wounded returning from hospital swelled the unit's strength to 650 men, a third of whom were British. One of those returning to the battalion was Albert Charlesworth, the metal polisher from Oldham who had fled to Barcelona after the rout at Calaceite. For two days he had wandered round the Catalan capital, before guilt got the better of him. 'I realized what I had done,' he admitted, 'and went to the Brigade Office and asked to be sent back to the battalion.' On his return Sam Wild put him on punishment duty. 'I was digging trenches for two days,' Charlesworth recalled.[2] It was back breaking work and took its toll. Charlesworth became ill and was sent to hospital to recover.

On 14 April, Harry Pollitt paid the battalion a surprise visit. Walter Gregory thought the CPGB leader looked faintly ridiculous. 'He cut a rather curious figure in the Spanish countryside in his blue three-piece suit ... collar and tie, but he also had a commanding presence.'[3] Pollitt's speech was well received. 'He reminded us how often during the first seven years of the Soviet Republic its death had been prophesised,' the battalion diary recorded, 'and pointed to its strength to-day as the answer to those who thought the days of the Spanish Republic were numbered.'[4] Two weeks later, 1 May dawned bright and glorious. Battalion command had laid on a series of events for the men's entertainment. Sam Wild made an opening speech and was later presented with a wrist watch from Brigade HQ, 'in appreciation of his courage and excellent leadership during the Belchite-Caspe action'. The gesture prompted 'a big cheer' from the men.[5] In between such morale-boosting events, serious training was also taking place. Command's insistence on regular practice of night time operations crossing rivers in inflatable boats convinced the men that they would soon be back on the offensive. In June Pandit Nehru, the future prime minister of India, visited and later a delegation of trade union members and students, including a young Ted Heath, arrived. After a final fiesta with local villagers who once again defeated the British at football, the battalion received the order to move to the front line. 'The word passed round – *We are going to cross the Ebro.*'[6]

The offensive was one of the biggest ever launched by the Republic, and around 80,000 men took part. Grizzled veterans stood alongside the latest civilians to be called up, Catalan boys of sixteen and middle-aged men. Despite the re-opening of the French border, they had precious little equipment. There were barely enough rifles to go round, only 22 T26 tanks and no more than 150 field guns, many of which dated from the previous century. Planes were also in short supply. Facing the assault force on the west bank of the Ebro were 40,000 Nationalist troops, mostly Moroccan veterans from Yagüe's Corps.[7]

Early in the morning of 25 July the attack began. The first to cross the river were Republican commandos. Paddling silently across the 100-yard stretch of water in rubber boats, they landed undetected and slit the throats of the Nationalist sentries, before fastening lines to the west bank for the main assault boats to follow. Six divisions then crossed at sixteen points along a 50-mile front, whilst thousands of engineers constructed a dozen pontoon bridges that would carry the heavy equipment and supplies. Although the XVI International Brigade suffered heavy casualties crossing in the south, in the centre and to the north the advance went well. In just over twenty-four hours, the lead units had seized 300 square miles from the enemy, who fell back in disorder. Over 5,000 prisoners and huge quantities of matériel were taken. By the second day, however, the advance had begun to falter. The planes of the Condor Legion, Spanish Air Force and Italian Legionary Air Force, made countless bombing and strafing runs against the crossing points and the government columns winding their way to the front. The Republican air force, by contrast, was by now a spent force and put up little resistance. As soon as he learnt of the attack, the Nationalist commander, Colonel Yagüe, ordered his reserves to dig in at the town of Gandesa. It was there, 15 miles west of the Ebro, amidst the rolling wooded hills of southern Catalonia, that the battle would be won or lost. The British Battalion were amongst the Republican troops sent against them.[8]

Walter Gregory, now in charge of the battalion's 2nd Company, had been with the British as they splashed ashore on the west bank of the Ebro that morning. 'It was a marvellous moment,' he recalled. 'We were on the move again ... taking the initiative and ... on top of the world.'[9] The feeling would not last long. En route to Gandesa, Gregory's company suffered its first casualty. Whilst the majority of the enemy had retreated in face of the Republican attack, a few Nationalists had remained behind, setting up machine-gun posts on isolated hill tops to delay the advance. It was one of these that shot Gregory's clerk:

> When I heard that George [Stockdale] had been wounded, I rushed to him ...
> [and] found him lying among the sweet smelling herbs that grow in Aragon.
> He was in a very bad way. A bullet from a concealed machine-gun nest had struck

him in the head, just above the left eye, and had cut a dreadful groove in his skull from front to back leaving his brain exposed. George tried to speak and I knelt to listen. I put my ear to his mouth but all I heard was the sound of death as his last breath rattled in his throat.[10]

On the evening of 26 July, the day after the crossing, the battalion reached the outskirts of Gandesa. Wild was ordered to take Hill 481, a prominent defensive feature riddled with trenches, machine-gun posts, pillboxes and anti-tank guns which had to be captured before the main strike on the town could go in. At dawn the next day the 1st Company made the first attack. Supported by heavy artillery and frequent air strikes, the Nationalist position proved impregnable and the men were driven off with heavy casualties. Nevertheless, for six days the British launched further attacks. Rushing up the slopes, they were cut down and forced back each time.[11]

On 30 July, it was Gregory's turn.

> Just before dawn we started our cautious ascent, crawling from rock to rock, keeping as low as possible, and trying to leave the loose shale undisturbed, lest the sound ... alert the enemy to our presence. We had moved but a short distance ... when we were greeted by a fusillade of rifle and machine-gun fire and ... each man sought cover for himself ... we were [soon] pinned down [and] ... it was ... simply a matter of returning fire whenever ... it was safe enough ... to discharge a few rounds ... at the heights above.

Like the men who had gone before them, the 2nd Company were trapped. They could no longer advance and had to wait in the blazing sun all day before nightfall would offer a chance to retreat. 'What a prospect!' Gregory recalled:

> Twelve hours of lying on the rocky soil, every fragment of which seemed intent on burying itself in our bodies, of being continually shot at, of having nothing to eat or drink [and] of being driven half-mad by the ceaseless attention of the most malevolent flies in the whole of Spain.[12]

As it turned out the Nottinghamshire man would not have to wait quite that long. 'Around midday,' he remembered, 'I felt a blow in my neck which hurled me round and threw me flat on my back.'[13] Gregory was bandaged by two of his comrades and sent to the rear. The wound proved minor, however, and he was soon back at the front.

On 3 August, following one last desperate attempt to capture the hill, which the men had nicknamed 'the Pimple', the battalion was put into reserve. Three days later they were withdrawn from the sector, but on 11 August they were back in action again, this time on the defensive. The Republican advance had been halted and 100,000 Nationalists, supported by 300 guns, 500 aircraft and 100 tanks, had been ordered to drive them back across the Ebro. The British Battalion was tasked with holding the appropriately named Hill 666, one of the Sierra Pandols, a range of heights south-east of Gandesa. They held on for two weeks, under constant artillery barrage, but the casualties kept mounting. On 24 August after the most ferocious bombardment yet, two Nationalist infantry battalions launched a night attack. Somehow, the British held firm and forced them back. During the action, Wild was wounded in the hand by a shell splinter, but refused to leave the front line. The next morning the battalion was withdrawn once more. Their 'rest' positions were within range of the enemy artillery, however, so their ordeal continued. By now, rumours that the International Brigades were to be disbanded were sweeping through the Republican lines. In a forlorn attempt to curry international favour and shame Mussolini and Hitler into recalling their troops, the Republican Prime Minister, Juan Negrín, had decided on the policy as a last resort to save his crumbling Republic. Meanwhile, Pollitt made one final visit to the battalion, as always handing round letters and packages from home and packets of British cigarettes. Then, before the recall order could be put into effect, the battalion were called into action one final time. The Nationalists were attacking in strength in the Sierra Pandols and every man was needed to plug the growing gaps in the line. As the British were about to be repatriated, it was deemed that only those who chose to go would be taken to the front. 'Sam Wild paraded us and called for volunteers. Needless to say,' Tommy Bloomfield, one of the machine-gun company captured at Jarama, recalled, 'all the lads went back in.

That was a hard decision to make knowing it meant you could die instead of going home.'[14]

On 23 September the battalion took up positions. After five hours of air attack and heavy artillery bombardment, during which a shell fell on the British sector every second, the enemy infantry attacked. Supported by tanks they advanced on the positions flanking the British line, which were manned by Spanish units and the Canadian Mackenzie-Papineau battalion, who fell back in the face of overwhelming odds. The British were then cut to pieces by enfilading fire and the tanks rolled in. Three were knocked out, but the British suffered horrendously. Casualties were heavy and dozens of prisoners were taken. Walter Gregory was amongst them.

> [The] tanks went on beyond our position, [then] suddenly I heard shouting away to my right and saw that the lads ... were standing with their hands raised in submission. I remembered [sic] thinking 'What the hell is going on here? ... why are these idiots acting so bloody stupidly?' The answer was all too obvious when I saw that enemy troops had managed to work their way round behind my right flank ... I took the precaution of hastily removing my jacket ... since in one of its pockets was a pass entitling Teniente Gregory to visit all parts of the Eastern Front. I did not want to be taken into captivity with that ... on me for I was certain it ... would have earned me a short, quick march to the nearest wall and the position of honour at a firing squad.[15]

After Gregory's capture, the remnants of the battalion, which numbered just 137 men, withdrew, leaving the Nationalists holding their former positions.[16]

The action was the last the battalion would endure in Spain, but two final duties remained. On 17 October all the foreign troops in the 35th Division, to which the British were attached, were paraded and reviewed. Several received promotions or commendations, amongst them Sam Wild and Tommy Bloomfield, two of a dozen Jarama veterans still in Spain. At the end of the month, the battalion was taken by lorry to Barcelona for the International Brigades' farewell parade. Both President Azaña and Prime Minister Negrín were there as well as numerous other VIPs and the remnants of the Republican air force flew overhead to provide cover from marauding Nationalist planes. Fred Thomas of the British Battalion remembered the day well:

> Trucks took us through crowded streets, with flags and bunting everywhere, the people were cheering and throwing flowers, crowding every window and balcony. We finally dismounted ... at the Sarria Road, starting point of the procession. There the brigades of many different nationalities were drawn up nine abreast. Spanish troops lined the route as, led by military bands, we set off. Everywhere thousands packed the broad streets, time after time men and women broke through the cordon to hug and kiss us, holding up small children and babies to be kissed in return, smothering us in affection as they cheered and cheered. For an hour and a half we made our slow way through some of the principle [sic] streets in one long glut of emotional excess. I was not the only Brigader ... reduced to tears: we, who were leaving the fight, were yet receiving the heartfelt homage of the Spanish people. In the street of the 14th April the march ended, and ... the speeches [began]. From a platform ... Dr Negrín [the Minster of Finance] ... addressed us and the vast crowds. Then came President Azaña followed by the chief of the Army of the Ebro. Finally we recognized the spare figure of the indomitable 'La Pasionaria' who quickly had the crowd roaring their approval.[17]

La Pasionaria, or Dolores Ibarruri, the Spanish Communist Party's most renowned figure, honoured the occasion with a memorable speech, which concluded with the following lines:

> Comrades of the International Brigades! Political reasons, reasons of state ... are sending you back, some to your own countries and others to forced exile. You can go proudly. You are history. You are legend. You are the heroic example of democracy's solidarity and universality. We shall not forget you, and when the olive tree of peace puts forth its leaves again, mingled with the laurels of the Spanish Republic's victory – come back![18]

BACK TO BRITAIN
(OCTOBER 1938–THE PRESENT DAY)

The 305 volunteers remaining in Spain after the Ebro offensive did not leave for home until 6 December 1938, six weeks after the farewell parade in Barcelona. British bureaucracy was responsible for the delay. The volunteers were an embarrassment to Neville Chamberlain's government. Their existence was a reminder that a considerable section of society was against Franco and believed the policy of Non-Intervention was a sham. Nevertheless, after considerable legal wrangling and pressure from sympathetic Labour rebels, the British Consul in Barcelona eventually gave them permission to return home. A number of delegates were sent to their quarters at the Catalan town of Ripoll to give them the good news. 'They were very snotty,' one volunteer remembered, but another recalled the event more fondly.[1] 'Finally the great day came,' he explained. 'A large consignment of civilian clothing arrived and the task of changing into civvies was begun.'[2]

After boarding 'an old freight train' at Ripoll, the men were taken to the town of Puigcerda on the French border where they got out and crossed over the frontier on foot.[3] 'There was a barrier across the platform,' Albert Charlesworth recalled. 'On the other side ... we could see British Army staff.'[4] Determined to make a good impression, Sam Wild ordered the men to form up in three ranks and they marched across in style.[5] The officials 'made sure we got on the train on the other side ... [and] we were locked in ... for the journey through France'.[6] Approaching the outskirts of the French capital, the train was diverted. The

Parisians had prepared a grand welcome for them, but their government was determined to thwart their plans. Like the British they too were embarrassed by the presence of the Brigaders and wished to avoid any undue publicity. At Dieppe dock workers presented the volunteers with a 'huge wreath of red poppies ... as a token of their support', then the men boarded the boat-train for home.[7]

On the evening of 7 December the volunteers arrived at Victoria Station. To their surprise, a huge crowd had gathered to welcome them. With Sam Wild at their head, bearing the battalion colours, they formed up and marched into the street. Flanked by 20,000 spectators who burst into rapturous applause as they passed, Wild led them past the Houses of Parliament to deliver a petition to Number 10 demanding support for the Spanish Republic. 'On reaching Downing Street,' Tommy Bloomfield recalled, 'a cordon of police halted us and said we could go no further.' Wild was not so easily discouraged. With the walking wounded acting as a barrier between the police and the rest of the men, he pushed his way through, telling 'the inspector in charge that he was going to deliver the petition come hell or high water.' The police had met their match. '[They] didn't care to have the stigma of batoning wounded veterans of Spain,' Bloomfield explained, 'so common sense prevailed'. The cordon split and Wild was allowed through.[8]

Afterwards the Brigaders boarded a fleet of buses which took them to a rally in the East End. Clement Attlee, Sir Stafford Cripps and Willie Gallacher, the communist MP for West Fife, all made speeches. Will Lawther, president of the National Union of Mine Workers and elder brother of Clifford Lawther, the amateur boxer with the 3rd Company who had been killed on the first day at Jarama, also took the podium. Later, Sam Wild spoke in return. 'We intend to keep the promise we made to the Spanish people,' he said, 'that we [will] ... continue to fight in Britain for the assistance of Spain.'[9] Once the speeches had been made, the rally broke up. In the next few days, similar scenes were played out in towns and cities across Britain as the Brigaders returned home.[10]

For those captured at Calaceite or in the final offensive at the Ebro the war was not yet over. Walter Gregory would have to endure several weeks of captivity before he eventually made it home. His ordeal began with interrogation by a smartly dressed Nationalist officer:

> He asked me a lot of questions about where I had come from and how long I had
> been in Spain. I lied about everything! I denied being a company commander and
> insisted that Bill Briskey [the leader of the 3rd Company who had been killed at
> Jarama] was my officer ... I was adamant: I had only just arrived in Spain. I had
> had the misfortune to be captured on my first day in action.[11]

Talking to his comrades in a holding cell afterwards, Gregory learnt that they
had all reacted in the same way, but, unfortunately their 'fabricated stories had
not been synchronised'.[12]

   Afterwards the prisoners were used as stretcher bearers then bundled aboard
a train to Zaragoza. On arrival, Gregory was separated from his comrades.
Whilst they were marched to a civilian prison, he was taken to a military
barracks. The next few weeks were a trying time for the young Briton, who
came to believe that he would be executed by firing squad. 'I began to steel
myself to go to my death with as much dignity and defiance as I could summon.'
His bravado dissipated after dark, however, as his thoughts turned to his family
back in Nottinghamshire. 'Would they learn of my death,' he wondered as he lay
awake in his cell, 'or would they simply assume when many months had passed
with no news ... that I had died somewhere in Spain.' A few days later the
moment he had been dreading seemed to have arrived when three guards
escorted him to the parade ground:

> As I left my cell I was engaged in a titanic struggle to make my limbs operate and
> to stop my bowels from functioning... Somehow I managed to pull myself together
> ... but I was convinced that my strong defiant cry of 'Viva la Republica' as I faced
> the firing squad would come out as a hoarse whisper. It ... looked as if the romantic
> exit ... which I had conceived in my cell was going to turn into a sad and rather
> ridiculous parody.[13]

In fact, Gregory was fated to live for another fifty years. Rather than being led
to his death, he was actually being transferred to a rambling prison in San Pedro
de Cardeña, home to hundreds of other captured Brigaders. His life as a
prisoner of war soon became routine. 'We were confined to our quarters except

at meal times, when we were permitted to go into the courtyard and collect our food.' No exercise was allowed and washing facilities were entirely inadequate. In the cramped conditions disease spread quickly and the men were plagued by lice. 'We were alive with them,' Gregory recalled. A few weeks after his arrival, Gregory and his fellow Britons were moved once more, this time to a jail at San Sebastian near the French border. As it was run by civilian staff, conditions were far superior. Exercise was permitted and their diet was improved. One month later, with no prior warning, the sixty British inmates were gathered together and taken to the town of Irún, where they were released into French custody. 'As we walked past the [Spanish] guard,' Gregory recalled, 'he quietly said, "*Adios*. God be with you." I could not resist replying, "*Adios, Hasta la Vista*."'[14] Gregory would not see Spain again for forty-two years.

Although most of the British prisoners were released a few months after their capture, Frank Ryan, the former IRA fighter who had been captured at Calaceite, would never see his homeland again. Like Gregory, Ryan was taken to San Pedro, where he continued to provide leadership and guidance for the British contingent. On one occasion, when a prisoner had been caught stealing food from his comrades, Ryan headed the subsequent court martial and sentenced him to have his rations confiscated as a result. Uniquely, Ryan refused to hide his rank from the Nationalists and was fiercely defiant throughout his captivity. On 15 June 1938, he was sentenced to death for commanding a squad of International Brigaders who had executed Nationalist prisoners at the battle of Brunete. After the trial he was led away in handcuffs. His comrades at San Pedro never saw him again and the rest of his story is shrouded in mystery. Years later it was discovered that Ryan had been taken to Germany, where the Nazis hoped to use his IRA connections to foster rebellion in his homeland. As a result of harsh treatment whilst in captivity in Dresden, he became seriously ill and died in June 1944.[15]

For those who made it home, their first battle was adapting to peacetime Britain. Many found the calm difficult to cope with after the bombs and bullets of the front line and several suffered from what would now be termed Post Traumatic Stress Disorder. 'The experiences of many people leave unseen scars, on the mind, in the heart', as Tony Hyndman explained. 'If this is true, my scar is Spain.'[16] John 'Bosco' Jones, the young Londoner who had been described as 'cheerful' by his former comrades, was another psychological casualty. By the time he got home in the autumn of 1938, Jones was on the verge of a nervous breakdown:

> Physically I looked marvellous. I was brown as a berry but inside I was shaking like a jelly. My nerves had partially gone. I went to a doctor and told him what I had been through... He told me to get a job doing something a little bit dangerous, such as a window cleaner.[17]

With nothing better to go on, Jones took the advice. To his surprise, it worked. 'Going up and down ladders I had one or two falls, and I think that helped me to recover. It was only after a few months of doing this that I was better again.'[18]

For Jason Gurney, who had been wounded in the face and right hand during the trench fighting at Jarama, rehabilitation was somewhat more complicated. Although his facial injuries proved superficial, the damage to the sculptor's hand was more serious:

> The outer two bones in the palm ... were completely smashed. I ... [had] to reconcile myself to the fact that ... I would only be able to use two fingers and the thumb of my right hand. It might have all been a good deal worse. The one serious aspect of the thing was that I clearly would not be able to continue my work as a sculptor, and I did not know what the hell else I wanted, or would be able to do.[19]

When Walter Gregory returned to Britain in early 1939, the trials and deprivations of the last three years in Spain suddenly overwhelmed him. 'The long journey ... and the exhilaration of experiencing freedom must have used up ... [my] last vestiges of stamina,' he explained. After arriving at Victoria his mother and sister accompanied him to the family home, where he 'sank into ... bed with a sense of great relief and ... almost unbearable weariness'.[20] Whilst in prison he had dreamed of such a moment, but once it arrived, feelings of disappointment and guilt overwhelmed him:

It was only now that I came to appreciate fully just how hard a time my mother and sister had experienced during my ... absence. My mother had borne the trials ... with customary fortitude and had never ceased to believe ... that I would return ... safe and sound ... [but] my sister ... had been ill for long periods. She and I had been very close throughout our childhood and she had been worried about me greatly, especially when there had been long gaps between my letters home.[21]

A few weeks later, Gregory received an unexpected visitor. It was Mr Winfield, the father of a friend who had been killed at Teruel. 'Would I call at his home to talk to his wife, he asked, as she was still dreadfully upset by Bernard's death.' Gregory agreed, and, with heavy heart, made the trip one evening after work. The hour that followed was one of the hardest of his life.

I was subjected to a barrage of questions ... that only a mother could ask. Did Bernard have a nice coffin? Were there flowers on his grave?... I had not been prepared for questions such as these... Bernard had been buried at the height of a ferocious battle. There had been no time or materials to make a coffin ... no flowers grew in the snows of Teruel and Bernard's comrades [had been] ... too busy fighting for their own lives to be able to attend a funeral service, had there even been one.[22]

Faced with his comrade's grieving mother, Gregory lied. He could not bring himself to 'tell the poor ... woman the realities of life in action and invented for her solace a truly memorable funeral'. Finally released from the awful scene, Gregory headed straight to the nearest pub 'for a few stiff drinks'.[23]

Bernard's mother was not the only relative left mourning an empty grave. On 2 May 1937 a memorial service was held in Manchester for the nine volunteers from the city who gave their lives at Jarama. Towards the end of proceedings, after several speeches by local politicians, Leda Beckett, the speedway champion's widow, made her way to the lectern. Struggling to hold back the tears, she addressed the crowd. 'My husband, like hundreds of others, went to Spain and faced death, not because he was reckless, but because he loved life and believed that people can live freely and happily only if they take power into their hands.'[24] In the years that followed, Leda Beckett rebuilt her life, eventually remarrying and moving to India. Her second husband, Dr Anand, was the brother of Mulk Raj Anand, a respected novelist who had also volunteered for the International Brigades.[25]

Upon his return to England in November 1937, Tom Wintringham was forced to make some difficult decisions. Although his relationship with his wife had remained friendly, Wintringham's philandering ensured that his marriage was effectively over. Facing up to the fact, he moved into a North London flat with his American journalist girlfriend, Kitty Bowler, and began writing about Jarama. The resulting memoir, *English Captain*, published by Faber and Faber in 1939, was a great success. It was the beginning of a new career for the former *Daily Worker* journalist, who proved a prolific author. Over the next five years, he produced nine books which 'were much in demand by a general readership'. Although his shoulder had not yet fully recovered and he would have to endure one final operation in the summer of 1939, Wintringham had landed on his feet on his return from Spain. Unlike many of the men he had commanded at Jarama, he was mentally fit and his financial future was secure.[26]

Politically, however, Wintringham faced considerable difficulties. The CPGB issued an ultimatum shortly after his return from Spain: he was to break off his relationship with Kitty Bowler or be expelled from the Party. Following her brush with André Marty in Albacete, Bowler was considered a Trotskyite spy. Despite the injustice of the attack, Wintringham remained enthralled by the party and begged to remain. He still refused to choose, however, and the decision stood. In March 1938, following a final appeal, he was expelled from the CPGB for good.[27]

Whilst Wintringham fell from grace, another former commander of the British Battalion was still very much in favour. One month after his return to England in April 1938, Fred Copeman married his fiancée Kitty at Lewisham Registry Office. Present at the ceremony were Kitty's father, Tom Mann, Harry Pollitt, Charlotte Haldane and George House. Suffering from complications resulting from his burst appendix and the shrapnel wounds he had suffered at Brunete, Copeman 'was still not feeling too well' and as 'too much excitement brought on fits of fainting', he was forced to sit on the sidelines whilst his bride danced the night away with his former comrades from the Brigades.[28] Pollitt's presence at the ceremony was significant. With his chiselled jaw, unshakeable working class credentials and reputation as a hero of the International Brigades, Copeman was the Communist Party's poster boy. And despite his waning enthusiasm following Aitken and Cunningham's dismissal, Pollitt was determined to make use of him. After he had recovered from his wounds in late 1938, the former mutineer was asked to join the British delegation travelling to the Kremlin to celebrate the anniversary of the Bolshevik seizure of power. Copeman reluctantly agreed.[29]

The journey took them through Nazi Germany. Signs of Hitler's hold on the country were everywhere. 'Even the ticket collector on the train gave the Nazi salute and clicked his heels,' Copeman recalled. Although understandably nervous, the delegation was determined to show at least token opposition to Hitler's regime. 'Bob Taylor ... Chairman of the Scottish T.U.C. [Trades Union Congress], produced a handful of badges normally worn by members of the Union', which the men stuck to their caps in defiance of Hitler's ban. Although a minor gesture, Copeman approved: 'I personally liked it very much ... it revived everyone's spirits.' After leaving Germany the train continued east through Poland, before entering the Soviet Union. 'The last we saw of Polish territory,' Copeman remembered, 'was a floodlit cemetery right on the border itself' – an apt metaphor for the fate that the country was soon to endure.[30]

For men who had swallowed Stalinist propaganda whole, initial impressions of Russia were disappointing. The clanking train that took them to Moscow was a museum piece, the Hotel Metropole, once the capital's finest, was now a shadow of its former grandeur and beyond the gleaming central thoroughfares, the city's streets were dark and squalid. The next day carefully orchestrated trips to the Bolshoi, an auto plant and a road construction party produced more favourable impressions. 'At two in the morning I went to bed feeling quite happy,' Copeman recalled. 'A few little things had got me thinking, but in the main we had seen a lot of good things.'[31] On the anniversary of the revolution, the international delegations returned to the Bolshoi for a grand rally. Stalin himself led the party hierarchy onto the stage. For Copeman, the appearance of the party leader was the biggest disappointment so far. 'I had expected him to be a great Georgian type with a huge black moustache, but in actual fact he was a little, short, stumpy man – but obviously Stalin.' As Copeman later put it, 'the gilt was wearing off the ginger-bread – and I didn't like the taste of the biscuit underneath.'[32] The big man needed to brace himself. Far worse was yet to come.

A few days later, on a trip to the drab Comintern headquarters, Copeman met La Pasionaria, the Spanish communist who had spoken so eloquently at the International Brigades' farewell parade in Barcelona. The way the Soviets had treated her since epitomized their approach to the Spanish Republic. '[The] meeting ... hurt me deep down,' Copeman admitted. 'I expected to find her on the stage at the Bolshoi Theatre, holding the hand of Stalin, and being introduced as one of the greatest living Communists. [Instead] I found her alone in a little room closely guarded by units of the Red Army.' It was a defining moment and opened Copeman's eyes to the realities of the Party:

> No doubt when Spain again became important in international politics ... [La Pasionaria] would be permitted her true place in the leadership of the Spanish Communist Party. Now, however, Spain to the Soviet[s] had become an embarrassment. The Brigade was beginning to pass into history. Future Soviet policy would wish to forget it. Her new-found friends had no time for La Passionaria [sic]. The Soviet-Nazi pact had already become an immediate possibility. This woman, with her deep convictions and loyalty to principles, was likely to become a political problem. I was continually learning that callousness was essentially part of Communist doctrine.[33]

The final straw came soon after Copeman's return to England. Working at the CPGB's headquarters in London one morning, he was approached by a leading communist who presented him with a tailor's receipt for suits purchased by former Brigaders whilst attending a post-war rally in Liverpool. Copeman had understood that the Party would cover the cost, but he was now told that the matter would have to be taken up with Pollitt. Incensed at the man's pettiness in refusing to pay a bill of £3 10 shillings for men who had risked their lives actively pursuing a cause that the party had been deeply allied to, Copeman saw red. 'I tore into him like a thunderbolt,' he explained. The man ran from the office with a bloody nose swearing he would get his revenge. The next day Copeman was called into a meeting with Pollitt. Believing that he would be given full support, Copeman was flabbergasted when Pollitt suggested he should take extended leave. 'I decided there and then that this was the end of the Communist Party for me.' Copeman was true to his word. He would never see Pollitt again.[34]

For many of the volunteers the fight to save the Spanish Republic continued long after their return to Britain. Whilst Azaña's crippled regime struggled on into the spring of 1939, the campaign to raise awareness and funds for the fight and attempts to pressurize the British government into changing their policy of Non-Intervention continued. Early in 1939, two trucks took returned British Brigaders on a tour of the country to speak at rallies and meetings in clubs, factories and town halls urging support for Spain. The campaign continued until the Republic's final days and a lorry carrying food, driven by a former Brigader, actually crossed the French border as Catalonia was falling. The supplies were handed out to the growing stream of refugees. One of those involved was George Leeson, the Royal Navy veteran who had been captured with the machine-gun company on the second day at Jarama. After his release, Leeson worked in Paris with the Spanish Aid Committee, an organization that raised money for the Republican refugees who had escaped over the border into southern France. Leeson was appalled by their treatment at the hands of the French government. Herded into concentration camps and surrounded by armed guards, the refugees rarely had sufficient food supplies and the only water available was brackish. Many were wounded and disease spread rapidly. In March 1939, one month before the end of the war, the International Brigade Association was formed, its purpose to continue to promote the Republic and support its adherents even after Franco had crushed the last vestiges of resistance in Spain. The end of the war finally came in April 1939. By then Britain and France had officially recognized Franco's regime. Nevertheless, the Brigaders continued to fight the Republic's corner and for the rights of those captured by the Nationalists in their final advance. Outside of the Brigaders' circle, however, the final days of the Republic went largely unnoticed. By late

1939 a far more pressing concern demanded the British people's full attention. Hitler was on the move. The Second World War had begun.[35]

The war years proved a frustrating time for the British veterans. Although keen to continue the fight against fascism, many were not allowed to join the armed forces. Having served in Spain, they were seen as 'Reds' not to be trusted. George Leeson, as a veteran of the Royal Navy, thought himself an ideal candidate. 'I was called up,' he remembered, and 'taken for my medical exam.' Having passed with 'a grade 1' and impressed the interviewing officer, he thought it would only be a matter of time before he began. In fact, he never heard from the recruiting office again. Frustrated, Leeson decided to take matters into his own hands. 'I wrote a letter to the admiralty saying I'd ... been a seaman gunner and I would like to volunteer and then I wrote to the merchant marine.' Both organizations told him they did not accept volunteers and that he should wait at home for his call up papers to arrive. Needless to say, they never did. As a fit man in his twenties in a London stripped of its youth, Leeson stood out like a sore thumb. 'Occasionally ... I would be stopped ... by the police,' he recalled. 'Why haven't you been called up?' they would ask him. 'Don't ask me, ask them,' was his reply.[36] Leeson was not alone in being rejected. Sam Wild's efforts to join up were similarly frustrated, whilst Jock Cunningham, although allowed into the Army, was thrown out a week later, when his commanders learnt of his involvement in Spain.[37]

Other Brigaders were allowed to serve. Leeson believed that whether or not they were barred seemed to depend on the whims of the individual recruiting officer. James Maley, the Celtic fan captured on the second day, joined the Royal Artillery in 1942 and later saw action against the Japanese in Burma with the 2nd Battalion of the King's Own Scottish Borderers. Walter Gregory was also accepted. After joining the British Navy in 1941, he saw action with the North Russian convoys, at the Dieppe raid and during the 'race up the Channel' against the German capital ships *Prinz Eugen*, *Scharnhorst* and *Gneisenau*.[38] Albert Charlesworth, the metal polisher from Oldham who fought at Jarama with the 4th Company, was also permitted to fight. Desperate to escape his job as a foreman in a munitions factory (a reserve occupation which was nigh-on impossible to leave once the war

223

had begun), Charlesworth took the only way out: volunteering for RAF pilot school. A few months later he was called up. After training in Aberystwyth he was given his wings and flew for the rest of the war. 'I was out in India supply dropping in Burma,' he recalled. Unlike many of his former comrades, he found that his experiences in Spain were never an issue, as the RAF had a more relaxed recruitment policy than the Army and Navy. When his 'leftist tendencies' did eventually become apparent after some time in India, his commanding officer treated the whole matter as a joke. 'From then on I was known as the Red Baron,' Charlesworth explained.[39]

David Crook, the Jarama veteran who had worked for the KGB in Barcelona, also served in the RAF. After the communists had wrested control of the Catalan capital from the anarchists, Crook had been sent to China where he continued spying on international Trotskyists for the Kremlin. Having spent so much time in 'bad company', his fanaticism for Stalin began to crumble, resulting in his expulsion from the ranks of the KGB; Crook then decided to return to Britain. His journey home was a war-time epic. After escaping Shanghai shortly before the arrival of the Japanese, he passed through Pearl Harbor. The attack on the US Pacific Fleet had occurred ten days before. The image of the wounded made a dramatic impact on the Englishman. 'Many ... were pitiable human cinders,' he recalled, 'burnt in the flaming oil which spread over the water.'[40]

After picking up 150 survivors, Crook's ship steamed on. On Christmas Day 1941, it passed under the Golden Gate Bridge and arrived at San Francisco, where a casual encounter with 'a journalist acquaintance' would shape Crook's destiny:

> When he heard that I was going home to join up ... [he] gave me some advice. 'Join the RAF,' he said. 'That's the most democratic of the three forces. The British army and navy will sling a lot of bullshit at you. I know. I've just come from the UK.'[41]

After San Francisco, Crook continued his journey by Greyhound bus to New York, where he fell in with a group of International Brigade veterans who had fought in the Abraham Lincoln Battalion. His former comrades were busy trashing Hemingway's recently released novel, *For Whom the Bell Tolls*. They had a litany of complaints: 'it makes the hero of the Spanish Republic an American, denounces the Communist André Marty, describes Republican not fascist atrocities and subordinates the whole story to an unlikely love affair.' Their subsequent review appeared under the title 'Three Nights in a Sleeping Bag'. 'I acknowledged they had a point,' Crook admitted, 'while confessing that I had found the book moving.' After weeks of trying and failing to get passage across the Atlantic, a friend suggested that he travel to Nova Scotia and sign up with one of the merchantmen plying the U-boat plagued route between Canada and Britain. Crook travelled north and signed up and after an uneventful voyage reached England, a country he had not seen for over three years.[42]

After a tearful reunion with his father and a hurried wedding to his Canadian sweetheart Isabel, Crook joined the RAF. During the training period, he reflected on his attitude towards the Stalin–Trotsky divide. With the battle of Stalingrad in full flow, Britain was awash with pro-Soviet propaganda and his affections swung back to his former employers. 'I identified with this and suppressed the memory of my Shanghai flirtation with Trotsky in a surge of love for Stalin,' he explained.[43] The next three years saw him posted to India's North West Frontier, Sri Lanka, Burma and Singapore, where his knowledge of Spanish, German, French and Chinese made him suitable for intelligence work, specifically recording intercepted Japanese codes.

Another veteran of Jarama joined Churchill's SOE (Special Operations Executive). Due to his experience before the Civil War in the Merchant Navy, Joe Garber was recruited to take part in maritime expeditions smuggling arms to Albanian partisans. Later in the war, Garber worked with Haganah, a Jewish paramilitary organization set up by the British which operated out of Palestine. In what was an exceptionally varied career, he also became involved in the Stalinist spy ring known as the Red Orchestra, whose agents, placed throughout occupied Europe, provided Moscow with vital information throughout the war.[44]

Other veterans found different ways to contribute to the war effort. Giles Romilly, Tony Hyndman's friend and a nephew of Winston Churchill, worked as a war correspondent for the *Daily Express*. In 1940, whilst reporting from the town of Narvik in Norway, he was caught up in the Nazi invasion and arrested by the Wehrmacht. Classified as a special prisoner due to his family connections, Romilly was imprisoned at Oflag IV-C, a Bavarian castle better known as Colditz. He was later transferred to Oflag VII-D (Tittmoning Castle), where he managed to escape alongside two Dutch officers by abseiling down the walls. Hitler tasked 3,000 men with their recapture. Nevertheless, the escape was entirely successful. Whilst Romilly pretended to be deaf and dumb, the Dutch officers, who were fluent in both German and French, bluffed their way past various German guards. Eventually, the trio worked their way through occupied Europe and reached Allied lines.[45]

André Diamant, the French-Egyptian Jew who had taken command of the 1st Company at Jarama, was also captured by the Nazis. Having failed to recover from the wound he had sustained at Brunete, Diamant had had his leg amputated and was repatriated to France when the International Brigades were disbanded. After the Germans occupied Paris in the summer of 1940, he was betrayed to the Gestapo. He was arrested and executed as an undesirable soon after.[46]

Forty-one years old at the outbreak of hostilities, Tom Wintringham was too old to be called up. Not one to be left out, the former 'English Captain' devised another way of fighting fascism. By the summer of 1940, after the debacle at Dunkirk and with Hitler's troops firmly in control of France and the Low Countries, a wave of defeatism was rolling over Britain. A few figures stood against the tide. As well as those of Churchill and J.B. Priestley, the name of Tom Wintringham came to be associated with this spirit of resistance. Through his books, columns in the *Picture Post* and *Daily Mirror* and broadcasts on the BBC, he encouraged the British people to arm themselves and learn how to fight. The Nazis were coming, or so the country believed, and everyone had to be ready to repel them. On 10 July, with the financial backing of *Picture Post*, Wintringham opened a private training school at Osterley Park in London to teach the basics of guerrilla warfare to members of the Local Defence Volunteers, the forerunner of the Home Guard. Using the experience he had gained in Spain, he held workshops on ambush, sabotage and hit and run raids, whilst the Canadian, Bert 'Yank' Levy, Wintringham's former comrade from Jarama, taught classes on hand-to-hand combat techniques. Although no longer a member of the Communist Party, Wintringham was still a passionate believer in the people's struggle and his lectures were often coloured by his political beliefs. Well aware of Wintringham's revolutionary ideals, but also alive to the effectiveness of his training methods, the government settled on a policy of the gradual absorption of Osterley Park into the Home Guard scheme. By early 1941, after marrying Kitty at a civil service in Dorking, Wintringham realized he no longer had effective control. As a result, in June he resigned as chief training instructor and joined the Home Guard as an ordinary recruit instead.[47]

In 1942 with the threat of invasion dispelled by the successful outcome of the Battle of Britain, Wintringham turned his attention to politics and founded the Common Wealth Party, a socialist organization based on three key principles: Common Ownership, Morality in Politics and Vital Democracy. Over the next three years party members stood in various by-elections and won six seats, although Wintringham himself missed out, narrowly losing at North Midlothian to the Conservative MP, Sir David King Murray by just 869 votes. In the 1945 general election, the party was less successful, with just a single victory out of 23 candidates. After the war Tom and Kitty moved to Broxted and on 26 January 1947, Kitty gave birth to a son. In 1948 they moved again, this time to Edinburgh, where Tom continued to work as a journalist, broadcaster and author. Whilst Tony Hyndman would write that his former captain was haunted by his experiences at Jarama and 'blamed himself for the promotion of Bert [Overton] and the tragic fiasco that followed', in his latter years Wintringham appears to have found a certain peace of mind.[48] A passage in a letter to his son, O.J., written on the latter's twentieth birthday seems to bear this out. 'Happiness, I feel superstitiously,' it begins, 'should never be mentioned in a world such as this that you inherit. Then sometimes it may creep up on you without noticing you are there; and if you politely do not stare at it, may remain about the place.' Not long after writing the letter, Wintringham suffered a heart attack while working on his sister's farm in Lincolnshire. He died shortly afterwards aged fifty-one.[49]

In his later years it seems that Fred Copeman also found inner peace. After quitting the Communist Party in 1938, he 'converted to Moral Rearmament, and later joined the Catholic Church'.[50] When the Second World War came, Copeman helped organize a Civilian Defence Force tasked with preventing casualties from German air-raids in London. He gave several lectures to the Royal Household at Buckingham Palace and in November 1948 was made an officer of the Order of the British Empire. 'I had never dreamed that I should be offered such an honour,' he later confessed. Nevertheless, Copeman was immensely proud: 'life,' he wrote, 'has some amusing turns – Workhouse, Mutineer, Brigade, now O.B.E.'[51] Following his award, Copeman remained active in politics. He was a prominent trade unionist throughout his life and a Labour Party councillor for Lewisham Borough. He died in London in 1983. Kitty and their four children survived him.

Other veterans never got over their involvement in Spain. After the row at King Street in the summer of 1937 and his subsequent dismissal from the army, Jock Cunningham walked out on the Communist Party and tried to put the war behind him. Disgruntled and disillusioned, he took to a nomadic lifestyle, working temporary jobs all over Britain for a few weeks at a time before moving on. He never spoke publicly about his involvement in the war or what had happened at the meeting in King Street and aside from a few close friends like Donald Renton who had fought with the 2nd Company at Jarama, he had little contact with his former comrades. It seems he was bitter about the whole affair and a sense of betrayal lingered. On one occasion at a rally for Aid Spain in Aberdeen, he heckled the speaker Bob Cooney. 'Are ye still at that game yet? Ye'll never get anywhere,' Cunningham called out, before being ushered out of the hall. Cooney had been a commissar in the British Battalion in the latter stages of the war and it may well have been his political connections that provoked the Scot's ire.[52] In 1969 Jock was admitted into Mearnskirk Hospital on the outskirts of Glasgow for a long overdue operation. Whilst removing the machine-gun bullet that had been lodged in his chest for over thirty years, doctors discovered he was in the advanced stages of lung cancer. Cunningham died a few weeks later.[53]

Giles Romilly was another veteran of Jarama who never got over the war. After his escape from Nazi Germany, he went on to write a memoir of his experiences entitled *The Privileged Nightmare* which was published in 1954 and later reissued as *Hostages at Colditz*. The book sold well and he continued to write for the rest of his life, but never achieved the same commercial success. In 1967, whilst researching a book on the 'great American novel' in Berkeley, California, he 'took an overdose of pills ... in a lonely hotel room'. He was pronounced dead at the scene.[54]

In their latter years the surviving veterans began to reflect on their time in Spain. Many felt a sense of bitterness towards the Communist Party, which they believed had betrayed them. Following such calculating examples of Realpolitik as the Molotov–Ribbentrop pact of 1939 and the Soviet invasion of Hungary sixteen years later, they left the party in their droves. Others remained loyal until the bitter end. Patrick Curry was still extolling the virtues of Stalinism in 1976, whilst Tom Spiller, the New Zealander from Overton's 4th Company, also continued to toe the Party line. A fellow socialist who knew him in the mid-1970s recalled that:

> ... he always spoke his mind. Anyone at an SUP (Socialist Unity Party) meeting who ventured the mildest criticism of Uncle Joe in his presence would catch an earful of the industrial transformation of Russia, the arming of the Spanish Republic, the siege of Leningrad, the breakout at Stalingrad and the Red Army's final triumph in Berlin.[55]

Regardless of whether or not they underwent a political epiphany, almost all the veterans felt that they had taken part in something remarkable. Jason Gurney summed up these feelings in the final pages of his posthumously published memoir, *Crusade in Spain*.

> There is no longer any point in trying to untangle the web of lies and confusions which lay behind that ghastly Civil War. There were individuals on both sides who committed every possible form of cruelty and beastliness. And nobody ... came out of it with clean hands. We, of the International Brigades, had wilfully deluded ourselves into the belief that we were fighting for a noble Crusade because we needed a crusade – the opportunity to fight against the manifest evils of Fascism,

in one form or another, which seemed then as if it would overwhelm every value of Western civilisation. We were wrong, we deceived ourselves and were deceived by others: but even then, the whole thing was not in vain. Even at the moments of the greatest gloom and depression, I have never regretted that I took part in it. The situation is not to be judged by what we now know of it, but only as it appeared in the context of the period. And in that context there was a clear choice for anyone who professed to be opposed to Fascism. The fact that others took advantage of our idealism in order to destroy it does not in any way invalidate the decision which we made.[56]

In 1976, the same year in which Gurney's final thoughts were published, George Leeson, one of the machine-gun company captured on the second day at Jarama, was interviewed about his time in Spain.

[It was] the greatest experience of my life, because nothing like that will ever be seen again ... I've never had any regrets that I went. I know a lot of people have said ... [we] were stooges for the Spanish Communist Party ... [but] I don't care, because I still think that the struggle ... was worthwhile... If I were on my death bed and someone said what was the most valuable thing that you've ever done in your life, I shall say the day I decided to go to Spain.[57]

A few months before Leeson's interview, in November 1975, Francisco Franco died. On hearing of his old adversary's demise, Tom 'Kiwi' Spiller bought a round for all the punters in his local, but it was not until eight years later, after Spain had developed into a liberal democracy, that Spiller decided the time was right to return. After flying to Barajas airport in Madrid, he took the bus to Morata de Tajuña and made his way back to the battlefield to lay a wreath for his 'cobber', Fred Robertson, who had been killed during one of the final bayonet charges on 14 February, forty-six years before. His duty done, Spiller returned to New Zealand. He died the following year.[58]

One of the last British survivors of Jarama was James Maley, the Celtic fan who had been captured with the 2nd Company on the afternoon of 13 February. Like Spiller and Patrick Curry, Maley remained faithful to the communists until the end. After a lifetime of political activism and trade union membership, the father of nine passed away shortly after midnight on 8 April 2007. He was ninety-nine years old. Six days later Celtic beat Saint Johnstone 2–1 in the semi-finals of the Scottish cup. Before kick off two 30ft banners were unfurled in the stands. 'James Maley R.I.P.' announced one. *'No Pasarán!'* (they shall not pass) read the other.[59]

APPENDIX 1:
THE BATTLEFIELD TODAY

The battlefield of Jarama has barely changed. The White House no longer exists and a cement factory now dominates the north-eastern horizon, but beyond this the ground remains much the same as when the volunteers went into action. The best way to reach the site is by car. From Madrid take the A3 towards Valencia, turn off onto the M311 just after Vaciamadrid and turn right on the M302 signposted to San Martín de la Vega. On a hill overlooking the junction to the south-west is a memorial to the International Brigades. The battlefield can also be reached by public transport. Take the La Veloz bus from Plaza Conde De Casal (Metro Conde de Casal) to Morata de Tajuña. Ask the driver to drop you off at the San Martín turnoff (M302) or stop at Morata. The battlefield is an hour's walk west on the M302.

The British fought across the plateau and olive groves to the left of the M302 as you head towards San Martín. After nearly a mile you will see the Sunken Road bisecting the olive groves on the left. Half a mile along you will reach a track turning off to the right, which leads to a small plateau. A memorial to the British Battalion now points towards the hills where they fought and died on 12 February 1937. Nothing remains of the White House, but the Conical Hill is immediately recognizable. To the right is the ridgeline where Fry set up his machine guns. A few hundred yards further on is the knoll from where the Moors raked the British lines. Beyond, the skyscrapers of Madrid still shimmer through the haze.

APPENDIX 2:
ORDER OF BATTLE
JARAMA – 11 FEBRUARY 1937

This order of battle is intended only as a guide to the forces involved at Jarama, rather than a comprehensive list. The main source has been Jesús González de Miguel, *La Batalla de Jarama: Febrero de 1937, Testimonios desde un Frente de la Guerra Civil*.

REPUBLICAN FORCES
1st Division
19th Mixed Brigade

23rd Mixed Brigade

XI International Brigade (five battalions)

- Edgar André Battalion (Austro-German)
- Commune de Paris Battalion (Franco-Belgian)
- Thaelmann Battalion (Austro-German)
- 2 x Spanish battalions

Artillery Group

Cavalry Squadron

Sappers

Transmissions unit

Field Hospital

2nd Division

18th Mixed Brigade

24th Mixed Brigade

XII International Brigade (five battalions)

- Dombrowski Battalion (Polish-Balkan)
- Garibaldi Battalion (Italian, Albanian, Spanish)
- André Marty Battalion (Franco-Belgian)
- Madrid Battalion (Spanish)
- Prieto Battalion (Spanish)

Cavalry Squadron

3rd Division

17th Mixed Brigade

45th Mixed Brigade

48th Mixed Brigade

Reserve Group

XV International Brigade (six battalions)

- Abraham Lincoln Battalion (American) (NB: the Abraham
  Lincoln Battalion did not reach the front line until 16 February 1937)
- Dimitrov Battalion (Balkans)
- Franco-Belgian Battalion
- British Battalion
- 2 x Spanish battalions

Sappers

Transmissions unit

Transport section

Services unit

Artillery

5 batteries (3 guns each) – Schneider 75mm Mod.1906

3 batteries (3 guns) – Krupp 77mm FK 1q6

1 battery (3 guns) – Krupp 105mm FH 16

1 battery (3 guns) – Krupp 105mm FH 98/09

2 batteries (3 guns) – Vickers 105mm Mod.1922

16 batteries (3 guns) – QF 1,143mm

27 batteries (2 guns) – Schneider 155mm Mod.1917

1 battery (1 gun) – Krupp 155/26

NATIONALIST FORCES

General Luis Orgaz Yoldi

Colonel José Varela

1st Brigade

Infantry

1st Regiment

3rd *Tabor* of Tiradores of Ifni (Moroccan)

7th *Tabor* of Regulares of Alhucemas (Moroccan)

1st Melilla Battalion (Moroccan)

2nd Regiment

7th *Bandera* Spanish Foreign Legion

Tercio of Requetes of Alcazar (Carlist Militia)

1st Battalion of Argel (Spanish)

Artillery

1 battery of the Support Group – 65/17

4th Battery of the 3rd Light Regiment – Schneider 75/28

7th Battery of the 3rd Light Regiment – Schneider 75/28

Anti-tank

1st Section 2nd Battery of the Anti-tank Group – 5x Pak 35/36 37mm

Sappers

2nd Brigade

Infantry

3rd Regiment

11th *Bandera* Spanish Foreign Legion

1st *Tabor* of the Mehal-la of the Rif (Moroccan)

4th Regiment

1st *Tabor* of Alhucemas (Moroccan)

7th *Tabor* of Tetúan (Moroccan)

Bandera of Falange of Morocco (fascist militia)

Artillery

1 battery of the Support Group – 65/17

3rd Battery of the 13th Light Regiment – Schneider 75/28

4th Battery of the 13th Light Regiment – Schneider 75/28

2nd Battery of the Cueta Group – Vickers 105/22

4th Battery of the Cueta Group – Vickers 105/22

Anti-tank

1 section of the 4th Battery of the Anti-tank Group – 5x Pak 35/36 37mm

Armoured Cars

2nd Company (with the 2nd Section detached) of the Battalion of Armoured Cars – 11 x Panzer I

Sappers

3rd Brigade

Infantry

5th Regiment

1st *Bandera* Spanish Foreign Legion

1st Battalion of the Cazadores of Cueta

6th Regiment

1st *Tabor* of the Tiradores of Ifni (Moroccan)

2nd *Tabor* of the Regulares of Melilla (Moroccan)

Cavalry

2nd Regiment

Commander Ricardo Balmori Díaz

1st & 4th squadrons (+ 1 section of machine gunners) of the Cazadores of Farnesio No.10

3rd Squadron of the Cazadores of Villarrobledo No.1

3rd Squadron (+ 1 section of machine gunners) of the Group of Regulares of Melilla No.2

3rd Regiment

Commander Manuel Jurado Andrés

2nd Squadron of the Group of the Regulares of Alhucemas No.5

3rd, 4th and 6th squadrons (+ 1 section of machine gunners) of the Cazadores of Calatrava No.2

Artillery

1st battery of the Support Group – 65/17

9th Battery of the 13th Light Regiment – Schneider 75/28

Arjona Battery – Schneider 75/28

7th Battery of the 14th Light Regiment – Schneider 75/28

6th Battery of the 12th Light Regiment – Vickers 105/22

4th Battery of the 14th Light Regiment – Vickers 105/22

Anti-tank

2nd Section 1st Battery of the Anti-tank Group – 5 x Pak 35/36 37mm

Armoured Cars

1st Company of the Battalion of Armoured Cars – 15 x Panzer I

Sappers

4th Brigade

Infantry

7th Regiment

1st and 3rd *Tabores* of Regulares of Tetúan (Moroccan)

2nd Expeditionary Battalion of Tenerife

8th Regiment

6th *Bandera* Spanish Foreign Legion

7th *Tabor* of Regulares of Melilla (Moroccan)

Cavalry

1st Regiment

Commander Velasco

3rd Squadron of the Regulares of Alhucemas Group No.5

3rd and 4th squadrons (+ 1 section of machine gunners) of Cazadores of Numancia No.6

1 section of machine gunners of Cazadores of Villarrobledo No.1

Artillery

3rd Battery of the Support Group – 65/17

10th Battery of the 13th Light Regiment – Schneider 75/28

4th Battery of the 15th Light Regiment – Schneider 75/28

Light Battery of the Artillery Academy – Vickers 105/22

5th Battery of the 14th Light Regiment – Vickers 105/22

Anti-tank

1st Section 1st Battery of the Anti-tank Group – 5 x Pak 35/36 37mm

Armoured Cars

3rd Company of the Battalion of Armoured Cars – 11 x Panzer I

Sappers

5th Brigade

Colonel Francisco García Escámez

9th Regiment

5th *Bandera* Spanish Foreign Legion

Bandera of Falange of Valladolid (fascist militia)

10th Regiment

2nd *Tabor* of Regulares of Cueta (Moroccan)

2nd Battalion of Toledo

Artillery

1 battery of the Support Group – 65/17

2nd Battery of the 13th Light Regiment – Schneider 75/28

5th Battery of the 14th Light Regiment – Schneider 75/28

1st Battery of the Cueta Group – Schneider 105/11

5th Battery of the 2nd Mountain Regiment – Schneider 105/11

Anti-tank

2nd Section 2nd Battery of the Anti-tank Group – 5 x Pak 35/36 37mm

Armoured Cars

2nd Section 2nd Company of the Battalion of Armoured Cars – 5 x Panzer I

Sappers

Condor Legion

2 x heavy machine gun battalions

A detachment of Mark I Panzer tanks

1 battery of 88mm guns

Detached Artillery Group

1st Group – 155mm

2nd Battery of the 1st Heavy Regiment – Schneider 155/13

4th Battery of the 1st Heavy Regiment – Schneider 155/13

Reserves

8th *Bandera* Spanish Foreign Legion

2nd Battalion of Serrallo

C Battalion of Cueta

C Battalion of San Fernando

Engineers

1st and 4th units of the Engineers Group of Zaragoza

NOTES

Preface
1. Lewis, p.8.

Introduction
1. Mikhail Bakunin was a former Russian army officer of noble birth. After resigning from the service in 1835 at the age of twenty-one, he travelled to Moscow to study philosophy. There he began moving in radical circles. Later he moved to Dresden and Paris, where he met Karl Marx and acquired a fleeting passion for communism. By now Bakunin's radical views and involvement in popular uprisings had brought him to the attention of the authorities and in 1851, after an idealogical split with the communists (with whom he disagreed about the use of absolute authority) he was deported to Russia and imprisoned in the notorious Peter-Paul Fortress. There he remained until 1857, when, thanks to the appeals of his mother, made directly to Nicholas II, he was released and sent into permanent exile in Siberia. Escaping under the noses of the Russian Imperial Fleet, he travelled through Japan via the United States to London. There he worked on the radical journal *Kolokol* ('The Bell') before moving onto Italy where he met Garibaldi and began to develop his Anarchist ideology. In 1866 he published *Catechism of a Revolutionary*, a virtual manifesto for his new movement, which advocated 'the absolute rejection of every authority'. In 1868 Bakunin joined the Geneva section of the First International, a communist-led movement dedicated to the unification of the radical left. His expulsion by followers of Marx in 1872 illustrated the growing divergence between the two main blocks of left-wing thought. The Social Democratic section, headed by the communists, envisioned the revolution bestowing all political power in the hands of the working classes, whereas the 'anti-authoritarian' section advocated the abolition of the state entirely. Bakunin saw Marx's doctrine of 'The Dictatorship of the Proletariat', an intermediary stage of the revolution which would lead to a classless society without government, as a doomed philosophy. '[The Marxists] maintain that only a dictatorship ... can create the will of the people, while our answer to this is: no dictatorship can have any other aim but that of self-perpetuation, and it can beget only slavery in the people tolerating it; freedom can be

created only by freedom, that is, by a universal rebellion on the part of the people and free organization of the toiling masses from the bottom up'. Bakunin believed in absolute liberty, rejected religion and advocated 'collective anarchism' (a system by which the workers directly managed the means of production and divided the proceeds equally amongst themselves). Bakunin remained active in revolutionary politics until his declining health forced him into hospital in Bern, Switzerland, where he died in 1876.

2. Rankin, pp.79–80.
3. Othen, p.49.
4. Rankin, p.80.
5. Thomas, *The Spanish Civil War*, p.361.
6. Baxell, pp.57–61. From October 1936 the Thaelmann Battalion was part of the XII Brigade, but joined the XI Brigade in November 1936. This reshuffle saw the Germans swap places with the Garibaldi Battalion, as the latter had no rifles.
7. Rust, p.22.
8. Arthur, p.222.
9. Scurr, p.24.
10. Cunningham (ed.), p.30.
11. Thomas, *The Spanish Civil War*, pp.474–75.
12. NMLH, CP/IND/POLL/2/6; *Daily Worker*, 19 January 1937.
13. IWM Sound, Tunnah, 840/5.
14. NMLH, CP/IND/POLL/2/6.
15. Baxell, pp.65–66.
16. Alexander, pp.85–89.
17. Levine, p.37.
18. Alexander, pp.85–89.
19. Beevor, pp.221–33.
20. González de Miguel, p.762.
21. Archivo Militar, Avila. Armario 31, Legajo 1, Carpeta 7, Rollo 275, Documento 6.
22. González de Miguel, pp.113–15; Beevor, pp.232–34.
23. González de Miguel, p.762.
24. Baxell, p.75.

Dramatis Personae

1. Gurney, p.62.
2. Thomas, *The Spanish Civil War*, pp.35–36.
3. MML 21/E/1.
4. Gregory, pp.30–31.
5. MML, 50 O'R 3.
6. Gurney, p.84.
7. IWM 10358 / 1 of 3; Comintern Archives 545 / 6 / 121 / f.46.
8. Copeman, p.82.
9. *Daily Worker*, 17 March 1937; Gurney, p.114; Copeman, p.89.
10. Comintern Archives – 545 / 6 / 124 / f.1; Wintringham, p.196.

11. Graham (ed.), *The Book of the XV Brigade*, p.54; Wintringham, p.226.
12. Strongos, p.133.
13. Gurney, p.72.
14. Ibid., pp.93, 109.
15. Gurney, p.69.
16. IWM Sound, Jones, 9392/3.
17. Comintern Archives – 545 / 6 / 162 / f.38; IWM Sound, Tunnah, 803/ 2 of 4.
18. http://www.jewishvirtuallibrary.org/jsource/History/spanjews.pdf.
19. *The Guardian*, 18 April 2007.
20. Thomas, *The Spanish Civil War*, p.443; Gurney, p.54.
21. Gurney, p.64; Wintringham, pp.103 and 69.
22. Wintringham, pp.148 and 66.
23. Cunningham (ed.), p.33; Wintringham, p.229.
24. Gurney, p.183.
25. Ibid., p.66.
26. Acier (ed.), p.113; Alexander, p.100.
27. *Daily Worker*, 16 March 1937; Hopkins, p.340.
28. Crook, *Memoirs*, http://www.davidcrook.net/simple/contents.html; Comintern Archives – 545 / 6 / 215 / f.26.
29. Copeman, p.79; Cunningham (ed.), p.34; Gurney, p.63.

PART ONE
Part one opener quote 'A Crowd of Boy Scouts': IWM Sound, Curry, 799/1.

Chapter 1

1. Toynbee, *Friends Apart*, p.91.
2. Wintringham, p.145.
3. Ibid.
4. Gurney, pp.88–91.
5. Comintern Archives – 545 / 6 / 93 / folio 1; MML D7 E/1 p.2.
6. NMLH, CP/IND/POLL/2/6; *Daily Worker*, 19 January 1937; MML D7 E/1 p.2.
7. MML 50 O'R 3.
8. Ibid.
9. Stradling, *The Irish and the Spanish Civil War*, p.136.
10. Acier (ed.), p.124; *The Irish Democrat*, 13 November 1937.
11. Gurney, pp.71/2.
12. *The Irish Democrat*, 13 November 1937.
13. Comintern Archives – 545 / 6 / 187 / folio 3; *The Aberdare Leader*, 27 February; *Daily Worker*, 31 December 1936; MML, Box 50 / Mi 1.
14. Gurney, pp.99–101.
15. Gurney, p.63
16. Comintern Archives – 545 / 6 / 91 / folio 80; Wintringham, p.148.
17. Comintern Archives – 545 / 1 / 20 / folio 33.

18. Wintringham, p.146.
19. Gurney, p.102.
20. Memoir of Tom Spiller; MML, A12/F/Spi. *The Manchester Guardian*, 9 December 1938; Comintern Archives 545 / 6 / 182 / folio 34; Hopkins, p.344; Alexander, p.96; Acier (ed.), pp.117–18; Wintringham, pp.171–72.
21. Alexander, p.33; Wintringham, pp.16 and 115; Stradling, *Wales and the Spanish Civil War*, pp.127, 146 and 195; Acier (ed.), p.100; Strongos, *Spanish Thermopylae*, p.178; IWM Sound, Tunnah, 840/6; Comintern Archives – 545 / 6 / 91 / folio 71.
22. Comintern Archives – 545 / 6 / 99 / folio 6, 545 / 6 / 91 / folio 43 and 545 / 6 / 100 / folios 7, 12 and 13.
23. Hopkins, p.340.
24. *The Guardian*, 22 May 1992.
25. *The Sunderland Echo*, 10 April 1937; *North Mail*, 29 December 1936.
26. MML, Box A15/2.
27. Cunningham (ed.), p.33; Mitford, p.95.
28. Baxell, p.22; Brandon, p.214; Comintern Archives – 545 / 6 / 99 / folios 2, 3 and 6; MML, Box 50, Gy/2; Coward, pp.2–6; Gray, p.29.
29. Derby (ed.), p.46.
30. O'Connor, p.i.

Chapter 2

1. Toynbee, *Friends Apart*, p.90.
2. Levine, pp.29–30.
3. *The [Reading] Evening Gazette*, 11 March 1937.
4. Gregory, pp.19 and 21.
5. Comintern Archives – 545 / 6 / 162 / folio 38; IWM Sound, Leeson, 803/1.
6. IWM Sound, Charlesworth, 798/1.
7. IWM Sound, Jones, 9392/3; *The Aberdare Leader*, 27 February 1937.
8. The story of the Mitford sisters is a tragic tale that encapsulates the political upheavals of the 1930s. Whilst Jessica was a communist, two of her sisters were on the opposite side of the ideological divide. Diana married Oswald Mosley, the leader of the British Union of Fascists, whilst Unity met Hitler on a trip to Germany before the outbreak of the Second World War. After war was declared she tried to commit suicide, suffered brain damage as a result and died six years later from complications. For more on the Mitford sisters see Jessica's marvellous memoir, *Hons and Rebels*.
9. Cunningham (ed.), pp.32–33.
10. Gurney, pp.38–39.
11. Gary, p.37; IWM Sound, Maley, 11947/1.
12. *North Mail*, 29 December 1936.
13. Lewis and Gledhill (eds), p.36.
14. Gurney, p.39.
15. Gurney, p.39; Gregory, pp.23–25.
16. IWM Sound, Leeson, 803/1.

17. Derby (ed.), p.47.
18. MML, Sexton's Memoirs, A15/2.
19. Gurney, p.41.
20. Crook, *Memoirs*.
21. Comintern Archives – 545 / 6 / 198 / folio 24.
22. Gregory, p.25.
23. Lewis and Gledhill (eds), p.37.
24. Grey, p.41.
25. Ibid.; Gurney, p.42.
26. Gregory, p.25.
27. Ibid.
28. Watson and Corcoran, pp.54–55.
29. Crook, *Memoirs*.
30. IWM Sound, Wild, 10358/1.
31. Graham (ed.), *The Book of the XV Brigade*, p.30.
32. Gurney, p.45.
33. Crook, *Memoirs*.
34. IWM Sound, Copeman, 794/1
35. *TCD: A College Miscellany*, 27 March 1937.
36. Corcoran, *The Rev. Robert Martin Hilliard, Journal of the Kerry Archaeological & Historical Society*, 5:2, 2005.
37. Gurney, p.69.
38. Ibid., pp.47–52.
39. Gregory, pp.26–27.
40. Gurney, p.47.
41. Ibid., p.52.
42. Ibid., p.53.
43. Gregory, p.28.
44. Gurney, p.53.
45. Lewis and Gledhill (eds), p.39.
46. Beevor, pp.180–81.
47. Gurney, pp.54 and 58.
48. Cunningham (ed.), pp.33–34.

Chapter 3

1. Gurney, p.58.
2. Copeman, p.79.
3. *A Cause Worth Fighting For*, 9 minutes.
4. Gurney, p.58.
5. Crook, *Memoirs*.
6. Gregory, p.29.
7. *North Mail*, 29 December 1937; Graham (ed.), *Battle of Jarama*, p.72.
8. Comintern Archives – 545 / 6 / 89 / folios 47–58 and 545 / 6 / 198 / folio 19; MML,

Sexton's Memoirs, A15/2.

9. Gregory, p.28.
10. Crook, *Memoirs*.
11. Comintern Archives – 545 / 6 / 134 / folios 2–5 and 545 / 6 / 99 / folio 4.
12. Gregory, p.31.
13. *The Aberdare Leader*, 17 and 24 April 1937.
14. Gregory, pp.31–32.
15. IWM Sound, Copeman, 794/1.
16. Comintern Archives – 545 / 6 / 93 / folios 23–27. 545 / 6 / 96 / folio 36. 545 / 6 / 97 / folio 7. 545 / 6 / 122 / folios 31–40.
17. Gregory, p.32; Gurney, p.81; Gray, p.74.
18. Gurney, p.61.
19. IWM Sound, Leeson, 803/2.
20. Wintringham, p.110.
21. *Daily Worker*, 20 January 1937.
22. Levine, p.33.
23. IWM Sound, Curry, 799/1.
24. Copeman, p.81.
25. Comintern Archives – 545 / 6 / 129 / folios 71–130.
26. *A Cause Worth Fighting For*, 13 minutes 44 seconds.
27. IWM Sound, Copeman, 794/1.
28. Alexander, p.69.
29. Copeman, p.82.
30. *The Aberdare Leader*, 24 April 1937.
31. Copeman, p.82.
32. Gurney, pp.81–82.
33. Baxell, pp.71–73.
34. Gurney, p.83.
35. Cunningham (ed.), p.36.
36. Crook, *Memoirs*.

Chapter 4

1. Wintringham, p.116.
2. Gregory, p.30.
3. Gurney, p.79.
4. Comintern Archives – 545 / 6 / 120 / folio 78.
5. Crook, *Memoirs*; MML, A12/Wi/1.
6. IWM Sound, Jones, 9392/6.
7. *Daily Worker*, 19 February 1937.
8. Wintringham, p.102.
9. *Daily Worker*, 6 March 1937; Comintern Archives – 545 / 6 / 105 / folios 89–107.
10. IWM Sound, Curry, 799/1.
11. IWM Sound, Copeman, 794/1 p.11 and 794/2 p.13.

12. Ibid., 794/1 and 12; Copeman, p.11.
13. Wintringham, p.185.
14. Gurney, p.84; MacDougall (ed.), p.61.
15. Crook's diary, MML, D4 Cr/3 p.11; IWM Sound, Tunnah, 840/9.
16. Wintringham, p.185.
17. Ibid., p.160; NMLH, CP/IND/POLL/2/6; Cooper and Parks, p.33; Gurney, p.112; Comintern Archives – 545 / 6 / 139 / folios 1–8.
18. *The Irish Democrat*, 13 November 1937.
19. The Junkers 87 (Stuka) dive bomber, the 88mm anti-aircraft / anti-tank gun and the Me109 fighter plane were all first tested in Spain.
20. *The Irish Democrat*, 13 November 1937.
21. Graham (ed.), *Battle of Jarama*, p.66.
22. Gurney, p.102.
23. MML D7 E/1 p.3.
24. *The Irish Democrat*, 13 November 1937; Westwell, p.26.
25. *The Irish Democrat*, 13 November 1937; Gurney, p.99; IWM Sound, Copeman, 794/13.
26. *The Daily Worker*, 16 March 1937; Gurney, p.114.
27. Comintern Archives – 545 / 6 / 122 / folios 44 and 45; *The Daily Worker*, 16 March 1937; Gurney, p.114.
28. MacDougall (ed.), p.61.
29. *The Irish Democrat*, 13 November 1937.
30. Ibid.
31. MML, Spiller's Memoirs, A12/F/Spi.
32. IWM Sound, Charlesworth, 798/4.
33. IWM Sound, Copeman, 794/2.
34. Wintringham, p.148.
35. Ibid.; Purcell, p.7.
36. IWM Sound, Maley, 11947/1; Gray, p.37.
37. MML, Box D7 E/1, p.6.
38. Wintringham, p.160; NMLH, CP/IND/POLL/2/6.
39. Wintringham, pp.148–49.
40. Ibid., p.149.
41. Archivo Militar de Avila, Zona National, Rollo 275, Armario 31, Legajos 1, Carpeta 7, Documentos 3 and 6.
42. Archivo Militar de Madrid, Zona National, Rollo 9, Legajos 16/17, Carpeta 9, Folios 2, 5, 7, 10–12; Rollo 10, Legajos 19, Carpeta 8, Folios 13, 17, 27; Rollo 78, Legajos 1, Carpeta 22, Folios 14, 16, 21–22.
43. Thomas, *Brother against Brother*, p.53.
44. Ibid., pp.2 and 4–5; Scurr, pp.21–24; Sánchez Ruano, p.197.
45. Othen, pp.31, 33–34, 39 and 196.
46. *Manchester Guardian*, 12 March 1937.
47. Othen, pp.193–94; MML, A12, Kr/3.
48. MML, A12, Kr/3

49. IWM Sound, Copeman, 794/9.
50. *Daily Worker*, 16 December 1936.

Chapter 5

1. IWM Sound, Copeman, 794/2; MML, 50, Gy/2; IWM Sound, Gregory, 8851/2; Gregory, p.45.
2. *The Irish Democrat*, 13 November 1937.
3. Wintringham, p.151.
4. IWM Sound, Curry, 799/1.
5. IWM Sound, Tunnah, 840/9.
6. Comintern Archives – 545 / 6 / 105 / folios 89–107.
7. IWM Sound, Jones, 9326/6.
8. Ibid.
9. *The Irish Democrat*, 20 November 1937.
10. IWM Sound, Leeson, 803/2.
11. Copeman, p.89.
12. Gurney, p.108.
13. *The Irish Democrat*, 20 November 1937.
14. MML, Box 21, B, 30.
15. Gregory, p.45; Wintringham, p.167; IWM Sound, Charlesworth, 798/1.
16. Gurney, pp.107–08.
17. Ibid., p.43.
18. Wintringham, pp.152–53.
19. Ibid., p.155.
20. Ibid., p.156.
21. *The Irish Democrat*, 20 November 1937.
22. IWM Sound, Fanning, 850/3.
23. Crook, *Memoirs*.
24. Hopkins, p.189.
25. *The Irish Democrat*, 20 November 1937.
26. Wintringham, p.157.
27. Ibid., p.157 8.
28. MML, D7 E/1.
29. Comintern Archives – 545 / 6 / 198 / folio 24; MML, Sexton's Memoirs, A15/2.
30. Gurney, p.99.
31. Wintringham, p.158
32. Corkhill and Rawnsley (eds), p.75.
33. IWM Sound, Leeson, 803/2.

PART TWO
Part 2 opener quote: 'Death Stalked the Olive Groves', Cunningham (ed.), p.36.

Chapter 6
1. IWM Sound, Curry, 799/1.
2. Copeman, p.89.
3. IWM Sound, Copeman, 794/2.
4. Wintringham, pp.13, 78–79 and 170; MML, A12/F/Spi; *The New Zealand Herald*, 25 April 2009; Gurney, p.107.
5. NMLH, CP/IND/POLL/2/6.
6. Wintringham, pp.13 and 169; MML A12.F/Spi.
7. Wintringham, p.167.
8. *The Sunderland Echo*, 10 April 1937.
9. Gregory, p.45; Wintringham, pp.173–74.
10. Wintringham, p.171.
11. Ibid., pp.166, 169 and 170–71.
12. Gregory, p.47; Gurney, p.107; Wintringham, p.176; IWM Sound, Charlesworth, 798/1.
13. Wintringham, p. 229
14. Ibid., p.174; NMLH, CP/IND/POLL/2/6.
15. IWM Sound, Jones, 9392/6.
16. Graham (ed.), *The Book of the XV Brigade*, p.50.
17. IWM Sound, Copeman, 794/2; Graham (ed.), *Battle of Jarama*, p.2; Arcier (ed.), pp.116–17; *The Irish Democrat*, 20 November 1937.
18. *The Irish Democrat*, 20 November 1937; Comintern Archives – 545 / 6 / 114 / folio 37; IWM Sound, Charlesworth, 798/1.
19. Graham (ed.), *The Book of the XV Brigade*, p.62; *The Daily Worker*, 6 and 16 March 1937; MacDougall (ed.), p.61; Alexander, p.96.
20. Wintringham, p.196.
21. MML, D7/E1.
22. IWM Sound, Copeman, 794/2.
23. Copeman, pp.90–91.
24. Wintringham, p.181.
25. Gurney, p.64; Wintringham, p.99.
26. Wintringham, pp.98–99.
27. Ibid., pp.181–82.

Chapter 7
1. *The Guardian*, 10 December 1990
2. IWM Sound, Aitken, 10357/3.
3. Alexander, p.74.
4. IWM Sound, Copeman, 794/13; Comintern Archives – 545 / 6 / 97 / folio 12 and 545 / 6 / 90 / folio 7; Wintringham, p.160.
5. IWM Sound, Copeman, 794/13.

6. Wintringham, p.184.
7. *The Guardian*, 8 May 2004; Gurney, p.67.
8. http://www.webspotter.com/popboffin/chapter4.htm.
9. Cunningham (ed.), p.35.
10. Wintringham, pp.186–87.
11. Ibid., pp.187–88; *Daily Worker*, 31 December 1936.
12. Graham (ed.), *The Book of the XV Brigade*, p.63.
13. Coward, p.7.
14. Wintringham, p.189.
15. Ibid., p.189; MML, D7, E1.
16. MML, D4/Cr3, p34.
17. *The Aberdare Leader*, 27 March 1937.
18. Crook, *Memoirs*.
19. Watson and Corcoran, p.56.
20. Wintringham, p.190.
21. Ibid.
22. Ibid., pp.190–91.
23. MML Box C 10/8.
24. IWM Sound, Copeman, 794/13.
25. Graham (ed.), *The Book of the XV Brigade*, p.63.
26. MML, D7, E1, p.23.
27. *Daily Worker*, 18 March 1937.
28. Ibid.
29. Hopkins, p.189.
30. Crook, *Memoirs*.
31. Graham (ed.), *Battle of Jarama*, pp.67 and 72.
32. *The Guardian*, 22 May 1992.
33. Hopkins, p.344.
34. Wintringham, p.78.
35. Graham (ed.), *Battle of Jarama*, p.67.
36. *The Guardian*, 10 November 2000.
37. Gregory, p.48.
38. IWM Sound, Gregory, 8851/2.
39. Ibid.; Gregory, pp.47–49.
40. IWM Sound, Fanning, 850/3.

Chapter 8

1. IWM Sound, Tunnah, 840/7.
2. IWM Sound, Garber, 12291/10.
3. IWM Sound, Copeman, 794/2.
4. Ibid.
5. Copeman, p.93.
6. *The Guardian*, 10 November 2000.

7. Watson and Corcoran, p.56.
8. Archivo Militar de Avila, Zona National, Rollo 275, Armario 31, Legajos 1, Carpeta 7, Documento 3; IWM Sound, Copeman, 794/2 and 13.
9. *The Guardian*, 10 November 2000.
10. IWM Sound, Garber, 12291/10.
11. IWM Sound, Tunnah, 840/7.
12. IWM Sound, Copeman, 794/13.
13. Wintringham, p.193.
14. IWM Sound, Tunnah, 840/7.
15. Copeman, p.93.
16. Wintringham, p.193.
17. MML, Box A15/2.
18. Wintringham, pp.193–94.
19. Ibid.
20. IWM Sound, Tunnah, 840/7.
21. IWM Sound, Copeman, 794/2.
22. Cunningham (ed.), p.35.
23. Cook, p.75.
24. Cunningham (ed.), p.35.
25. Alexander, p.97; MML, Box D7, E1, p.2; Comintern Archives – 545 / 6 / 134 / folios 2–6 and 545 / 6 / 99 / folio 4 and 545 / 6 / 89 / folio 6.
26. Gregory, pp.49–50.
27. IWM, Wild, 10358/1.
28. Crook, *Memoirs*.
29. Ibid.
30. MML, Box 50, BK1.
31. *The Irish Democrat*, 20 November 1937.
32. *Daily Worker*, 18 March 1937.
33. Gurney, pp.113–14.

Chapter 9

1. Graham (ed.), *The Book of the XV Brigade*, pp.41–46.
2. González de Miguel, pp.762–63.
3. MML, Box D7, E1; Wintringham, pp.194–96.
4. Gurney, p.116.
5. Ibid.
6. MML, Box A15/2.
7. Wintringham, pp.197 and 198.
8. Ibid., p.198.
9. IWM Sound, Curry, 799/1.
10. Gurney, p.71.
11. *Daily Worker*, 16 March 1937.
12. *Manchester Guardian*, 9 December 1938.

13. Cunningham (ed.), p.35; Wintringham, pp.198–99; MML, Box A15/2 p.13.
14. Cunningham (ed.), p.35.
15. Wintringham, p.199.
16. Ibid., p.201.
17. MML, Box A15/2 p.13; MML, Box D7, E/1 p.4.
18. Wintringham, p.200.
19. Copeman, pp.93–94.
20. Ibid., pp.94–95; IWM Sound, Copeman, 794/2 pp.20/1.
21. Wintringham, p.201.
22. Comintern Archives – 545 / 1 / 2 / folios 85– 87; IWM Sound, Tunnah, 840/7.
23. MacDougall (ed.), p.37.
24. MML, D7 E1 p.16.
25. Wintringham, p.203
26. Ibid., pp.203–04.
27. MML, D7 E1 p.16.
28. MacDougall (ed.), p.37.
29. Copeman, p.95.
30. IWM Sound, Tunnah, 840–9.
31. Gurney, pp.117–18.
32. Ibid.
33. Ibid.
34. Wintringham, p.206.

Chapter 10

1. MML, D7, E1, p.16.
2. Wintringham, p.207.
3. Gurney, p.118.
4. Wintringham, p.207.
5. Ibid.
6. Ibid.
7. Copeman, p.95.
8. Wintringham, p.209.
9. AMM, Archivo Nationalista, Rollo 9, Armario 16/17, Carpeta 9, Documento 7–12; Wintringham, pp.209–10.
10. MML, D7, E1, p.16.
11. Ibid.
12. Wintringham, p.109.
13. Beevor, p.188.
14. Wintringham., p.212.
15. Gurney, p.119.
16. Wintringham, p.211.
17. MML, Box A15/2, p.15.
18. *Herald Scotland*, 3 February 2001.

19. *Daily Mail*, 13 and 15 February 1937.
20. Gurney, p.32.
21. See Wintringham's biography (by Purcell) for further details. Also the Comintern Archives in Moscow – 545 / 6 / 216 / folios 74–108.
22. Purcell, pp.122–24.
23. MML, D7, E1, p.4; Wintringham, p.211.
24. Comintern Archives – 545 / 1 / 2 / folios 85–87; MML, Box A15/2, p.15.
25. Wintringham, p.212.
26. http://www.grahamstevenson.me.uk/index.php?option=com_content&view=article&id=549:dave-springhall-&catid=19:s&Itemid=131
27. Gurney, p.119.
28. Wintringham, p.213.
29. Ibid., p.214.
30. Ibid., p.233; Comintern Archives – 545 / 1 / 2 / folios 85– 87.
31. Wintringham, p.174; http://www.anb.org/articles/20/20-01892.html
32. Wintringham, pp.214–15.

Chapter 11

1. Wintringham, p.216.
2. Ibid., pp.216–17.
3. Ibid., pp.218–219.
4. Graham (ed.), *Battle of Jarama*, p.18.
5. Wintringham, p.220.
6. NMLH, CP/IND/POLL/2/6.
7. Wintringham, p.219.
8. Ibid., p.221.
9. MML, D7 E1, p.23.
10. There is some confusion as to when exactly Charlesworth was wounded. In his own account in the Imperial War Museum's archives (IWM Sound, 798 1/4), he places the incident on 12 February. Records in the Comintern Archives in Moscow (545 / 6 / 114 / folio 32), however, state that it happened on the 13th. As the latter were made some forty years closer to the incident in question I have favoured them here.
11. Wintringham, pp.221 and 222.
12. Ibid., p.222.
13. MML, D7 E1, p.17.

Chapter 12

1. IWM Sound, Leeson, 803/3.
2. Wintringham, pp.222–23.
3. Ibid., p.223.
4. IWM Sound, Graham, 1187/2
5. MML, 21/F/6.
6. MML, D7, E1, p.17.

7. IWM Sound, Leeson, 803/4; Comintern Archives – 545 / 1 / 2 / folios 85–87.
8. Wintringham, p.224.
9. Baxell, p.81; Strongos, p.178.
10. MacDougall (ed.), pp.26 and 36; MML, D7 E1, p.18; Comintern Archives – 545 / 1 / 2 / folios 85–87.
11. Wintringham, p.224.
12. MML, D7 E1, pp.18/9.
13. Ibid.
14. Gurney, p.121.
15. http://www.spectacle.co.uk/archive_production.php?id=211
16. Wintringham, p.225.
17. http://www.spectacle.co.uk/archive_production.php?id=211
18. *The Sunderland Echo*, 10 April 1937; IWM Sound, Jones, 9392/4.
19. Gurney, p.122.
20. Ibid.
21. MacDougall (ed.), p.37.
22. Ibid., p.38.
23. MML, 21 F/6; MacDougall (ed.), p.26.
24. MacDougall (ed.), p.26.
25. MacDougall (ed.), p.48; MML, 21 F/6; Comintern Archives – 545 / 1 / 2 / folios 85–87.
26. Wintringham, p.228.
27. Gurney, p.123.
28. Cook, p.67.
29. Ibid.
30. MML, D7 E1, p.9.
31. MML, A15/2, p.16.

Chapter 13

1. Comintern Archives – 545 / 6 / 93 / folio 1.
2. Wintringham, p.229; MML A15/2, p.16.
3. Comintern Archive – 545 / 6 / 95 / folio 42; Baxell, pp.56–59.
4. Copeman, p.82.
5. IWM Sound, Greenhalgh, 111879/6; IWM Sound, Jones, 9392.
6. IWM Sound, Aitken, 10357/2.
7. Cook, p.68.
8. IWM Sound, Aitken, 10357.
9. Gregory, pp.50–52.
10. Purcell, pp.138–39.
11. Gurney, p.123.
12. *The Aberdare Leader*, 1 May 1937.
13. IWM Sound, Jones, 9392.
14. MML, A15/2, p.16.
15. IWM Sound, Aitken, 10357.

16. MML, D7, E1, p.9; IWM Sound, Aitken, 10357.
17. MML, A15/2, p.16.
18. Wintringham, p.238.
19. MML, D7, E1, p.10.
20. IWM Sound, Aitken, 10357.
21. MML, D7, E1, p.4.
22. Gurney, pp.123–25.
23. Wintringham, p.230.

Chapter 14

1. *The Aberdare Leader*, 1 May 1937.
2. Wintringham, pp.230–32.
3. Ibid., p.231.
4. MML, D7, E1, p.11.
5. Ibid.
6. Ibid.
7. MML, A15/2, p.16.
8. Comintern Archives – 545 / 6 / 106 / folios 4–5.
9. MML, D7, E1, p.11.
10. IWM Sound, Aitken, 10357.
11. MML, D7, E1, p.6; Comintern Archives – 545 / 6 / 90 / folio 5.
12. IWM Sound, Economides, 10428/3.
13. *The Aberdare Leader*, 8 May 1937; MML, A15/2, p.16.
14. MML, D7, E1, pp.6–7.
15. Ibid.
16. Rust, p.49; MML, A15/2, p.17.
17. MML, A12, F/Spi.
18. IWM Sound, Garber, 14277/4.
19. MML, A12, F/Spi.
20. *The Aberdare Leader*, 1 May 1937.
21. MML, D7, E1, p.12.
22. Ibid.
23. MML, D7, E1, p.12; Wintringham, p.232; *The Aberdare Leader*, 1 May 1937.
24. Lewis and Gledhill (eds), p.46.
25. Copeman, p.96.
26. MML, D7, E1, p.13.
27. MML, A12, F/Spi.
28. MML, A15/2, p.16.
29. Graham (ed.), *The Book of the XV Brigade*, p.63.
30. IWM Sound, Economides, 10428/3.
31. MML, A12, F/Spi.
32. Ibid.
33. Ibid.

34. MML, D7, E1, p.24.
35. MML, A15/2, p.17.
36. MML, D7, E1, p.24.

Chapter 15

1. Cook, p.68.
2. MML, D7, E1, p.14.
3. Graham (ed.), *Battle of Jarama*, p.68.
4. MML, D7, E1, p.24.
5. MML, A12, F/Spi.
6. MML, D7, E1, pp.13–14.
7. Wintringham, p.232.
8. IWM Sound, Garber, 14277/4.
9. Graham (ed.), *The Book of the XV Brigade*, p.58.
10. Ibid., p.60. MML, D7, E1, p.14.
11. Graham (ed.), *The Book of the XV Brigade*, p.60.
12. Ibid., p.60.
13. MML, D7, E1, p.14.
14. Wintringham, p.233.
15. Graham (ed.), *The Book of the XV Brigade*, p.60.
16. *The Aberdare Leader*, 1 May 1937.
17. Graham (ed.), *The Book of the XV Brigade*, p.60.
18. MML, D7, E1, p.15.
19. Graham (ed.), *The Book of the XV Brigade*, p.60.
20. MML, A12, F/Spi.
21. Derby (ed.), p.47.
22. *The New Zealand Herald*, 25 April 2009; http://c20c.wordpress.com/2008/04/.
23. Graham (ed.), *The Book of the XV Brigade*, p.61; Wintringham, pp.233–34.

PART THREE

Chapter 16

1. Gray, pp.209–10. Chapayev was a hero of the Red Army during the Russian Civil War.
2. Baxell, p.84; Gregory, p.57.
3. NMLH, CP/IND/POLL/2/6.
4. Rust, pp.67–68; IWM Sound, Aitken, 10357/2.
5. Baxell, p.85.
6. Comintern Archives – 545 / 6 / 134 / folios 2–6 and 545 / 6 / 99 / folio 4.
7. Comintern Archives – 545 / 6 / 114 / folio 37; 545 / 6 / 99 / folios 8 and 28; see also 545 / 6 / 88 / folios 1 and 2.
8. Comintern Archives – 545 / 6 / 151 / folio 35.
9. Cunningham (ed.), p.37.
10. Ibid., pp.37–38.

11. Comintern Archives – 545 / 6 / 151 / folio 35.
12. Crook, *Memoirs*; *Manchester Guardian*, 9 April 1937; Comintern Archives – 545 / 6 / 148 / folio 26.
13. Beevor, pp.305–06.
14. Crook, *Memoirs*.
15. Comintern Archives – 545 / 6 / 99 / folios 2 and 3.
16. Gray, p.62.
17. Ibid., p.58.
18. Comintern Archives – 545 / 6 / 100 / folios 7, 12 and 13.
19. Gray, p.62.
20. Ibid., p.60.
21. Alexander, p.184.
22. MacDougall (ed.), p.50.
23. Graham (ed.), *The Book of the XV Brigade*, p.199.
24. Gray, pp.62–64.
25. Gurney, p.167.
26. Ibid.
27. Lewis and Gledhill (eds), pp.55–56.
28. NMLH, CP/IND/POLL/2/6.
29. Comintern Archives – 545 / 6 / 107 / folios 4–7.
30. Ibid.
31. NMLH, CP/IND/POLL/2/6.
32. Gregory, p.62; Copeman, pp.125–26; Baxell, p.86; Graham (ed.), *Battles of Brunete and the Aragon*, p.9.
33. Copeman, p.131.
34. Graham (ed.), *Battles of Brunete and the Aragon*, p.14; Gregory, pp.69–71.
35. Copeman, p.132.
36. *The Reading Standard*, 18 November 1937. This article is based on the story of Frank Hillsey, a former soldier from Reading who claimed to have served in the British Battalion. Although many of the details he provided are convincing, others are demonstrably false and there is no record of him in the Moscow files. After discussing the matter with Bill Alexander, a former commander of the British Battalion in Spain, the authors of *We Cannot Park on both Sides* (a book on the volunteers from Reading) have suggested two possible explanations for this. 1. Hillsey served under an alias (as several volunteers did), and exaggerated his story for dramatic effect. 2. He did not actually serve in Spain, but got his information from a veteran.
37. Copeman, p.132.
38. IWM Sound, Graham, 11877/3.
39. Thomas, *The Spanish Civil War*, p.692.
40. Baxell, p.85.
41. Graham (ed.), *The Book of the XV Brigade*, pp.175–76.
42. Alexander, p.129; Lewis and Gledhill (eds), p.77; Thomas, *The Spanish Civil War*, p.693.
43. IWM Sound, Charlesworth, 9427/3.

44. Graham (ed.), *The Book of the XV Brigade*, p.189; Comintern Archives – 545 / 1 / 5 / folio 34; *The New Zealand Herald*, 25 April 2009; http://www.nzhistory.net.nz/war/spanish-civil-war/new-zealanders-in-spain

45. Copeman, p.135.

46. Comintern Archives – 545 / 2 / 70 / folio 56; 545 / 6 / 99 / folio 6 and 545 / 6 / 88 / folios 1 and 2.

47. Copeman, p.137.

48. Alexander, p.131.

49. Comintern Archives – 545 / 6 / 121 / folio 46.

50. Copeman, pp.139–40.

51. Ibid.

52. Baxell, p.95.

53. Copeman, pp.139–40.

Chapter 17

1. Gregory, p.88.

2. Purcell, p.152.

3. Graham (ed.), *The Book of the XV Brigade*, p.243.

4. Alexander, p.149.

5. Baxell, p.98.

6. Ibid.; Graham (ed.), *The Book of the XV Brigade*, p.298.

7. Graham (ed.), *The Book of the XV Brigade*, p.298.

8. Copeman, p.142.

9. Ibid., p.145.

10. Alexander, p.161.

11. Baxell, p.101.

12. Alexander, p.82.

13. Baxell, pp.144–45.

14. Gray, p.180.

15. Baxell, p.101.

16. Beevor, pp.361–62; Alexander, p.170; Baxell, p.103.

17. IWM Sound, Graham, 11877/5.

18. Rust, p.147.

19. Gregory, p.106.

20. Baxell, p.103.

21. Gregory, p.108.

22. Baxell, pp.104–05 and 120.

23. IWM Sound, Charlesworth, 798–3.

24. Gregory, pp.109–12.

25. Rust, p.158.

Chapter 18

1. Beevor, p.389.
2. IWM Sound, Charlesworth, 9427/3.
3. Gregory, p.113.
4. Rust, p.164.
5. Ibid., p.167.
6. Ibid., p.171.
7. Beevor, pp.389–91; Thomas, *The Spanish Civil War*, p.816.
8. Thomas, *The Spanish Civil War*, pp.816–18; Beevor, p.391; Baxell, pp.109–10.
9. Gregory, p.121.
10. Ibid., p.122.
11. Baxell, pp.111–12.
12. Gregory, pp.125–26.
13. Ibid., p.26.
14. Alexander, pp.210–11; Baxell, p.112; Beevor, p.398; Gray, p.189.
15. Gregory, p.134.
16. Alexander, p.214; Baxell, p.112.
17. Baxell, p.114.
18. Alexander, p.240.

Epilogue

1. Lewis, p.51.
2. Clark, p.117.
3. Ibid., p.118; Alexander, p.241.
4. IWM Sound, Charlesworth, 9427/3.
5. Clark, p.118.
6. IWM Sound, Charlesworth, 9427/3.
7. Williamson, p.62.
8. Gray, pp.201–02.
9. Alexander, pp.241–42.
10. *North Mail*, 29 December 1937.
11. Gregory, pp.138–39.
12. Ibid.
13. Ibid., pp.142–43.
14. Ibid., pp.150–52.
15. Baxell, p.133; Alexander, p.194.
16. Toynbee (ed.), *The Distant Drum*, p.129.
17. IWM Sound, Jones, 9392/6.
18. Ibid.
19. Gurney, p.174.
20. Gregory, p.153.
21. Ibid.
22. Ibid., pp.154–55.

23. Ibid.
24. *Manchester Guardian*, 3 May 1937.
25. MML, Box 21 /E/ 1
26. Purcell, p.159.
27. Ibid., pp.160–63.
28. Copeman, p.152.
29. Ibid., pp.154–55.
30. Ibid., p.155.
31. Ibid., p.159.
32. Ibid., pp.161 and 74.
33. Ibid., pp.170–71.
34. Ibid., pp.179–80.
35. Alexander, pp.247–49; IWM Sound, Leeson, 803/3.
36. IWM Sound, Leeson, 803/3.
37. IWM Sound, Wild, 10358/2.
38. Gregory, p.178.
39. IWM Sound, Charlesworth, 798/4.
40. Crook, *Memoirs*.
41. Ibid.
42. Ibid.
43. Ibid.
44. http://www.jewishvirtuallibrary.org/jsource/History/spanjews.pdf.
45. For more details of Romilly's wartime adventures see: Romilly and Alexander, *Hostages of Colditz*, (New York, Praeger, 1973).
46. Colman, p.6.
47. Purcell, pp.169–208.
48. Toynbee (ed.), *The Distant Drum*, p.130.
49. Purcell, pp.209–50.
50. Gurney, p.71.
51. Copeman, p.201.
52. MacDougall (ed.), p.120.
53. Information supplied by DeeDee Cunningham.
54. Toynbee (ed.), *The Distant Drum*, p.130.
55. Derby (ed.), p.49.
56. Gurney, pp.188–89.
57. IWM Sound, Leeson, 803/3.
58. Derby (ed.), p.50.
59. *Herald Scotland*, 14 April 2007; *The Independent*, 18 April 2007.

BIBLIOGRAPHY

Archives
Imperial War Museum, London (IWM)
Marx Memorial Library, London (MML)
National Museum of Labour History, Manchester (NMLH)
Archivo General Militar, Madrid
Archivo General Militar, Avila, Spain
Comintern Archives, Moscow

Newspapers and Magazines
The Aberdare Leader (1937)
The Daily Telegraph (1937)
Daily Worker (1936, 1937)
The [Newcastle] Evening Chronicle (1937)
The [Reading] Evening Gazette (1937)
The Evening Standard (1937)
The Glasgow Herald (1937)
The Guardian (1990, 1992, 2000)
Herald Scotland (2001)
The Independent (2007)
The Irish Democrat (1937)
Journal of the Kerry Archaeological & Historical Society (2005)
The Manchester Guardian (1937, 1938)
The New Zealand Herald (2009)
North Mail (1936, 1937)
The Oldham Evening Chronicle (1937)
The Reading Standard (1937)
The Scottish Daily Express (1937)
The Sunderland Echo and Shipping Gazette (1937)

260

TCD: A College Miscellany (1937)
The Times (1937)

Documentaries
Yesterday's Witness: A Cause Worth Fighting For, BBC, 1973

Primary Sources
Acier, Marcel (ed.), *From Spanish Trenches: Recent Letters From Spain* (New York, Modern Age Books, 1937)

Arthur, Max (ed.), *The Real Band of Brothers: First Hand Accounts from the Last British Survivors of the Spanish Civil War* (London, Collins, 2009)

Clark, Bob, *No Boots to my Feet: Experiences of a Britisher in Spain* (Newcastle, People's Publications, 1984)

Colman, Jud, *Memories of Spain* (privately printed, 1995)

Copeman, Fred, *Reason in Revolt* (London, Blandford Press, 1948)

Corkhill, David and Rawnsley, Stuart (eds), *The Road to Spain: Anti-Fascists at War 1936–1939* (Dunfermline, Borderline Press, 1981)

Coward, Jack, *Back from the Dead* (Liverpool, Merseyside Writers, 1986)

Cox, Geoffrey, *Defence of Madrid: An Eyewitness Account from the Spanish Civil War* (New Zealand, Otago University Press, 2006)

Crook, David, *Memoirs*, http://www.davidcrook.net/simple/contents.html

Cunningham, Valentine (ed.), *Spanish Front: Writers on the Civil War* (Oxford, OUP, 1986)

Graham, Frank (ed.), *The Book of the XV Brigade: Records of British, American. Canadian and Irish Volunteers in the XV International Brigade in Spain 1936–1938* (Newcastle, Frank Graham, 1975)

Graham, Frank (ed.), *The Battle of Jarama 1937: The Story of the British Battalion of the International Brigade's Baptism of Fire in the Spanish War* (Newcastle, Frank Graham, 1987)

Graham, Frank (ed.), *Battles of Brunete and the Aragon* (Newcastle, Frank Graham, 1999)

Gregory, Walter, *The Shallow Grave: A Memoir of the Spanish Civil War* (Nottingham, Five Leaves Publications, 1996)

Gurney, Jason, *Crusade in Spain* (Newton Abbot, Readers Union, 1976)

Hooper, David, *No Pasarán* (London, Avon Brooks, 1997)

Levine, Maurice, *From Cheetham to Cordova: Maurice Levine, a Manchester Man of the Thirties* (Manchester, Neil Richardson, 1984)

Lewis, Greg, *A Bullet Saved My Life: The Remarkable Adventures of Bob Peters, An Untold Story of the Spanish Civil War* (Ebbw Vale, Warren and Pell, 2006)

MacDougall, Ian (ed.), *Voices from the Spanish Civil War: Personal Recollections of Scottish Volunteers in Republican Spain 1936–39* (Edinburgh, Polygon, 1986)

Mitford, Jessica, *Hons and Rebels* (London, Indigo, 1996)

O'Connor, Peter, *Soldier of Liberty: Recollections of a Socialist and Anti-Fascist Fighter* (Dublin, MSF, 1996)

Romilly, Giles and Alexander, Michael, *Hostages at Colditz* (London, Sphere, 1973)

Stratton, Harry, *To Anti-Fascism by Taxi* (Glamorgan, Alun Books, 1984)

Thomas, Frank (ed. Robert A. Stradling), *Brother Against Brother* (Stroud, Sutton, 1998)

Toynbee, Philip (ed.), *The Distant Drum: Reflections on the Spanish Civil War* (London, Sidgwick and Jackson Ltd, 1976)

Toynbee, Philip, *Friends Apart: A Memoir of Esmond Romilly & Jasper Ridley in the Thirties* (London, Sidgwick and Jackson Ltd, 1980)

Williamson, Howard, *Toolmaking and Politics: The Life of Ted Smallbone – An Oral History* (Birmingham, Linden Books, 1987)

Wintringham, Tom, *English Captain* (London, Faber and Faber, 1939)

Secondary Sources

Alexander, William, *British Volunteers for Liberty: Spain 1936–1939* (London, Laurence and Wishart, 1982)

Baxell, Richard, *British Volunteers in the Spanish Civil War: The British Battalion in the International Brigades, 1936–1939* (Abersychan, Warren and Pell, 2007)

Beevor, Antony, *The Battle for Spain: The Spanish Civil War 1936–1939* (London, Phoenix, 2007)

Brandon, Piers, *The Dark Valley: A Panorama of the 1930s* (London, Jonathon Cape, 2000)

Cook, Judith (ed.), *Apprentices of Freedom* (London, Quartet Press, 1979)

Cooper, Mike and Parks, Ray, *We Cannot Park on Both Sides* (Reading, Reading International Brigades Memorial Committee, 2000)

Derby, Mark (ed.), *Kiwi Compañeros: New Zealand and the Spanish Civil War* (Canterbury, Canterbury University Press, 2009)

González de Miguel, Jesús, *La Batalla de Jarama: Febrero de 1937, Testimonios desde un Frente de la Guerra Civil* (Madrid, La Esfera de los Libros, 2009)

Gray, Daniel, *Homage to Caledonia: Scotland and the Spanish Civil War* (Edinburgh, Luath Press, 2009)

Hall, Christopher, *Disciplina Camaradas: Four English Volunteers in Spain 1936–39* (Pontefract, Gosling Press, 1996)

Hills, George, *The Battle for Madrid* (London, Vantage Books, 1976)

Hoar, Adrian, *In Green and Red: The Lives of Frank Ryan* (London, Brandon, 2004)

Hopkins, James K., *Into the Heart of Fire: The British in the Spanish Civil War* (California, Stanford University Press, 1998)

Larrazabal, Jesus Salas (trans. M.A. Kelly), *Air War over Spain* (London, Ian Allan, 1974)

Lewis, Brian and Gledhill, Bill (eds), *Tommy James: A Lion of a Man* (Yorkshire Art Circus, 1985)

Manchester Dependants' Aid Committee, *Clem Beckett – Hero and Sportsman* (Manchester, 1937)

Othen, Christopher, *Franco's International Brigades: Foreign Volunteers and Fascist Dictators in the Spanish Civil War* (London, Reportage, 2008)

Purcell, Hugh, *The Last English Revolutionary: Tom Wintringham 1898–1949* (Gloucestershire, Sutton, 2004)

Rankin, Nicholas, *Telegram from Guernica* (London, Faber and Faber, 2004)

Rust, Bill, *Britons in Spain: The History of the British Battalion of the XV International Brigade* (London, Lawrence and Wishart Ltd, 1939)

Sánchez Ruano, Francisco, *Islam y la Guerra Civil Española: Moros con Franco y con la Republica* (Madrid, La Esfera de los Libros, 2004)

Scurr, John, *The Spanish Foreign Legion* (London, Osprey, 1985)

Stradling, Robert A., *The Irish and the Spanish Civil War, Crusades in Conflict 1936–1939* (Manchester, Manchester University Press, 1999)

Stradling, Robert A., *Wales and the Spanish Civil War: The Dragon's Dearest Cause?* (Cardiff, University of Wales Press, 2004)

Strongos, Paul Philippou, *Spanish Thermopylae: Cypriot Volunteers in the Spanish Civil War: 1936–1939* (London, Warren and Pell, 2009)

Thomas, Hugh, *The Spanish Civil War* (Penguin, London, 2003)

Watson, Don and Corcoran, John, *An Inspiring Example: The North East of England and the Spanish Civil War* (Newcastle, The McGuffin Press, 1996)

Westwell, Con*dor Legion: the Wehrmacht's Training Ground* (London, Ian Allan, 2004)

INDEX